THE POMERANIAN HANDBOOK

A Complete Guide to The Cutest Canine in The Cosmos

GW00674535

DENISE LEO

The Pomeranian Handbook

Formatting by Rik – Wild Seas Formatting

ISBN-13: 978-0-9924878-9-8
ISBN-13: 978-0-9924878-8-1

Foreword

The Pomeranian Handbook started life as a very basic pamphlet on Pomeranian puppy care for Dochlaggie owners. It has since evolved, after many years, into a full-fledged reference book on the Pomeranian.

These amazing dogs have given me tremendous joy over many decades. I can't imagine life without dogs, especially my beautiful Poms.

Thank you to my wonderful family for supporting my Pomeranian addiction.

Denise Leo

Denise Leo with her granddaughters and Pomeranians.

Contents

Introduction 1

Part 1 – Meet the Pomeranian 4

The Pomeranian's Ancestry 5

Pomeranians and Royalty 8

About the Pomeranian 11

Pomeranian Sizes 15

Part 2 - Pomeranian Purchase 19

Owning a Pomeranian 20

I Just Want a Pet Pom. Do I Need to Buy from a Show Pom Breeder? 24

Differences Between Show Pomeranians and Pet Pomeranians 27

Purchasing Your Pomeranian 29

Buyer Beware – Bogus Breeders Abound 30

Puppy Buyer Etiquette 31

How to Avoid Scammers 32

Finding Good Breeders 34

Are Pomeranians Good with Other Dogs? 43

Pomeranians for Apartment Residents and Working Owners 44

Two Puppies or One? 44

Gender-Specific Pomeranian Personalities 45

How Much Does Age Influence Your Choice of a Dog? 46

What Type of Pomeranian Do You Want? 49

Part 3 – New Puppy Care 53

Bringing Puppy Home 54

Managing a Happy Homecoming 58

Hints for "Pom-Proofing" Your House 59

Introducing a New Puppy to Your Household 60

Tips for Helping Your Pom Settle in On Night One 62

Introducing a New Puppy to Other Pets 64

Caring for Your New Pomeranian 67

Crates and Exercise Pens for Your Pomeranian 68

Tips on Your Pom's First Vet Check-Up 70

Establishing Rules of the House 71

Naming your Pomeranian 72

Your Pomeranian's Documents 73

The Correct Way to Lift and Hold Your Pomeranian 75

Part 4 - Feeding — 78

Feeding Your Pomeranian — 79
Learn How to Read Dog Food Labels — 85
The Non-energy Providers — 87
Switching from Puppy Food to Adult Dog Food — 90
Why Keeping Your Pomeranian Trim is Vital — 91
Tips on Handling a Fussy Eater — 93
What are the Best Treats for My Pomeranian? — 94
What Can Pomeranians Eat? — 95
Which Human Foods Should My Pomeranian Not Eat? — 96
Feeding Pomeranians Raw Food — 99

Part 5 - Grooming — 104

Grooming Your Pomeranian — 105
Bathing your Pomeranian — 105
Brushing your Pomeranian — 111
Handling Mats In Your Dog's Coat — 114
Important Pomeranian Hair Care Tips — 115
Pomeranian Trimming — 118
Nail Trimming — 123
Tear Stains — 125
Pomeranian Grooming Chart — 126
Pomeranian Shedding — 127
Shaving a Pomeranian — 130
Pomeranian Puppy Uglies — 132
Dental Care Tips for Pomeranians — 134

Part 6 – Health — 138

Pomeranian Health Concerns — 139
Choosing Your Pomeranian's Veterinarian — 144
Tips on Your Pom's First Vet Check-Up — 146
Intestinal infections — 147
Understanding Vaccinations — 148
Dealing with Fleas — 149
Worms — 152
Pomeranian Allergies — 157
Pomeranian Reverse Sneezing — 162
Winter Care — 166

Summer Care — 170

More Than You Ever Wanted to Know About Rectal Sacs — 174

Pomeranians In Heat — 176

Neutering Facts — 179

Pomeranian Spaying Aftercare — 180

Caring for Your Senior Pomeranian — 183

Questions When Choosing Pet Insurance for Your Dog — 189

Emergency First Aid Tips for Your Dog — 190

How Long Do Pomeranians Live? — 193

Part 7 – Training — 197

When Should You Commence Pomeranian Puppy Training? — 198

How to Give Treats When Training – Yes, It Matters! — 199

Socialising Your Pomeranian Puppy — 200

Pomeranian Exercise Requirements — 202

Potty Training and Crate Training — 209

Marking — 215

How to Talk to Your Pomeranian — 217

The Language of Pomeranians — 220

Taking Training to the Next Level — 222

Dealing with Behavioural Problems — 225

You Can Do Lots of Activities with Your Pomeranian — 232

Part 8 – Behaviour — 238

Pomeranian Intelligence — 239

Why Do Pomeranians Spin in Circles? — 246

How Long Can Pomeranians Be Left Alone? — 247

Pomeranians and their Toys — 248

Pomeranians And the Outdoors — 252

How to Avoid Pomeranian Dog Park Dangers — 259

Why Does My Pom Eat Poop? — 261

Traveling with Your Pomeranian — 263

Boarding Your Pomeranian or Using a Pet Sitter — 269

Important Tips to Follow if Your Pomeranian is Lost — 270

Looking After A Rescue Pomeranian — 271

Part 9 – Breeding and Showing — 278

Breeding and Exhibiting Pomeranians — 279

What is the Pomeranian Breed Standard? — 283

Characteristics of the Pomeranian 284

Pomeranian Colours and Patterns 298

Coloured Pomeranians 303

Dog Stud Services – Contracts, Compensation, Fees and Stud Selection 306

A Week-by-Week Guide to Your Dog's Pregnancy 309

Putting Together Your Own Whelping Kit 314

Weaning 317

The Different Stages of Puppy Development 320

An Overview of Puppy Development 325

Selecting a Pomeranian Show Puppy 330

Training a Pomeranian Show Dog 337

Final Thoughts 341

Introduction

Are you thinking about getting a Pomeranian? Perhaps you definitely want one, but you don't know how to find the ideal one for you. Maybe you already own a fine specimen of this special breed and want to learn more about how to provide him with the best possible care.

Pomeranians fall into the category of "toy" dog, but nothing about his spirit is small. He'll have boundless enthusiasm and a high degree of intelligence. You'll also quickly learn just how loyal and loving a Pomeranian can be. Pomeranians are also known to have a mischievous streak. It's all in the name of fun and he'll clearly demonstrate his unconditional love for you every single day.

Small dogs frequently compensate for their small size with huge personalities and this trait is incredibly accurate with the Pomeranian. He's best described as a toy dog with a big dog's attitude and outlook; traits that have taken numerous decades of specific breeding to create. A Pomeranian carries himself with supreme confidence, whether he's walking in the local park or winning "Best in Show" in competitions.

This comprehensive book provides you with answers to everything related to one of the cutest breeds of dogs in the world. It will help you give your Pomeranian that 100% care he so richly deserves.

Learn everything you need to know to provide care for your precious dog (whether he's a show dog or a household pet). Your life together will start when you first think about buying this beautiful dog as a puppy, and continues through his adolescence, into adulthood and then into his senior years.

From the moment when you first bring your new puppy home, it will be a very rewarding experience - one that never gets old or boring. Yes, there's a lot of work involved in caring for any animal and you'll soon learn about the extra responsibilities you need to take on.

The great news is that you're not alone if you refer to this all-in-one manual for Pomeranians. It will be your best guide book while you're adjusting to life as a dog owner and all the new challenges that involves. After all, doesn't your newest best friend deserve the greatest possible care?

You'll need to learn everything about your Pomeranian and what's needed to provide him with the best possible care.

The list includes:

- What (and how much) food and treats to give him and how often.
- How to puppy-proof his new home, so he's always safe.
- Potty training.
- Tips on grooming your new puppy, including how often to bathe him, trim his fur, cut his toenails and much more.
- What are the best, and safest, toys for him to play with?
- Health issues and tips to help you assist your vet in caring for your precious Pomeranian.
- And on the list goes on.

You'll soon discover this comprehensive book is an important tool to help you and your family welcome your new dog to the household as warmly and positively as possible.

Pomeranian owners interested in breeding and exhibiting Poms will benefit from my extensive knowledge of the breed gained over more than 45 years. Breed type, movement, colours, breeding, selecting and training a show Pomeranian and more, are all topics explained at length.

I'm a well-known Pomeranian breed authority. I have been breeding and exhibiting Best in Show winning Supreme, Grand Champion & Champion Pomeranians since 1975.

NOTE: If you're thinking of purchasing, or already own, a Pomeranian and don't have a copy of this book, you're doing yourself and your Pom a huge disservice. You'll refer to this book throughout your Pomeranian's life.

Who better to educate you on all the ins and outs of ensuring your Pomeranian has the best quality lifestyle? I mix expertise with the kind heart and soul of a true pet lover and I hope you'll benefit greatly from my well-rounded knowledge and experience.

Please note: while I do discuss healthcare and behavioural issues, you should never use this information as a replacement for advice from qualified veterinarians. Their diagnoses or recommended treatment regimens should be followed. If you have any worries about the health of your Pomeranian, your first contact should be your regular vet or, if you don't yet have one, find a vet that works locally. Never ignore or avoid treatment and/or advice from your vet because of a piece of information you have read in any book.

For the purposes of continuity, this book will mainly refer to Pomeranians as "him" or other words denoting the male gender. However, unless otherwise specified, the female Pomeranian gender applies equally.

Part 1 – Meet the Pomeranian

The Pomeranian's Ancestry

Whether they're working dogs in the Arctic, real British Royalty, or even survivors of the first voyage of the ill-fated Titanic, the Pomeranian dog breed have appeared virtually everywhere in the world, and they are renowned for their strong character and gracious beauty.

If you have ever been an owner or you have simply enjoyed time around them, you will appreciate the fact that Pomeranians are among the most energetic, lovable and charismatic dogs on the planet. It is uncommon for breeds to have such a rich, deep history while, simultaneously, fitting the bill as one of history's most iconic breeds. Pomeranian dogs ideally suit the bill, which they display in all they do each day.

Perhaps you have wondered why your adorable Pomeranian behaves and looks like he does. Like every animal and person, their overall characteristics have been created over an exceptionally long time. To understand today's Pomeranians, it is necessary to do a deep dive into the history and origins of Pomeranians.

Many eons ago, in a land that bordered Poland, Germany and the Baltic Sea, there was a place called Pomerania. This was a derivation of "po more," a Slavic word, meaning "on the sea" or "by the sea." This Polish place is nowadays known as Gdansk.

The Pomeranian was once a larger dog and now is the smallest of the Spitz dog breeds. Dogs of the Spitz type have been displayed on various artefacts dating as far back as 400 B.C. The Spitz breeds are a dog family that lived in parts of Europe and Asia.

Dogs of the Spitz family have pricked ears, tails that curl up over their backs and a thick double coat. People have relied heavily on these dogs for many reasons including guarding homes, pulling sleds and protecting livestock. The smaller dogs were frequently cared for as pets.

In Germany, various older regional names for these Spitz dogs were translated into English and became the Wolf Spitz, Lion

Spitz, Bear Spitz and the Great (aka Gross) Spitz. The smaller dogs included the Fox Spitz and, a little later, the Mannheimer Zwerg-Spitz.

This breed evolved throughout some areas of Europe and was called various names, with several types having no relationship with Pomerania. In France, there was Lulu, Chien de Pomeranie or the Lou Lou. The Wolfshond was in Holland but, during the 1780s, this name was altered to Keeshond. Italy had numerous names for this dog, including the: Italian Spitz, Florentine Spitz, Cane de Quirinale, Lupino and Volpino. The Italian varieties were usually bright orange or yellow in colour.

The Swedish naturalist, Carl Linnaeus (1707-1778), spent a great deal of time classifying dogs of his era. He mentions the Canis Pomeranus and offered plenty of evidence to support his theory that these dogs were well known in Central and Northern Europe.

It wasn't until the 18th century that the Pomeranian (known then as the Wolf-dog), became firmly established in England, when the breed captured the interest of members of the English monarchy.

Despite a few imports, Pomeranians didn't make a big impact on the people of England until after 1870. In 1859, Newcastle was home to the very first English dog show and, in 1861, another one was held in the Belle Vue Zoo, Manchester.

Mr. Bennett owned a Pomeranian Fox Dog that won in his class as a non-sporting foreign dog. In the same year, Mr. J.H. Seed exhibited his dog (Jack) in Birmingham, after which the owner made the dog available for purchase at the price of 10 guineas.

December 1862 saw three Pomeranians exhibited, also in Birmingham, as part of the Third Annual Showing for Sporting and other dogs. They were classified in an extra class that accounted for small foreign dogs not used for field sports.

For the first time, in 1863, Pomeranians had classes of their own in London's Great International Dog Show.

Research, found in numerous old dog books, tells us the

glorious colours now available weren't even a spot on the horizon during the early development of the Pomeranian breed.

The Pomeranian Club was established in 1891. There was growing interest, by breeders, in reducing the size of the dogs they were breeding, but also in producing new colours. No longer did the whites and blacks rank top position in breeding programs and the show ring. Now there were other colours such as orange, sable, blue and chocolate as well.

During the late 1880s, Pomeranians started appearing in various shows in the United States of America. In 1900, the country's Kennel Club officially recognised the Pomeranian and the American Pomeranian Club was formed.

Before this official sanction, the breed had to participate in the Miscellaneous Class.

The American Pomeranian Club became a member club of the American Kennel Club in 1909. 1911z saw the very first Pomeranian breed show in the U.S.A. The total entry of 262, consisted of 138 Pomeranians entered under English Judge, Mrs. L.C. Dyer. Best of Breed was awarded to a black dog, Champion Banner Prince Charming, owned by Mrs. Frank Smyth.

During this period, shows provided classes for small, medium and big dogs, and it took the English Pomeranian Club much longer to settle on a suitable weight range for these amazing dogs. Finally, it was agreed that Toy Pomeranians weighed under 7lb. All the other Pomeranians were "oversized" with 20lb being the heaviest weight allowed.

The adorable Pomeranian dog was now known and loved throughout England. A great deal of the credit for this adulation goes to Queen Charlotte's granddaughter, Queen Victoria, whose enthusiasm for Poms thrust the breed directly into the public eye. Queen Victoria made the Pomeranians extremely popular, more so than during her grandmother's reign.

For a couple of years, Queen Victoria was listed as one of the leading breeders, along with Mrs. Thomas, Mrs. Gordon Lynn and Miss Hamilton. The Queen's "Marco" won the Club's gold medal. Mrs. Thomas brought dogs from Germany to improve the quality of her stock. Miss Hamilton owned dogs of different colours but concentrated on breeding whites.

Pomeranians were exchanged for large sums of money. There was a strong craze for breeding dogs that were as small as possible. Often through awfully close inbreeding, the results included apple heads, popeyed, unsoundness and weediness. The mortality rate during whelping was incredibly high. By 1916, the bigger Pomeranians no longer appeared in the shows, with only the "Toy" size remaining.

Pomeranians and Royalty

In 1761, after marrying King George the Third, Queen Charlotte brought her pet dogs to England. Her dogs were what was then called "wolf dog" in type and were either white or cream in colour, except for Fino, a black and white dog who was especially loved by the Prince of Wales.

Pomeranian dogs lived in the royal palaces and several of the Queen's peers received Pomeranians for themselves. The King's son carried on this royal tradition, and examples of this appear in paintings by Gainsborough and Stubbs. A lot of the information about these dogs is derived from various paintings.

The Pomeranian is named after the territory in Germany from which Queen Charlotte, imported her Pomeranians; Pomerania. At the time, Queen Charlotte referred to the breed as the "Pomeranian."

Queen Victoria's involvement with Pomeranians

Queen Victoria was Queen Charlotte's granddaughter, and she obviously inherited her grandmother's passion for Pomeranians. She was widely acknowledged as the most famous person who owned and exhibited Pomeranians during her lifetime.

Queen Victoria imported numerous dogs of many colours from different parts of Europe and her kennel at Windsor housed more than 30 Pomeranians.

Queen Victoria housed several different dog breeds in her Home Park Kennels. In February 1891, at Crufts dog show, the Queen first exhibited Pomeranians and Collies.

The people of England greatly admired and loved Queen Victoria, as well as her dogs, who became very popular. She absolutely loved her Pomeranians and they were of great comfort to her during the period after Prince Albert passed away.

The Queen's royal Pomeranians often travelled with her. The royal train contained a specially made compartment to house her dogs during her train trips. They were even protected by special policemen to guarantee their security and safety. When Victoria was on her deathbed, she asked for her favourite Pomeranian to keep her company.

Because people had an incredible fascination for the dogs involved in the Queen's life, there was a mammoth amount of information available to the general public.

So, there's plenty of accurate information about her dogs and their involvement in her life. Much of this information appeared in the New York Times, various British papers and magazines, as well as numerous canine-specific magazines.

While Queen Victoria was on holiday in Florence in 1888, she purchased foundation stock of Italian Spitz dogs, also called Volpino Italiano or Florentine Spitz.

Reading all about the Queen and her passion for Pomeranians, you should understand that the dogs she loved, back in her day, aren't classified as Pomeranians today by the English Kennel Club. There have been many improvements to breed type in the Pomeranian since Queen Victoria's day, and the Pomeranian is now in the toy group in non-FCI countries.

The type of dog bred and loved by Queen Victoria is now referred to as the German Spitz and is even shown in a different group in non-FCI countriesIf Queen Victoria was breeding dogs today, her mission to breed German Spitz dogs with the Italian Volpino dogs would probably be frowned upon. This was a common practice of many other Pomeranian breeders of that era, and it resulted in the appearance of many new colours in the breed.

The Queen stopped exhibiting her dogs after a number of them contracted distemper and died. She suspected one or more of her dogs brought the disease back to the kennel after they were involved in a dog show earlier that year.

Queen Victoria had a preference for Poms that weighed 6-12 lbs.

The Windsor Kennel name is now owned by Queen Elizabeth II.

Mrs. Langton Dennis (a successful breeder of this era) received an incredibly special reception when she brought her canines to Buckingham Palace.

When the German Crown Prince and Princess inspected Mrs. Langton Dennis's dogs, it was regarded as a huge compliment and they assured Mrs. Dennis that their small Pomeranians couldn't compare to the English ones when it came to the texture and harshness of their coats and that the German dogs lacked the quality that was apparent in the English dogs.

The German Princess later purchased several British dogs, the first from Mrs. Langton Dennis, (a Dragonfly dog) and the second one was an orange sable female that was bred by Miss Kirkwood. Her name was Offley Shining Light, (she was a daughter of Champion Offley Saucy Atom).

Many other Royals loved and owned Pomeranians. Both Joséphine de Beauharnais, (wife to Napoleon I of France), and Princess Ileana of Romania had a passion for Pomeranians.

About the Pomeranian

Supreme Champion Dochlaggie Dragon Heart.

Photo by Pedini

Although Pomeranians are small, they're significantly more than the delightful furballs they resemble. Their bright, almost twinkling, eyes are always wide open, greeting the world around them with boundless curiosity, and supreme confidence that no other creature is as charming and adorable as him. Pomeranians have a huge personality, matched only by the size of their fur coats and their amazing self-confidence.

Pomeranians are the smallest breed in the Spitz dog family, but they're endowed with courage that you normally would associate with dogs of a much greater size. They're always a favourite breed, despite weighing under seven pounds.

A Pomeranian can easily be compared to a bright shining star: he's highly intelligent, has an exceptional temperament when it comes to mixing with people and other animals, and as mentioned previously, his eyes shine like bright stars in the sky. He loves his family and is ecstatic when it comes to lap time, but he's always full of beans. Instead of sleeping on his favourite piece of furniture, he's more often wondering around the home with specific goals in mind.

A Pomeranian is a good pet for someone needing a small dog, perhaps due to living in a unit or flat. The good news is that he'll still possess the characteristics of his bigger ancestors, large herding and sled dogs, and he'll be just as active.

Because of his diminutive size, he can usually get sufficient exercise inside. However, he's much happier if he goes on long walks, frolics with any other tiny dogs, and chases leaves around when it's windy.

You can recognise a Pomeranian for a few distinct features. He has a fluffy, luxurious double coat, his ears prick up when he's alert, and he has a cute foxy face. He has a square body with a very fluffy tail that usually sits up and over his back. Around his neck appears a thick ruff of fur. There you have it; a proud Pomeranian that could easily manage life in snowy regions.

This fun-loving, inquisitive toy dog has a body that could easily sit in your handbag. However, he has four legs and usually prefers to walk as much as possible. While this breed can be described as sassy at times, Pomeranians are fiercely loyal, loving, ideal companions for lots of people seeking a dog with such qualities.

Now you have some understanding of what a Pomeranian dog

is all about, it's time to learn more about their temperament because no two dogs are alike, in the same way that no two people are alike.

Although Pomeranians are small dogs, only weighing 3 – 7 pounds, their personalities are as big as many larger dogs. Pomeranians are ideal as family pets, and generally are: playful, energetic, loyal, loving, lively, outgoing and quite intelligent.

Because Poms are intelligent and playful, they require lots of mental stimuli, so they're kept busy. They are fiercely independent and succumb to "small dog syndrome," a trait they share with numerous other small dog breeds. They require plenty of training to help them be social and to ensure good behaviour.

Poms respond well when they are being trained and enjoy such activities, so it generally becomes easier to train them as you add new elements to the teaching regime.

Pomeranians are an alert breed, acutely aware of environmental changes. If they bark when faced with any new stimuli, that can create the bad habit of too much barking without a valid reason. Because they're extremely defensive when it comes to new stimuli in their territory, they're likely to bark at any sounds outside, regardless of whether it's somebody walking past the house or a person coming to the front door.

These dogs sometimes use their intelligence as a tool to get everything they want from the person or family who own them. As extroverts, they love being the centre of attention. However, if you don't set rules for them to follow, they can be naughty.

They make fantastic watchdogs because they are very alert, partly because they are also very curious. They love being outside and, if possible, they will either peek through the curtains or sit on a window-sill and watch the world moving around outside. Your Pom will bark to warn you if somebody is at your front door.

Poms are lap dogs. This does not mean they will want to spend every day sitting in your lap. However, they will want to stay close to you as much as possible. Poms are normally inside dogs but that does not squash their desire to explore the world outside of their home. They love running around and, in extremely cold temperatures, they need protection to keep them warm.

If your dog has been cooped up inside all day, he will love it if you grab his leash and take him for a long walk or to the local dog park so he can run around. Poms love exploring new things, whether they're smells, visual things or sounds.

Many people wrongly believe that a pom is naturally a barker when he's actually not a habitual barker. He'll usually do it when he wants your attention, if there are strangers at your door or near you when you're out walking together. In general, Poms aren't the "yappers" that lots of people believe.

Pomeranian Sizes

Canadian Champion and Australian Supreme Champion

Shallany's Rebel With A Cause. Photo by Ffire

The Pomeranian breed is classified as a toy dog (meaning a small dog when compared to many other dog breeds). However, within the Pomeranian family, there are lots that are bigger than average and some that are smaller than the norm.

The breed sizes standard for Pomeranians

There are four distinct Kennel Clubs that have standards for all purebred dogs. The range of sizes for small Pomeranians is very big. There are four dog clubs that influence the world of the canines. They are the AKC, FCI, CKC and the KC.

American Kennel Club (AKC). The weight range for a standard full-size Pomeranian is 3 - 7 lbs. (1.36 - 3.175kgs). For show Poms, they prefer the dogs to weigh 4 - 6 lbs. Lots of Pomeranians do match these criteria but there are also smaller and bigger Poms, which I'll cover in more detail further down.

Although the dog's height isn't listed, most Pomeranians that are in the 3 - 7-pound category are usually 8 – 11 inches (20.32 – 27.94 cm) tall. This measurement goes from the top of his shoulder blades (his withers) down to the floor.

The Fédération Cynologique Internationale (FCI) has more than 80 countries as members. Weight isn't part of their standard. However, they stipulate the height of a Pomeranian should be 21 cms +/- 3 cms. This is measured from the top of his shoulder (aka withers) to the floor. This figure is slightly less than that of Pomeranians in the AKC.

The FCI's name for a 20 cm Pomeranian is German Toy Spitz. If he is over height, they label him as a German Miniature Spitz.

The Canadian Kennel Club (CKC) matches the same Pomeranian standards for weight and height as the AKC mentioned previously. Of course, there will be Poms that fall below or above the figures in the ideal standard size.

The Kennel Club (KC) is also known as the English Kennel Club. Pomeranian standards in this kennel fall into a smaller range and there is not much leeway for size variables.

Females should be 4.5 - 5.5 pounds (2 - 2.5 kg). Males should be 4 - 4.5 lbs. (1.8 - 2kg). These measurements would mean Pomeranians would match the standards of the American Kennel Club's Pomeranian.

When they're born, Pomeranian puppies only weigh a few ounces. They double in size and grow quickly.

Most of the puppy's growth happens within his first nine months of life. After that, he may gain a small amount of weight and his height will increase for another three months, when he will be a full-grown Pomeranian.

Smaller Poms

The bone and body structure can vary and, in some rare cases, the Pomeranian dog weight might even be lower than the minimum of 3 lbs.

Many never appreciate that a standard Pom's size is already tiny.

Pomeranians that are bigger than normal

In some litters, the breeder may get a puppy that is smaller than the average. This can also apply where some litters include a puppy that is slightly bigger than the average size. Some breeders aim for the top end of the standard weight range to produce dogs that are sturdier than their smaller counterparts.

Throwback Pomeranians

Pomeranians come in a variety of sizes, colours, cuteness, personalities and styles.

This adorably tiny dog is loved because he can usually watch the world go by from the safety of his mother's handbag or father's pocket.

However, it is easy to find a Pom that is much bigger than the norm. The term "throwback Pomeranian" is often used incorrectly to describe these big Pomeranian breed dogs. I personally do not like the gimmicky terms "throwback Pomeranian" and "teacup Pomeranian" being used in association with my beloved breed.

These are the only three reasons why a Pomeranian will be much bigger than the standard size:

1. He is overweight. It's a normal problem for the Pomeranian breed of dog and is even more likely in Poms that have bigger bones.
2. He might be a mixed dog breed. You may own what

looks like a purebred Pom but he could actually be part Pomeranian and the other part could be a bigger Spitz dog such as the Samoyed, Chow-Chow or Japanese Spitz, just to mention a few examples.

3. Genetics. Big Pomeranian puppies are often observed in colour breeding programs. Puppies from backyard breeders and puppy mills are often larger than the Pomeranian breed standard, owing to poor breeding practices.

Technically speaking, this term (or a breed of dog by this name) does not exist. Owners and non-preservation breeders seem to have latched onto this term to describe their big Pomeranian breed dogs.

What some refer to as a throwback Pomeranian is merely a Pom that is larger than the Pomeranian breed standard size. The dog's natural body structure can be up to four times bigger than what is expected.

Part 2 - Pomeranian Purchase

Owning a Pomeranian

Owning a beautiful Pomeranian may be the result of an impulse. It may be something you have dreamt about for many years. Perhaps you saw this cute dog on TV, in a magazine or at a dog show or maybe a friend or neighbour has one that has caught your eye. Maybe you've heard them rave about how special they really are.

Regardless of why you want a Pomeranian, you can't stop dreaming about owning one. However, it's not a good idea to simply go out and buy a dog on impulse. There are many good reasons to do a little homework first.

The main reason is that a Pomeranian isn't a stuffed toy, fashion accessory or ornament. He lives and breathes and will depend on you for the remainder of his life. You'll be responsible for feeding him, training him, cleaning up his messes, grooming him, walking and playing with him and keeping him company. It's likely that he'll live ten plus years, so he's not a Christmas purchase you can just "send back" because he's the wrong colour, size or type; or because you have simply grown bored with having to care for him.

A puppy is for life.

Before buying a Pomeranian, consider these points:

You should take a lot of time to consider this immense commitment from every angle, and whether you can afford it? This is an enormous financial and time commitment. It can be quite demanding, especially in the early stages when the learning curve may be intense and steep.

The initial purchase is relatively cheap compared to the long-term financial commitment required. Dogs are expensive to care for. You will need to pay for food, bowls, toys, leashes and collars, a crate and bed to sleep in, brushes and other grooming aids and a carrying bag. You must locate a good vet, preferably close by, and one who has a good knowledge of Pomeranians if possible. Locality is important as there may be emergency visits.

He'll need regular vaccinations, heartworm and deworming treatments.

Check-ups are also vital as your vet may catch certain problems before they become a major issue.

A dog *is* man's best friend, and it's for very good reasons. They thrive on attention and return your love tenfold, unconditionally. Although they may survive with no interaction with people, it's not ideal. Owning a dog means making him part of your life, not just when you feel like it, but all the time.

Do you work long hard days? Do you flop down in your favourite armchair and watch TV when you arrive home? If this describes you, then you shouldn't bring a dog into your home since you obviously have no free time. If you own a dog but leave him home all day and then ignore him when you get home—it's just not fair to the dog.

In some places, there are day-care facilities where dogs can have some fun. You may consider paying somebody to come and play with your dog each day. You might even think of getting a second dog, so they have each other for companionship. But doing these things is merely replacing you, so don't bother buying a dog if you can't shower your Pomeranian with love and attention every day. They thrive on it; without it they suffer greatly.

The ideal time to work out if a Pomeranian is right for you is *prior to taking him home.* Once you meet a puppy, you'll immediately be captivated and the next thing you know, you're paying the owner and taking him home. It's impossible to make a wise decision when you have puppy eyes looking up at you, practically saying, "take me home, please."

Dog ownership is a long-term, full-time, daily commitment on your part. You need to become a best friend, a playmate, a nutritionist, an expert at home repairs, a trainer, a therapist, a nurse/doctor, a disciplinarian and much more.

The pros and cons of owning a Pomeranian

Even though Pomeranians are exceptionally cute, they're not the most popular dog in the world. Toy dogs have become more popular in the last 20 years or so. Pomeranians are certainly not for everybody and here are a few pros and cons to help you decide.

The negatives

No dog is ideal for every scenario and person. Being small does have some benefits but it also has certain drawbacks:

- They can easily hurt themselves when jumping off furniture, getting stepped on or by being dropped.
- They're small enough to make you trip if they get in your way.
- They're not good for jogging and would slow you down if you hike.
- They won't offer good protection and can't participate in certain sports geared for bigger dogs.

- They're fragile and unsuitable for young children to play with.
- They're frequent barkers.
- Their coats need plenty of attention.
- It's harder to house-train a Pomeranian than it is bigger dogs.
- Birds of prey, wild animals and large dogs can kill Pomeranians.

The positives

There are many positives to owning a Pomeranian:

- A major reason for the increased popularity of Pomeranians, and other toy dogs, is that having smaller pets is more sensible in many cases.
- It costs less to care for smaller dogs in general.
- Their food bill is considerably smaller than that of a bigger dog.
- They don't eat a lot, so their toilet deposits are smaller in size.
- Your Pomeranian can sit in a small travel bag and go to places inappropriate for bigger dogs.
- They need less exercise, a smaller yard (if one at all) and fit easily into a busy person's schedule.
- When it's bad weather, they can do exercises inside. Fetch, tag and other fun games can be played inside on even the harshest of days.
- They can't shove you out of your own bed.
- A Pomeranian isn't strong enough to drag you for a walk, dive through an open window to bite the postman's leg, or kill any nearby cats.

Once you have weighed up all your options and decided a toy dog would be ideal for you, it's time to choose what type.

You have Yorkshire Terriers, Affenpinschers and everything in between.

However, a Pomeranian is unique and here are a few facts to ponder:

- Poms are unique in the way they stand out in comparison to other toy dogs.
- They're among the most adventurous, energetic toy dogs.
- They thrive on challenges and can do well in many dog sports.
- Pomeranians really love playing, and cuddling up once they're worn out.

I Just Want a Pet Pom. Do I Need to Buy from a Show Pom Breeder?

If you're looking for a pet, there are many ways to find one. It's quite common for people to suggest talking to a breeder who Is involved in shows as your best option. Some will say, if a pet is all you want, shows don't matter, and you can get a pet from anywhere.

Snobbery? You're certainly not being a snob if you consider your pet should be bred to the breed standard. It's far from being excessive and it's necessary to understand just why you're not a snob.

The main reason behind dog shows is to test dogs against the standards set for each specific breed. Evaluations are done on temperament, type, gait, appearance, movement and soundness. Breed type is a combination of each.

Temperament

Your dog's attitude towards other dogs, other animals, and humans is assessed. Here is the ideal temperament, direct from the breed standard for Pomeranians. "The Pomeranian is an extrovert, exhibiting great intelligence and a vivacious spirit, making him a great companion dog as well as a competitive show dog."

Type

This covers character, appearance, temperament, bone structure, condition and movement.

Gait

Ideally a Pomeranian should move freely, with no trace of incorrect structure or unsoundness.

Appearance

The average Pomeranian is a toy-sized, small dog with a wedge-shaped head directly in proportion to the size of his body. His dark, medium-sized eyes are almond-shaped. He has small ears that sit high and erect. His profusely coated tail is usually seen lying flat over his back.

Soundness

This is achieved when your Pom's physical and mental health are good, all faculties and organs function correctly, and everything is in balance.

The whole package

A Pomeranian is an energetic, proud dog. He's highly intelligent, enthusiastic, keen to learn and will be fiercely loyal to his family. A Pom is a great show dog. He's a fine companion because he's affectionate and loving. He's an independent, inquisitive, active and alert toy dog.

People who don't regard themselves as "dog lovers" or "dog people" often fall in love with this adorable, lively dog. He'll sometimes need a firm hand, especially during training, but he's a fast learner. If you introduce your new dog to other house pets or other dogs, he'll generally get on with them. He's also a great watch dog.

Now that you have a better understanding of dog shows, you're possibly still unsure why this is important, especially if you only want him for a family pet. You probably selected a Pomeranian for a few reasons. You have already put in the necessary research. Pomeranians are glamorous balls of fluff, highly intelligent and they're ideal companions because they can sit beside you, at your feet or somewhere close by because they love being with people.

Responsible breeders always try to keep these positive

attributes. For example, there can be timid Poms and aggressive ones. Dogs at either end of the spectrum should be taken seriously and temperament problems are often inherited.

If you had a Pom you wanted to show, but he's at either end of the temperament spectrum, the dog probably won't cope with the stress. He may be aggressive towards other dogs and people or he may retreat into himself. Don't gamble and buy a dog from anywhere except a preservation breeder.

A preservation breeder's dogs will have a proven consistency. Consider type and structure. Does that dog even resemble a Pomeranian? Can he move easily without any health issues? It's wiser to make a purchase from a breeder who has repeatedly proven their dogs move well. Don't rely on a seller who isn't interested in proving anything about their dog. Remember that the stakes are high because you want to provide good quality of life for the puppy and ensure your wallet doesn't get emptied for the wrong reasons. In any well-bred litter, it's possible there will be at least one puppy unsuitable for showing. He'll have certain imperfections but will still make a great pet. It's not obligatory that your puppy is show quality if your objective is a great pet.

Every day Pomeranian rescue facilities see Poms being brought in because of poor temperament or lacking breed type due to poor breeding practices. Many of these dogs will require extensive care by vets and some will need surgical procedures that cost a lot of money. Some people hand their dogs over because they couldn't properly care for them, whether it's due to temperament, finances or other reasons.

It's not snobbish, or elitist, or assuming some dogs are better than others. It's all about acquiring a puppy that matches everything you have been told about the breed. It's helping more puppies get the best care and start in life by being loved and giving love in return. Lastly, it's about preserving and loving the Pomeranian breed and everything good about them - today and into the future. Choose the best breeder to obtain the ideal dog to suit you. He'll be there to love and give love for as long as he lives.

Champion Dochlaggie Dae Dreamer. Photo by Pedini

Differences Between Show Pomeranians and Pet Pomeranians

If your puppy originated from a Show Pomeranian breeder, pet quality Pom pups and show dogs are often in the same litter. The differences between the two types of puppies are often very minor.

The breeder will closely watch the litter develop and evaluate how close a puppy meets the Pomeranian breed standard. You should obtain a copy of the "official breed standard" because it specifically lays out everything to look for when it comes to the look of your Pomeranian and whether it meets official breed standards.

Ethical show breeders strive to breed as close as possible to this breed standard, as well as doing health testing and proving their Pomeranians in the show ring prior to breeding.

The unfortunate (and very sad) truth is that "breeders" who don't show dogs usually just breed dogs to produce pups. Every recognised breed of dog has a breed standard. These have been drawn up over a long period of time and, over the years, the standards have been revised. Kennel clubs conduct shows to assist breeders to prove breeding dogs in the show ring prior to breeding.

Dog judges study the breed standard and look for sound dogs who conform, as close as possible, to the standard. In other words, the dogs who are sound, and look exactly how they're supposed to look, win the highest awards. Exhibiting their Poms gives breeders the opportunity to learn more about their breed, compare programs and make important contacts with other breeders.

Breed Clubs often run health and grooming seminars in conjunction with their shows. Show Pomeranians compete in the show ring to enable breeders to compare breeding programs. Show dogs compete so they can be judged and measured to see which ones are closest to the breed standard. It's an extremely important and essential breeding tool for breeders.

Show breeders are also called preservation breeders, since these people often dedicate their lives to the preservation of their chosen breed. Without this dedication, dog breeds wouldn't exist.

Show breeders select the best specimens to breed with. For example, a Pom breeder will decide which dogs meet the Pomeranian breed standard and which don't. Even very small issues such as a curly tail or a tooth out of line may mean he's better suited to be a pet. If a Pom puppy is designated as a show prospect, this means he has no discernible flaws.

Breeders will know which puppies may develop into show dogs and have a real shot at winning events. If you're purchasing a puppy from a show Pom breeder, there will be very little difference in the quality of the pups to the untrained eye. When you check out a show Pom and compare it to a pet Pom purchased from a non-show breeder, there will be significant differences.

It's essential to understand that Pomeranians are amazing dogs. The "flaws" that make them unsuitable to become show dogs aren't negatives. Nobody, human or animal, is perfect. Models and celebrities also have flaws. All dogs are loving and very special. Every Pomeranian is beautiful and should be cherished. Some Pomeranians are rescue dogs and carry scars from their past experiences. Poms of all sizes, shapes, colours, personality types, ages and unique quirks are beautiful creatures and will lavish you with unconditional love, and they deserve the same in return.

Purchasing Your Pomeranian

Your Pomeranian will be a cherished member of your family for many years.

Therefore, careful consideration should be an important part of choosing your special dog.

To prevent the many difficulties often experienced by new puppy owners, don't buy that adorable puppy in the pet shop window. Impulse purchases have absolutely no place in pet ownership. Other avenues to avoid are newspaper advertisements, dodgy online ads with very little information and a low-price tag, puppy mills, unregistered breeders and unregistered puppies.

Purchase your dog from a reputable, registered Pomeranian breeder; ideally, a breeder who's actively involved in exhibiting their Pomeranians, or check out your local Pomeranian rescue shelter. The ideal avenue for locating Pomeranian breeders is to contact the Pomeranian Breed Club and request referrals to breeders with puppies in your area. A quick search on the internet for "Pomeranian Club" will usually provide you with contact information about your nearest Club.

Another way to find that special dog is to check out local dog shows. If you meet and befriend local Pom breeders, they'll introduce you to any available puppies they have.

You can see what sort of environment they're being raised in, and they get to know you because they want to evaluate whether you'll be a good owner for one of their puppies.

Pomeranian breeders generally are happy to chat with you at any time during a show, except when they're about to enter the ring. Be smart and make time to talk with them when judging is finished and they're less stressed.

Sometimes prospective Pomeranian owners wanting to buy a typical high quality, correctly sized Pom will ask for a "teacup" or "mini-Pomeranian." Officially, neither variety exists. Purchasing your Pom from a registered show Pomeranian breeder will ensure that your dog will mature close to the breed standard.

Pomeranians bred by people who don't show their dogs may look adorable and very cute as young puppies. New owners are often captivated by the appealing ball of fluff, but they're purchasing a totally different dog to the "show" type Pomeranian.

These poorer bred puppies have problems when compared to the Pomeranian breed standard.

Many pet Pomeranian purchasers are dismayed when their Pom puppy doesn't grow up looking like the famous Pomeranian Boo.

Buyer Beware – Bogus Breeders Abound

If you meet a breeder who tells you one of his dogs is rare due to size, colour or because he has an unusual trait, the alarm bells should start ringing. While there are some colours that are more typical, there are no colours that are rare and, regardless of the colour(s) of a Pomeranian, it should not increase his value in any way.

The same applies to size. While the official Pomeranian standard says a Pom's weight should be 3 - 7 pounds, no dog within this range is worth more money than another.

Avoid breeders who advertise their puppies as mini, toy, pocket, teacup or miniature Pomeranians. These advertisements are just sales tactics designed to trap the gullible.

Spend a little extra time selecting your Pom and purchase from a reputable show breeder.

Many Pomeranian lovers regard breeding high quality, healthy Poms as an obsession. Their lives are centred around their dogs and they compete in performance events and conformation shows. They're generally known as preservation or show breeders but that doesn't fully describe their complete dedication. Many of them view it as a calling and an essential aspect of their lives.

Lots of people assume breeders do it for money. Serious show breeders don't do it for that reason. It's purely because they love the Pomeranian breed. The amount of money they spend on their dogs far outweighs the amount they would ever get back.

Puppy Buyer Etiquette

- Stop searching for a puppy. Instead, focus your search on looking for a breeder of the type of Pomeranian you most desire and develop a relationship with that breeder.
- Be prepared to wait for your puppy. He's not something that can be picked up off a supermarket shelf. If your breeder of choice won't be breeding in the foreseeable future, ask if they could recommend another breeder.
- Introduce yourself properly. Your initial email needs to be of sufficient length to clarify exactly what type of Pomeranian you're seeking and, most importantly, include brief specifics about the lifestyle you're able to provide for the puppy. Avoid emailing lots of pages of

information about yourself or the required puppy during the preliminary contact. Most dog breeders are busy people and receive numerous emails, so ensure your first email isn't so long-winded that the breeder simply skims through it. Never, ever send "one-liners" requesting the price. Dog breeders tend to be extremely fast with the delete key when receiving this style of email.

- Avoid getting yourself on multiple breeders' waiting lists. Please be sure to conclude an encounter with one dog breeder prior to commencing enquiries with another one. Just about every breeder knows almost every other breeder because it's an incredibly small, close-knit community. We all know each other. The information that a "Mrs. So and So" is phoning or emailing all Pomeranian breeders shopping for a blue female puppy quickly becomes known to all breeders.

- Don't expect to be able to select your puppy. Most Pomeranian litters tend to be small, one to three pups being the norm. Most reputable breeders spend countless hours planning litters with a view to retaining a puppy for show or later breeding purposes. Any puppies available from this litter usually will be the ones not required by the breeder. Show breeders understand their chosen breed perfectly and, therefore, are extremely well equipped to match buyers with a suitable puppy.

How to Avoid Scammers

There are more scams than ever before. It's partly due to the internet and dishonest people's ability to manipulate information. They only care about what they want, namely the money in your pocket. A common scam begins with Pomeranian puppies advertised for sale. The dogs are real but aren't the property of the scammers. Photos are stolen and sometimes they're photo-shopped to look genuine.

Put yourself in the shoes of somebody who wants to buy a dog to care for. Now imagine you don't have much money, but you want a good quality breed such as a Pomeranian. So, you start looking out for ways to buy that puppy.

You log onto your computer because that's the fastest way to search for a dog. Unfortunately, it's also an easy way for disreputable people to con you. After looking through some ads, you see the cutest white Pomeranian puppy. It sounds great and the photos are amazing. Your heart is beginning to flutter.

Then you see the price - $250. You rub your eyes and shake your head in disbelief. I just hit the jackpot; you think to yourself. A beautiful, white Pomeranian puppy at a bargain price. You should grab it before someone else does. The dog would sell for $2500 or more from a true Pomeranian show breeder. This should set off alarm bells immediately.

But wait, shouldn't you investigate further? This is where the scammers outwit you. They usually only use an email address. The photos you see are captivating, so you email and ask for more. They say they don't have any more and tell you they have other buyers interested to put pressure on you to act.

Naturally, you'll ask why the dog is so cheap. They may say someone in the family is very ill and they need to raise funds or some other equally lame excuse. Then they'll say they're from a different country, so you have to wire them the money because their country doesn't accept PayPal or bank transfers. Be smart. When purchasing a puppy via the internet, only pay by direct deposit into a bank account.

You're told they'll ship the dog to your local airport once they have the money. But if you're foolish enough to send the money, they'll just keep asking for more for different expenses such as taxes, customs issues, insurance and cargo fees. Suddenly it doesn't sound so cheap. And they're prepared to walk away at any point keeping whatever you've already sent.

Before sending any money, ask for a video of the Pomeranian. Ask for the phone number of their vet so you can confirm details of health, vaccinations, etc. It's likely they'll say they can't give you that information and then they'll say they have other interested buyers but want to give you first choice seeing you replied before anyone else.

Ask for information and photos of the puppy's parents. Google them to see if they exist. Reputable, registered, show breeders usually have a website to confirm they're legitimate. Check the details to see if it's the same information as what they have told you. If there's a contact number, ring it to see who answers and where they're from.

Never buy a dog online without doing lots of homework. Only buy through a reputable, registered, show breeder. Ask for references and as much proof of ownership as possible. Genuine sellers will also ask you lots of questions because they want to ensure the puppy goes to a good home.

A Pomeranian puppy is a gorgeous pet but don't risk being scammed because your eyes light up at the thought of owning such a beautiful animal. Be smart and check the facts.

It's better to be safe than sorry. Scam artists are very clever. Every single day they, very easily, get people to part with their money. Make sure that you're not gullible enough to be one of them. Remember the old sayings, *"you get what you pay for,"* and *"if it seems too good to be true, it probably isn't true at all."*

Finding Good Breeders

You need to find someone who's willing to answer questions and is passionate about their dogs. You need to build a relationship with the breeder, not just buy a dog.

A genuine breeder will tell you about any health issues that may be expected in the breed. Things like: what his temperament is like, what the pup's parents and grandparents look like, and much more. The breeder will also become a friend and mentor to help you through the ownership transition period and down the line if you have questions of any type. A true breeder has the dog's best interests at heart, not only now but for the rest of his canine life.

You'll discover that you can belong to a large extended family of owners of this breeder's puppies and you can also learn how your puppy's doggie relatives are doing in their new lives.

Questions you can ask to help determine good breeders:

Can I visit the puppies in person?

Good breeders may stipulate this, so they can see how well you react to the dogs and how the dogs react to you. They're always willing to answer any questions you may have. Unless the breeder has a sick dog, there's no legitimate reason to say "no" to a visit. If they say "no," and don't offer any excuse, hang up the phone and ring the next breeder on your list.

Is the breeder a Pomeranian specialist?

Breeders who only deal with a single breed, are truly serious about what they're doing. They focus on the dog breed they're most enthusiastic about.

Are there always puppies available for purchase?

If the answer is "yes," the puppy you consider buying won't have received enough care and love from the breeder. The puppy needs to live in a home, not in a garage or kennel. On the other hand, a breeder may have been doing this successfully for many years and may have sufficient facilities and help from other experienced people. The puppy may have been socialised and cared for sufficiently. If that's the case, then there shouldn't be a problem with consistent breeding.

Are the dogs and puppies registered with the kennel club?

If the answer is "no," you can hang up the phone immediately. Good breeders register all their dogs.

What health issues do you screen for?

If they claim Pomeranians have zero health worries, the breeder is simply not telling you the truth. If you're told there have been a few medical issues, let him keep talking. No dog line is 100% free from all possible health risks.

Are you and your dogs involved in agility trials, conformation shows or obedience trials?

Are the pups' parents titled? If they do participate at shows, that signifies a huge commitment to Pomeranians. Titles also signify a commitment and the dogs are almost always high quality.

Ask to see the dog's pedigree which should be available to view on request. If you can't, the breeder isn't reputable.

There are a few items of paperwork you'll require if you do buy a puppy.

These are:

- A complete medical history, the registration papers and information about the pedigree.
- You'll also get a contract, a warranty and written information about how to care for your new puppy.

It's impossible for a breeder to guarantee everything related to a puppy. However, you should get a health warranty covering the first few weeks and, if the dog has a hereditary disease, a partial refund may apply.

Your contract must have a section outlining the process if, for whatever reason, you can't keep your puppy. Good breeders will say the puppy may be returned, so he doesn't end up in a dog shelter or get moved from owner to owner. If your puppy is an adult before you decide to send him back, a breeder won't generally give you a refund as adult dogs are harder to place in good homes.

Are there any breeding requirements?

Certain breeders will ask you to breed your dog when ready and either offer a free stud or request a share of your litter. It's a very bad idea. You should never be forced to breed your dog. You decide whether to neuter or spay *your* dog.

Does the breeder stipulate that you must neuter or spay the dog?

The reason for this concern is the "big picture" in terms of the breed and your puppy in particular. The puppy you buy will usually be ideal as a companion but probably not suitable for show or breeding. Instead of de-sexing the dog, you may choose to have limited kennel club registration. If you breed the dog, her puppies won't be eligible for kennel club registration.

When can I take my new puppy home?

The answer to this question will tell you whether the breeder is good or bad. The breeders who are only in it for the money are more than happy to sell the puppy immediately, so they don't have to spend any more money taking care of the dog.

Are there any previous buyers I can chat with?

Genuine breeders always keep in regular contact with prior buyers. If the breeder has no details, don't buy from them. Good breeders are very proud of the puppies they sell, and they know that same pride is shared with the new owners.

The breeder may ask if he can arrange for previous buyers to contact you, but this is simply a privacy issue. However, end the discussion if no information is forthcoming.

While you're asking specific questions of the breeder, you'll soon realise that he's assessing you as a potential new owner too. If he's not doing this, it can be an indication that he's not genuine. If his interest mainly involves how fast he can get your money and offload the puppy, that's the time to look for a better breeder.

A good breeder is keen to find one owner who'll look after the puppy for the rest of his life.

To help him decide if you're a good fit, he'll ask you numerous questions such as:

- Have you had prior experience caring for dogs and other pets and, more specifically, toy dogs?
- What is your home like? Do you have a family? Will the puppy be kept inside or outside?
- Can you afford to care for a new puppy? He'll outline costs such as food, exercise, grooming, training, health care and general safety concerns.
- He may ask you to de-sex your dog.
- He may request that you wait a couple of months until the next litter is ready. This will help weed out the impulse buyers.

Asking how much a puppy will cost is a difficult question to broach. If you ask that first, the breeder may think you're merely chasing a bargain instead of offering a loving home to a puppy for the rest of his life.

However, talking for a long time or returning more than once may be a waste of time if you can't afford the puppy.

The ideal time to ask about the puppy's cost is after you have learned enough about the puppies that you want to visit and see them for yourself, and after you have told the breeder a bit about yourself and your family, but before the actual visit.

Otherwise, you may be wasting the valuable time of the busy breeder and your time as well I can't give you an exact price that you'll pay for a Pomeranian. However, here are a few governing factors:

Location: More affluent locations generally mean the prices will be higher.

The puppy's age: Younger puppies are more adorable than older puppies and adults. Therefore, they generally cost more. The exception is an older puppy that possesses show qualities.

Show quality and pedigree: Puppies born from parents who have titles or have had health tests to prove they're free of any hereditary ailments will be more expensive.

Where you buy the puppy from:

Pet shop prices are usually the highest. Then there are the genuine show breeders and, finally, backyard breeders. Lowest prices are usually applied to adults.

Buying a puppy from a show breeder is usually the best bargain you can get in the long run. This is because his parentage has been tested for any hereditary problems and is cared for better than any other type of seller.

A rescue dog will give you every bit of extra love he possibly can.

A breeder could easily have a waiting list. He may ask for a deposit to secure your place on the list and this is a normal thing to do. However, ensure you get a receipt that covers agreements such as health and gender of the puppy, and if no puppies are available for you within a set time period, that you'll be guaranteed a full refund.

You may choose a puppy that's too young to be taken home. So, a deposit secures the puppy for you until he's ready. Take some photos of that puppy and make sure you can identify him when you return for collection.

Breeder visits

Once you have reduced your list of breeders, it's time to go and visit them. Most breeders don't have large-scale facilities and generally aren't geared towards unplanned visitors. They may just have a small kennel or could be doing it all from their home.

It's unfair to just drop in on breeders unexpectedly. So, make some calls and book appointments at mutually suitable times.

Then you're sure to get the best attention, but don't drag things out as the breeder will be very busy. So, choose only a couple of the best breeders on your list and book to see them.

Breeders don't like you going from one kennel to another and the possibility of spreading potential germs and diseases unwittingly. Wash your hands prior to your visit and, if asked, remove your shoes when entering.

The visit

When you visit the breeder, you'll see how he cares for the puppies, whether the puppies and other dogs look happy and healthy and, more importantly, if you and the breeder get along.

Check to see if his facilities are clean and that there's sufficient room for all the dogs. Good breeders will have more than ample room and any cages and pens will be kept as clean as possible.

Do his puppies get to spend time outside and can they play in the grass? If a puppy is solely raised inside, he may get used to the hard floor as a place to go potty and this will make it harder to housetrain him.

Do puppies spend time socialising with people? If the puppies are housed in a separate kennel, check whether they do get to socialise inside the home.

Do all the dogs seem healthy and friendly? Do their coats look clean and groomed? Some will like you more than others, but none should be growling and snarling at you.

As for their looks and temperament, apply leniency to older dogs, and to the dam who may have had her coat fall out after whelping and feeding a litter. Ask to see photos of the dam before she gave birth. She may dislike you being near her puppies, but she'll be fine with the breeder being there.

Ask these questions when you're with the breeder:

Why was this litter bred?

Good breeders choose specific dogs to mate so the puppies have the ideal qualities of both parents and the breeder will be extremely excited when explaining this. He may point out the excellent health of the parents, their pleasant temperaments and that they conform to the breed standard. Be wary if the breeder does not want to answer your questions or answers them in a reluctant manner.

May I see photos of the parents and any other relatives?

This is a loaded question as the excited breeder will bring out a dozen photo albums and rave about the various dogs within the pages.

How well do the parents match the breed standard?

For example, can the breeder identify a fox-like expression on one dog or a skull that's slightly too domed and has bigger ears? Any breeder who claims the dogs are perfect or tells you to simply ignore the standard should be crossed off your list immediately.

When can I take my gorgeous ball of fur home?

No puppy should be sent home with you prior to reaching eight weeks of age. Like other toy dogs, Pomeranians are often not let go until they're 10-12 weeks of age.

Pomeranians with Small Children

Lots of families wonder if a Pomeranian is a good breed for a pet if they have children, particularly if they're young children. There are a few factors to consider, with size being at the top of the list.

A Pomeranian is a good size for families who want a pet that isn't intimidating. He can be picked up easily by the children. They can take him for walks without having him escape. Bigger dogs can be too strong for children to handle.

However, small dogs can be fragile. You'll need to teach your children how to pick him up correctly, how to walk him, how to play with him without being rough, and other tasks that may potentially hurt your dog if not done properly.

The Pom isn't a dog that you can wrestle with in the way you would with a bigger dog.

Because Poms are fragile, it's not recommended that you get a baby puppy as a pet if young children are part of your family. Instead, consider an older puppy over the age of six months. Show breeders sometimes have older puppies available for good homes.

Toddlers are too young to understand the respect demanded by a Pom. If a Pom's toy is snatched from his grasp by a toddler, he may snap or bite as a defence mechanism. If a toddler behaves roughly or pulls on the Pom's tail or fur, he may bite.

Noisy young children may scare Pomeranians because they're not used to being around children who move suddenly, make loud noises, and generally have raucous fun. If a Pom feels scared, he may run and hide somewhere and refuse to come out.

Young children must never go near a Pomeranian puppy without being supervised by an adult.

Small children should always be careful when they're with the Pomeranian. Avoid picking him up because if done the wrong way, he may be dropped, and the result could be a broken leg or more serious injuries. While Pomeranians are terrific as pets, don't get a puppy under 6 months as a pet if you have children under the age of ten years.

Are Pomeranians Good with Other Dogs?

Adding a second dog to the household can bring plenty of love and joy to the entire family as well as being a wonderful companion to your existing Pomeranian, especially while you're at work and there are no people home during the day. However, you may be concerned about whether your Pomeranian will put up with not being the only dog in the household.

Why don't some Pomeranians get along when introduced to other breeds?

There are dogs with such a friendly nature that they get along with any dog they meet and you don't need to make any effort. Sadly, Pomeranians can often be bossy, aggressive and dominant, meaning they won't always play with others without causing trouble.

Never think a tiny Pomeranian can't possibly be a problem because, despite being small, he doesn't know that. This means he'll have no hesitation in challenging a dog three times his size. Imagine him facing off against a Labrador or German Shepherd, just to give you an image. If it wasn't so serious, it would come across as being ludicrous. Inside a Pomeranian's small body, a powerful spirit is trapped, so a larger dog can certainly harm him, even if it's unintentional. This is one good reason for ensuring your Pom is close to you when you go walking.

The specific breeds that Pomeranians will best get along with is a big question and it depends a lot on two factors: His socialisation level and temperament.

However, providing your Pomeranian doesn't have deep problems with aggression, and you'll need bucketloads full of patience, you should (given enough time), be able to teach your Pomeranian to get on well with almost every dog.

Pomeranians for Apartment Residents and Working Owners

Apartment residents definitely need to select a smaller breed of dog. A small dog doesn't require tremendous amounts of space to run around and play and a Pomeranian is an ideal dog for such conditions.

Pomeranian owners who work away from the home during the day might even consider purchasing two Pomeranians. Leave numerous toys around and a radio on and your Pomeranians will certainly be content to keep themselves entertained until you return home.

Your Pomeranian puppies will very quickly adjust to the routine of you coming and going to work. If possible, bring a puppy home while you're on holidays or on a long weekend, so your puppy has time to adjust to his new surroundings while you're at home during the day.

Two Puppies or One?

- Dog owners occasionally consider purchasing a playmate for their puppy. Buying two puppies together isn't recommended for many reasons:
- Bringing two puppies home from the same litter or an additional puppy from a different litter will most likely create relationship and bonding problems if you keep the two puppies together constantly. This situation occurs basically because they're the same species, so they'll form a powerful bond with each other instead of with their human family.
- The puppies may also teach each other their own particular skills and we know puppies often possess skills we wouldn't want taught. Rearing two puppies is incredibly time-intensive and takes lots of effort and hard work to do successfully.
- Puppies need to be separated 99% of the time. Double the time is required with two puppies because each

puppy should be trained, socialised and loved separately. You need to develop a close relationship with each puppy.

- It's extremely difficult, and very challenging, to train puppies alongside each other because the puppies will look to each other for direction. What happens is one puppy acquires assurance from the much more self-assured puppy.
- An additional difficulty may occur if you need to take one dog to the vet. The other dog will raise hell because he's not going with his best friend. You'll quickly give in instead of allowing the screamer to annoy the neighbours.
- Don't purchase a second puppy as a puppy sitter for the first dog. Wait until he's at least eight months old and you have the training under control

Gender-Specific Pomeranian Personalities

For many prospective Pomeranian owners, choosing a puppy involves deciding upon male versus a female. Although there's no right or wrong decision, it can be important, depending upon your household, your abilities, your goals and needs.

Female Pomeranians – pros and cons:

Female Pomeranians are expected to exemplify the "sweet" reputation befitting their breed; after all, how could they be otherwise? In fact, they're said to be typically very attentive to their owners, generally more obedient than their male counterparts, and reportedly easier to housetrain than male Pomeranians.

This, alas, is a myth. The female Pomeranian is no shy, wilting flower. Most rule their households, dominantly showing all "who's boss" over their territory. This goes for both human and animal companions. They can be standoffish and stubborn, especially when they need their "alone time."

With this being the case, never assume that training a female

Pomeranian is difficult. They love to get what they want, and if they realise the fastest way to get to their favourite resting spot is through compliance, so be it! They're extremely resourceful little divas and will do their owner's bidding to get what they want.

Ironically, most kennel fights occur between female Poms; thus, the term "bitch" is sometimes used as a double-entendre by exasperated female Pomeranian owners.

Male Pomeranians – pros and cons:

Despite their small size, male Poms can often exhibit machismo echoing their much larger dog cousins. However, unlike females, they're even-tempered, desiring nothing more than to snuggle and play with their human family.

Loyal to the core, male Pomeranians attach themselves quickly and forever. This includes other pets, even felines. They desire to have fun and play games their whole lives.

Training a male Pom must include plenty of praise and more than a few treats. His stomach and heart are the best ways to ensure he follows expectations when it comes to obedience and potty training. Without motivators of this sort, the male Pomeranian can become distracted, acting more like a naughty schoolboy than a well-behaved scholar.

Male Pomeranians who have been neutered don't tend to engage in secondary sexual behaviours (e.g., humping or marking). Typically, they should be de-sexed at approximately 6 months of age. Fees for neutering will vary between veterinarians but are about half the cost of spaying female Pomeranians.

How Much Does Age Influence Your Choice of a Dog?

How important is his age when you first claim new ownership and take him home to meet your human family? If you get a Pomeranian puppy who's at least eight weeks of age, it's actually not as important as you might think. Here are a few of the pros and cons of puppies versus adult Poms. Regardless of what you read, don't let age be the sole factor in any decision you make.

The positives and negatives of bringing an older dog home

When it comes to getting a new dog, most people immediately think of puppies, but adults can be just as appealing in their own ways. If you don't work from home, if you have children, or if your home is always hectic, an adult may fit into the environment more easily than a new puppy.

A lot of breeders have adults available because they used to be show dogs that were not quite successful enough or may be retired after being breeding dogs. Either way, they will quickly make you fall in love with them. Adults are also available from rescue groups.

If you select an adult dog instead of a puppy, you'll get what you see. You won't really know what sort of personality he has because he may start off being a bit shy and this is only natural when he's around strangers. However, it's nothing to be alarmed about, unless he growls or hides all the time.

Your new adult Pomeranian will already have some common sense (more than any puppy could have) and he'll understand enough to be curious about why you're keen on him. Will he accept a treat if you offer it? If so, then he's not upset. If he still seems a bit uneasy, ask the breeder if you can all go to a place that's regarded as neutral territory. It's common for dogs to be apprehensive if a stranger comes into their home.

Here are a few other benefits gained by loving an adult Pomeranian:

Affection:

Some new owners worry that a new adult pet won't form as strong a bond as a puppy will. However, don't be concerned. Pomeranians create strong bonds with their owners almost immediately. Then he'll feel like you have been his owner for his whole life. If your new dog is either aggressive or shy, he'll need a very experienced owner. You're not helping the dog or yourself by attempting a challenge you simply can't handle.

Behaviour:

Adult Poms have already been housetrained so you only need to get them used to your home and the ways they can get in and out when necessary. How well they're trained will depend on their previous owner. If you found your new pet living in a kennel, he's probably more disciplined than if he was allowed to run rampant through somebody's house, without any control.

He's well past the "chew everything and pull it apart" stage, although he may still occasionally destroy a toy. You don't need to feed your new adult dog every couple of hours, take him outside every few minutes so he can go potty and, if you're lucky, he may already know some tricks.

It's possible for an older dog to have developed bad habits such as: ignoring you when you call him, barking at shadows, and doing his business wherever he feels like. He may have come from a puppy mill where he was badly treated and may not have been trained to do anything. Before you take ownership of any adult dog, it's critical that you find out as much about his past as possible. You shouldn't take a dog home unless you're comfortable doing so because it's unfair to both you and the dog in question.

Health:

Is he healthy? As a dog ages, he's more likely to have some health problems. Get a vet to thoroughly examine him. If his health is a concern, the vet can most likely tell you if the problems will get worse.

Dealing with the loss of a pet:

You may have lost a pet, whether suddenly or after a long illness. Your friends and family will be divided on the topic of whether to replace the dog.

You'll never replace a pet because no two dogs are alike. Even if a new Pomeranian is the same age, lineage, gender and colour, every dog is unique.

- It's unfair if you keep comparing any new dog to a former pet. Your newest pet will never replace the hole that's left in your heart.
- If you can regard a new pet on his own merits and not as a replacement for your previous pet, then he'll help you fall in love with him in totally different ways. He'll create new memories to add to previous ones, not replace them.
- Once you're in the ideal mindset to choose a new Pomeranian, he'll become a healthy distraction that will help you during the grieving process.
- There's no better way to honour a family pet than to give your love to a new one.

What Type of Pomeranian Do You Want?

A pet Pom generally has at least one trait that stops him from being a suitable show dog. He may have minor issues such as larger ears or he's slightly larger than desired for show purposes. He may possess major problems for show purposes including not having much of a coat. One common issue in male Poms is when one or both gonads don't fully descend.

There's nothing wrong with the health of a pet-quality Pomeranian. He'll still have a great temperament. Acting as a companion or pet is regarded as the most significant task a Pom can fulfil, so owners will regard this type of dog as being of the highest quality.

The best breeders will generally sell puppies that are pet quality with the proviso that they are desexed, or they're sold with a limited registration. If your Pom turns out to be a higher quality dog, the breeder can move the limited registration to the main register. Reversing a desexing procedure can't happen but such dogs can still compete in most forms of competition, except for regular conformation shows.

Show quality

Show quality dogs need to be of excellent breed type and conformation with an ideal temperament. You'll also pay a lot more money for a show dog.

It's essential to note that breeders who don't show their own dogs generally won't produce show winning dogs. The dog's pedigree needs to contain many champions.

Expect to wait a long time for a show dog, compared to a pet puppy. If you definitely want a good quality show puppy, you probably should wait and find an older puppy. The odds are greatly increased of obtaining a winner if you do wait for an older puppy.

Pomeranians only have small litters (1-4 puppies at any one time) and often only a few of these puppies are top show quality.

If you're sure a show-quality dog is what you desire, think of these points:

As puppy develops, flaws may become apparent. He may keep growing and end up too big or he may develop coat issues. No dog is 100% perfect. Dog shows can be a lot of fun, but they only represent a tiny amount of the overall time spent with your dog. Never let it upset you. Try to compete in one of the other activities more suited to your Pomeranian.

Always be respectful of the breeder. If you do buy a good show dog, aim to compete in shows. Show breeders put in a huge amount of time and effort into producing show puppies. Their reward is the pride they feel when one of their puppies wins show awards.

You'll need to work hard to earn the respect and trust of a breeder. If you're a novice at showing dogs, breeders may feel unsure whether to trust a top-notch puppy to a newcomer. One method to gain their trust is to win an obedience title with a different dog. Maybe through the purchase of a pet dog before proceeding to obtain a show dog.

Breeding quality

Breeding-quality dogs come from the highest standard bloodlines. Occasionally they may have a minor fault that stops them from being the best show dogs (for example, being over-sized or having a curly tail).

However, these dogs have other merits that counteract the negatives.

No reputable breeder will sell you a Pomeranian of breeding quality if this is your first time owning a dog. You're obliged to prove your skills and knowledge with your first Pomeranian. A good breeder will not want you to merely breed his puppy with any dog you may have, regardless of quality.

Checking out pedigrees

Most pedigrees will only list information that dates back three or four generations. When you view the official document itself, you can read the pedigree backwards from one generation to the previous and so on.

Rescuing Pomeranians who have been abandoned

It's a sad fact that lots of Pomeranians don't have a loving family and a secure home environment. The most common reason is that the right dog is living in the wrong home. Sometimes an owner can't handle a lot of barking, gets tired of caring for a pet, or has a major life change that forces him to abandon his dog. Just like other dogs, Pomeranians can become homeless.

Regardless of whether the home is a loving one or not, Poms who have been rescued generally feel frightened, confused and anxious. They may try to cling to their new families or foster owners in fear of losing the people who recently rescued them.

However, with time, training, love and stability, the Pomeranian slowly gets used to the new environment and he becomes an indispensable, exceptional pet.

If you rescue a Pomeranian, it will have a wonderful effect on your overall life.

If you can't take home a rescue dog yourself, you can help the rescue people. Those groups always need cash, volunteers and supplies so they can groom, house, feed, bathe, train and transport the animals.

One of the biggest services the staff and volunteers offer is a temporary home, often called fostering, until a permanent home is found for each and every animal.

Part 3 – New Puppy Care

Bringing Puppy Home

That big day has arrived at last. You've puppy-proofed your home and his basket overflows with all the necessities. You're now ready, willing and able to bring your new addition into your home.

But, wait. Not yet! There are a few extra things to prepare before the big day comes. Find an ideal way to transport him from the breeder's home to yours. You must also devise a plan to introduce your new dog to his new home, and his human and animal family members (depending on who and what you have).

Of course, there's going to be plenty of excitement that you'll need to control. Think about everything and see it through the eyes of your little Pomeranian. He may feel anxious because he's leaving his mother and other members of his family (the only ones he has lived with since he was born). You plan everything because you want him to experience a happy day instead of a stressful, terrifying ordeal.

My suggestions will help you make this a memorable day for all the right reasons, instead of the wrong ones. I'll give you expert suggestions to help him feel safe and secure as he travels to your home on that first day. Meeting all the strange canines and humans, in the first few hours, is enjoyable but can be very taxing for your pup. Putting his head to rest, in his first night in these new surroundings, will help keep him calm so he'll get some good quality sleep.

Making sure puppy's first trip is a safe one

After you have chosen that special Pom puppy, it's planning time. Regardless of whether it's a local trip or you have to travel interstate, you must plan the collection time with the breeder.

Work out the collection time

It's best to arrive at the breeder's home as early as possible because you'll be there for a while and you don't want to still be driving when it's time for the puppy to sleep. The breeder will have a lot of information for you to digest (grooming, feeding, early training, etc.), and you need to understand everything. Ask the breeder questions if you don't understand something.

You may be given so much information that it becomes overwhelming and you get frazzled. It's a shame there's not a Pomeranian book that contains everything a new owner needs to know...hang on, there is!!! You're reading it. This book will become a training manual for you to follow so you'll be fine. Don't worry. It's all here in this "Pomeranian Owner's Handbook."

Make sure you confirm the time you'll arrive, so the breeder doesn't feed your new puppy just before you get there. The right timing can help prevent the risk of the puppy feeling car sick or having nervous diarrhoea.

If you work all week, plan to collect your new Pom either on Friday or just before you plan to have a holiday. This will enable you to spend a lot of quality time with him and you'll be able to take naps whenever he does. Hopefully, you won't be suffering from sleep deprivation on Monday morning when you return to work.

Things to take

Think you're ready to get in the car and head to the breeder's place? Wrong! With a little forethought, you can prevent your car from looking and smelling very unpleasant by taking some things with you. Your new Pom probably won't have spent much time in a car.

Necessities for the road trip

Another adult. Having somebody with you will help if your puppy doesn't settle down in the car and it's good to have company, especially if it's a long drive.

Carrier. You wouldn't take a newborn baby home cradling the baby in your arms. The same applies with new puppies. The trip's length doesn't matter; you should have a dog carrier with a blanket or two on the bottom. Also, take some spare towels in case there are any accidents.

Cleaning supplies. Paper towels and rinse-free shampoo will help if he has an accident.

Drinking water. Take a bottle of water or one that's empty but can be filled from a tap at the breeder's home. Some dogs get upset stomachs if the water changes and you don't need that happening in the car.

Money. While you're busy thinking about the needs of your new puppy, you must also have the money to buy him, whether it's a personal cheque (if the breeder approves it) ,or a bank cheque or cash.

Toys. Make sure you have a stuffed animal (to cuddle) or a chewable toy to keep him out of mischief. If it's a long trip, consider having more things to keep him amused.

Food. If your trip is more than a couple of hours, make sure you have some of the exact same food he's used to eating. Hypoglycaemia (low blood sugar) is a common worry in small animals, so never ignore a mealtime simply because you're driving.

Find out from the breeder what he feeds your new dog and either buy some yourself or ask him if you can buy a few days' worth to keep him going. Make sure your new Pom's first real meal is ready for him when you get home. Even if it's a short trip, it's likely that the breeder won't have fed the puppy before the trip to your home.

NOTE: Even if you believe you have the ideal food for your new dog, you should give him the exact same food he's used to eating for a while. He has enough changes in his life without altering what he eats as well. A new choice of food may cause an upset tummy as well as your training plans. If you wish to change his food, do it slowly to avoid tummy upsets.

Extra-small harness and leash. Be sure you have a secure harness and leash in case you need to take him outside. You certainly don't want him to escape, cross a busy road, hide under a parked car, disappear down a drain, or get into any other type of dog mischief you could imagine.

Warning: He probably has no idea how to walk when he's attached to a leash, so don't think he'll do a lot of walking or relieving himself.

You may have to travel, and stay somewhere near the breeder's home overnight, so bring plastic sheeting and an exercise pen.

It's possible the puppy you chose a few weeks ago doesn't resemble the one the breeder is giving you today. If you think this is the case, speak up. Genuine breeders would never swap puppies so, providing the breeder is trustworthy, this won't happen. The odds are high that he has simply altered as he has grown.

Flying to meet you

If your dog is being transported by plane, make sure you allow plenty of time to get to the airport and locate where he'll be. For example, if he's classified as air freight, he may end up in the air freight office, away from the main terminal.

If he arrives at the baggage area, ensure you're there to collect him with ample time to spare. You must have proper identification in case it's needed. He'll most likely have made a mess in the shipping crate so have plenty of towels and cleaning supplies available.

Managing a Happy Homecoming

When you arrive home, a new emotional thought hits you - today is the first day of the rest of your life and it will be very different from what it was. You now have a new, small family member controlling your every move and relying heavily on you, especially in the beginning. Your home will feel like it has been invaded by a tiny ball of Pomeranian fluff and, for every negative that may occur, you'll experience many wondrous pleasures with your Pom.

Did you notice the words small and tiny? Despite the temptation, you can't have a crowded, noisy welcoming party with neighbours and friends. Think about it and consider the view from your puppy's "close to the ground" perspective. Your new addition to the family is small (whether puppy or adult) and you have driven him home in your big car, to a place where *everything is unfamiliar*, including your large home itself, other big members of the family and, possibly, other animals of varying sizes, shapes and species.

Your fur-ball will need time to learn who the people really are, and to find a way to be brave in this new world he has entered. He can't deal with lots of noisy people, hands stretching out, and noses sniffing. On his first day and night, let him get used to you and the rest of the new family.

Investigating his new home

The first task you have is to familiarise your new Pom with his surroundings. Try and minimise distractions by other pets and people as much as possible so he can adjust to the normal smells and sights in his new environment.

Consider the following suggestions:

- Keep your children calm. They'll naturally be ecstatic to see your new Pom but either they stay quiet and watch or keep them in a different room.
- Secure any other pets. Make sure they're outside if possible or, if not, then keep them in a different room.
- Take him outside to the grassy area. Show him the spot

you have chosen to be his "bathroom." He most likely won't use it straight away but, over time, you'll train him to get used to going there.

- Once he has checked out his new potty area, take him into the home and let him play in the pre-chosen, pom-friendly space.
- Introduce your puppy to the areas he'll find most important: namely his sleeping and eating spaces. Put food in his bowl to put the idea in his head.
- He will be happy to finally be out of the crate, so he won't want to get back in it for quite a while.
- This new world might seem a bit scary, but he'll also want to explore. Don't even consider making him feel overwhelmed with a full house tour, even if it's only a one-bedroom unit. He has plenty of time to investigate his surroundings.
- Keep him company as he wanders around. He may never have been let loose in an apartment before, so it's highly likely he may get into mischief.
- Don't become distraught if he has an accident. Take him to his "bathroom" a few times as he wanders around.

Hints for "Pom-Proofing" Your House

A Pomeranian puppy is coming to your house. This means it's time to Pomeranian-proof your home. Precautionary measures should always be taken when bringing home any puppy. Otherwise, the experience is likely to be exasperating for everyone involved.

Helpful hints to keep your puppy safe from harm in your home:

Puppies love to chew (they go through a teething stage, just as human babies do), so pick up anything that looks "chewable." As silly as it sounds, it might be wise to crawl on your hands and knees through every room in the house. You'll gain the "dogs-eye" perspective. Trust me, it's different from yours.

You'll likely find plenty of things your Pomeranian would have discovered because his sightlines are much lower than yours.

Common tasks to carry out before bringing home your Pomeranian include:

- Removing children's toys, string, pillows, remote controls, books, papers, shoes, socks, electrical cords, purses and briefcases.
- "People food" should be removed from your Pomeranian's reach.
- Any chemicals must be kept away from a Pomeranian's inquisitive nose and mouth. Most household cleaners, anti-freeze and rat and snail baits are extremely dangerous to puppies.
- Keeping cupboards, pantries and closets shut when not in use.
- Stowing away garbage cans and wastebaskets so Pomeranians can't search through them for goodies.
- Checking all rooms often. People can become lax in their security, which could be hazardous for a Pomeranian.
- Closing doors to all areas of the house you don't want your dog to roam through without you present.
- Keeping any cat litter pans away from your puppy and up off the floor.

Check to see if your indoor/outdoor plants and flowers might be poisonous to dogs. Toxic plants include: Azalea, Belladonna, Bird of Paradise, Bulbs, Calla Lily, Cardinal Flower, Castor bean, Chinaberry tree, Daphne, Dumb Cane, Dutchman's breeches, Elephant ear, Hydrangea, Jack-in-the-pulpit, Jasmine, Jimsonweed, Larkspur, Laurel, Lily of the Valley, Mescal bean, Mushrooms, Nightshade, Philodendron, Poinsettia, Prunus species, Tobacco, Yellow jasmine and Yews.

Introducing a New Puppy to Your Household

As with any living creature, it's critical that your household is prepared for the Pomeranian's arrival. Your home must have the necessary supplies and puppy-proofing to ensure ease of transition for humans and animals alike.

Supplies to purchase in advance of your new puppy's arrival:

- Crate.
- Exercise pen.
- Bed and bedding.
- Toys.
- Extra-small harness.
- Water bowls and food dishes.
- Puppy pads, newspapers or a puppy potty.
- Puppy food and bottled water.
- Brush, comb and slicker brush.

The following are some tips and tricks to help you and your Pomeranian puppy make the new home transition safe and easy.

When you arrive home with your new puppy, he will be nervous, being in a new environment, away from his mother and littermates. During these first few days, stress can influence some Pomeranian pups considerably. Stress could make your puppy susceptible to hypoglycaemia.

Ask your breeder for some of the food he has been feeding the puppy or purchase the exact same brand of puppy food. Don't make any changes to his diet for at least a week and then gradually make changes to his diet.

The stress of leaving the puppy's mother and siblings will be traumatic for the Pomeranian puppy, without the added stress of a major dietary change.

Changes to the water your puppy is drinking can also upset a Pomeranian's tummy. Using bottled water for your Pom puppy is recommended. Too much excitement can cause exhaustion in a young Pomeranian. Resist the temptation to show off your new puppy to friends.

Your puppy is very much like a baby. What do babies spend most of the day doing? The answer is sleeping. Please ensure your new Pomeranian puppy gets adequate sleep. Young puppies need to sleep a lot.

Tips for Helping Your Pom Settle in On Night One

The first day and night in his new home can be very unsettling for a puppy. He'll meet other family members and your other pets, and must adjust to life in a brand-new environment. He'll have had a couple of meals, so he'll feel confident that he'll be regularly fed.

When it comes to bedtime, he'll most likely be too excited or nervous to sleep now that he's in your home. There are lots of ways you can make him more comfortable at the beginning of his new life with you and your family.

Set a specific time and routine for putting him to bed from the first night.

These tips will make that task easier to manage:

- Puppy should have his final meal 30 minutes prior to bedtime. For older dogs, this should be a snack instead of a meal.
- Ten minutes before bedtime, take him outside for a toilet break to avoid problems during the night.
- Finally, you should take him to where his bed is set up and ensure he's comfortable and has everything he needs.
- Go to bed yourself, or at least try.
- If your Pom is anxious because he's in a new home and can't sleep, read further to learn what to do for him.
- If he wakes up during the night, take him out to the bathroom again. This isn't play time so don't make it one. Otherwise, he'll want to play every night. Set your alarm clock so you decide when to take him to the bathroom instead of letting him dictate terms.
- This may occur a few times a night, at first, but should eventually settle down.

Reducing first night anxiety

At the end of the day, put your new puppy in his crate and wish him goodnight. Then turn off the lights and he'll be fine sleeping all night without any noise. This may be the case but it's common for pom puppies to feel lonely and afraid. So, he'll do what most puppies would do and that's cry and scream until he gets some attention from you. He wants to be reunited with his previous family.

It's impossible for you to imagine how your new Pom feels. He's dealing with that abrupt separation from his home and family; the two factors that have kept him secure for his whole life until that point.

Breeders should separate puppies for short periods before being sent to a new home. This helps reduce the feelings of abandonment your puppy may experience when he's uprooted and given to new owners.

Older poms generally also feel nervous when moved to a new home. Put yourself in your dog's shoes. If you were suddenly forced to move to a different place with new people, you'll also feel anxious and stressed.

These tips will help settle separation anxiety

Create a crate or space your new puppy can call his home. Include things he likes such as his toys, a blanket, cushion, water, snacks and food, so he'll feel more comfortable.

During the night, don't always come running whenever your Pom puppy makes any sound. If you do, he'll learn how to get you to come and you'll end up coming and going frequently. Don't ignore him either. That will make him feel more isolated and may contribute to feelings of anxiety.

This certainly doesn't mean you should come running at the slightest sound. It means you attend to his primary needs, comfort him and then place him back in his crate. This is similar behaviour to the way you treat a new human baby.

If your puppy's crate or space is at the other end of your house, it's natural that he'll feel alone and lonely during the night while everybody is asleep.

In the early stages of getting him settled into your home, you may need to create a temporary bed in your bedroom for a few nights, until he gets comfortable and calms down at night.

However, there's no reason to allow the puppy to sleep in (or on) your bed. It's unwise due to safety concerns (among other things).

Introducing a New Puppy to Other Pets

You and your family may be thinking about getting a new addition to the household in the form of a puppy. However, you need to really think it through before making any decisions. Your current pets (regardless of whether they're cats, dogs or both) won't be happy when you first bring that puppy home.

A young puppy will need lots of attention because he's a stranger to you and your human and animal family. A puppy can really annoy other pets because he'll do whatever he wants, and that includes stealing their toys, going potty wherever he desires, and making a general nuisance of himself.

It can take six months, or even longer in some cases, to train your puppy properly as well as getting him used to your other pets and the way the household is run.

Tips on easing tension

It's wise to make a confined area for your puppy. If it's currently the area where you feed your pets, change the feeding area so it's away from the puppy and is in a quiet place. This needs to be done a week prior to bringing puppy home so your pets get used to the change.

The same thing applies with caged pets and litter boxes. By doing this planning, you'll help eliminate potentially negative thoughts about this new family addition.

Your pets need to be fussed over more than normal so they don't feel as though you're ignoring them.

Here are a few tips to help you achieve this:

- You have to feed your puppy three times daily, so do the same with your other pets and split their meals so they're not getting more than usual.
- Feed your existing pets before your puppy.

- You should play with, give treats to, and generally respect, your current animals so they don't feel ignored because of the "intruder."
- If your pet is a dog, allow him to enter/exit rooms first.
- If your current pet comes to you while you're attending to the puppy, turn around and give him immediate attention, ignoring puppy while doing so.
- Never allow puppy to attempt to grab your attention if you're busy with other pets.

How to introduce your puppy to older dogs

If you have had one or more dogs for a few years, they'll feel territorial and won't like having to share your home with this little "intruder." At first, it's best to have your dogs and the puppy in separate neutral spaces outside and then introduce them slowly.

You should remain calm and your current pet needs to be the main focus of your affection. Follow these tips:

- Choose the time for the introduction when your current pet is relaxed and calm.
- You really need two people. You have your dog on a leash. Somebody else has the puppy on a leash. That's how you keep control of the situation.
- Give your dog plenty of treats as you solely focus on him.
- After you feel your dog will accept this new family member, ask the other person to carry puppy into your home.
- If you're worried about how your dog will react once both he and the puppy are inside your home, put the puppy in his playpen or crate. Give your dog 100% of your attention and pretend puppy isn't even there.
- Remain calm while the dog and puppy check each other out, and you stay focused on your dog. If interactions start getting rough, your dog will use body language to tell puppy who's boss. Watch as it happens, while remaining cool and ever vigilant.
- Another way of doing it is to start outside again and allow

the dog and the puppy to "say hello." Then indicate to your dog that he can lead puppy into your home.

- If you're seriously worried that your dog may cause harm to the puppy, you can muzzle him or grip his leash tightly, so you can pull him back if necessary.

Cats need to be introduced too

Most cats prefer not to have puppies in the same house. If your cat has a lot of confidence, he'll most likely wait patiently until the puppy gets near enough, so he can give the puppy a good slap across the snout. Don't over-react but ensure your cat does not harm puppy. Stay relaxed or you can make your pets feel stressed.

Put the puppy in his crate and have a toy or two in there for him to play with. Let your cat do what he wants. Never force a cat and puppy to be friends. In time, they'll either become great friends or the cat will simply stay out of reach.

Photo by Shadow's Farm Photography

Caring for Your New Pomeranian

A backyard is a great place for an adult Pomeranian to romp and exercise, but you'll need to ensure the yard is secure before leaving your puppy to his own devices. Remember that Pomeranians are small and very clever. He could easily slip through a hole in a fence or small space in a wall. Additionally, be aware that if your Pomeranian can escape through a nook or cranny, it means other animals can enter via those nooks and crannies.

Though you may have a lovely outdoor spot for your Pomeranian to play in, you should always keep this breed in the home. They're not meant to live in outdoor kennels. Besides, they can become very lonely if they're without their human companions! Plan a comfy place for your new puppy to sleep indoors. If your intention is to have an outdoor dog, you should purchase a different breed.

A bed for your Pomeranian should include bedding that can be removed and washed when needed. The bed can be placed anywhere in the house that's comfortable; just make certain that your puppy begins sleeping there from the first night you bring him home. This provides consistency, a must for any dog training.

Pomeranians who are left alone for hours at a time can become very bored and, as a result, may make their own fun. If your Pomeranian is forced to make his own entertainment, tissues and toilet paper could be at the receiving end of much annihilation. Consequently, you need to have playthings for your Pomeranian.

Toys are a Pomeranian's joy, but it's critical to buy only those items that won't be choking hazards. Be careful of toys that have plastic pieces like eyes, that could be easily torn off and swallowed by your Pomeranian. Don't buy a toy that can be easily (or quickly) torn and ripped apart.

Walks are always fun with a Pomeranian. Collars are not the best choice. A harness is a much safer, more comfortable option. Purchase a good quality harness and leash so you can both get your daily workouts as safely as possible.

Food and water bowls need to be a small and shallow size. Choose only those made from a non-plastic material and clean them daily. Fresh, clean water should be available night and day.

You'll need to buy a pet carrier if you don't already own one. This will ensure security for you both when travelling is necessary (such as to the veterinarian or for any car journeys).

One of the primary things a brand-new owner needs to learn about a Pomeranian is the fact that, in contrast to all other dog breeds, it's essential to always stroke their hair upwards. In simple terms, in the reverse direction to which the hair grows. Furthermore, the hair should always be brushed in the reverse direction. Doing this may feel unusual to start with but, after a very short time, you'll be doing this totally naturally.

Pomeranians have always been brushed and patted in the reverse direction. This practice is believed to prevent the coat becoming flat, as well as making the dog's coat appear more voluminous.

It's essential to learn to pick up a Pomeranian correctly. Your pet should never be picked up by the scruff of the neck, or by the neck itself. Owners who hold Pomeranian puppies by wrongly inserting a thumb beneath the Pomeranian's elbow will certainly in a short period stretch the ligaments of the shoulder and your Pomeranian will become "out at the elbow." Gently pick your puppy up by wrapping both hands around his upper body and legs, supporting his hindquarters and holding his front legs close to his body.

Crates and Exercise Pens for Your Pomeranian

Given their appearance, it may not be obvious that Pomeranians, like all canines, are descended from wolves. In the wolf "family," the den is a clean, safe place. It's snug, comfortable and must be kept free from faeces.

Your house is most likely too big to be considered a den. However, you can create the essence of a den by investing in a crate or exercise pen that can be placed somewhere in your residence.

Crates and exercise pens have a wide variety of uses:

As a housetraining tool

Your Pomeranian won't urinate or defecate in the crate. An exercise pen can have one area set up as a potty area with either a litter tray, potty pads or newspaper.

As a playpen

Playpens are useful for pups when they're home alone. A Pomeranian can be placed in the exercise pen whenever you must leave the house.

As a discipline tool

If your pet has an accident or has decided to make a toy out of your new chair, you may want to put him or her in the crate or exercise pen for a "time out."

As a sanctuary

At times your Pomeranian will enjoy having his own space. This isn't to say that you should allow the crate to become a prison cell. After your Pomeranian has been housebroken, you should leave the apparatus open during daytime hours. Don't be surprised if your Pom chooses to nap there or just "hang out" occasionally.

As your puppy grows to adulthood, you'll probably find yourself using the crate or exercise pen less and less. Still, don't be tempted to do away with it. As long as you don't use it as a place to confine your dog for long periods of time, there's nothing wrong with having it in place, should your Pomeranian need it. Over-use can create serious behavioural problems. Think of the crate as your child's crib, a safe place to sleep but not a place for your puppy to grow up in or be punished for long periods of time.

A word about crates

For the uninitiated, crating a pet often sounds barbaric. How could they possibly put their sweet, darling Pomeranian into a "cage?" Rest assured that no guilt needs to be experienced by owners who crate their dogs. What would seem like "confinement" to humans isn't seen that way by dogs. A dog views his crate as his fortress of solitude, not as a jail.

Tips on Your Pom's First Vet Check-Up

As soon as you get your new Pomeranian puppy home, you should ring and book a complete check-up with the vet. The breeder's contract may even include a specified period in which this needs to be done.

The initial appointment needs to be successful

The initial visit to the vet carries more importance than any further visits. Your puppy needs to realise the vet visits can be fun. To ensure this happens, follow a few tips. Take all the records from the breeder when you go to the vet. Also, provide a stool sample from your puppy so the vet can check for the presence of parasites.

Place your puppy in a small crate or travel bag during the trip. While sitting in the waiting room, ensure he's as close to you as possible and make sure he doesn't bark at other animals. Other owners will appreciate this as they may have sick pets.

Have some of his favourite treats for the vet to use to make him comfortable during the exam. It's wise to avoid cavity searches and needles during the first visit unless crucial. If injections are required, ask the vet to use the smallest gauge needle possible so the puppy barely feels it.

During this visit, the vet will give you advice regarding common problems for puppies and treatment options. He'll also want to talk to you about the puppy's schedule for vaccinations.

In this first exam, the vet will do a number of things to test your puppy's health:

- He'll listen to your pet's heart to ensure there aren't any unusual issues.
- Your puppy will be weighed.
- His gums and teeth will be thoroughly checked.
- His eyelids and eyes will also be checked.
- Knees might be checked to see if there are any signs of patellar luxation.
- Some vaccinations may already be due, and he'll administer them as gently as possible. The time frame will vary depending on the age of your puppy.

Before you leave his clinic, ask all the questions you may have and make the next appointment for further vaccinations.

If your puppy is very nervous, you can visit the clinic sometimes just to sit there and get him used to the waiting room. If he has some visits where nothing "bad" occurs, he'll grow more comfortable with the vet and other staff. They'll always appreciate this extra attention as it makes their job much easier for all future visits.

If you buy an adult Pomeranian, he still needs a check-up within a few days. The vet will check him out thoroughly, in much the same way as he would for a puppy, but will most likely also do a heartworm check.

Establishing Rules of the House

One of the most enjoyable aspects of welcoming a Pomeranian into your family is that you can go overboard in spoiling him. You may believe Pomeranians can't be overindulged. However, this notion isn't quite accurate. You don't want that little toothy fur ball to scare friends away and you certainly don't need your household and life to be ruled by that cute little Pom.

Training your Pomeranian to stay off the furniture

Many Pomeranian owners allow their puppies to get up on the furniture, often with muddy paws, where they leave fur everywhere and chew cushions. If you refuse to let your four-legged friend climb up on your furniture, you can try these steps:

Have furniture that's too tall for your puppy to jump on. Teach your Pom that he can't be on the furniture at all. It's easy to start letting him jump on the furniture when he gets older.

However, it's much harder to ban your dog after you have already set a bad precedent. If your Pom puppy gets on the furniture without your permission, you can't tell him off because you didn't train him properly. Instead, you can find a better spot for him to enjoy. It needs to be more appealing than the sofa if that's possible.

A deluxe-style dog bed would be ideal, if it also has a great view of what's going on. Train him to head for that spot and give him a treat if he goes and sits in his bed without being told to do so. As he moves towards his dog bed, say the cue "place" and once he has settled there, produce his treat.

Naming your Pomeranian

A very important aspect of the new relationship is choosing a name for your Pomeranian puppy. The earlier your Pomeranian has his very own name, the better. Discuss naming your puppy with your breeder prior to bringing him home.

If the breeder has already named your puppy and you wish to change that name, consider the following. There's a method that makes it easy to do without making the puppy confused. Begin by adding your new name to the name chosen by the breeder.

After you have used both names for several days, you can stop using the old name completely and only use the name you selected for your new puppy. This method prevents the puppy from realising his name was altered.

While it might be nice to have a long fancy name for your puppy, a short one or two-syllable name will be most recognisable by him. This name will also be very recognisable with one or two syllable commands such as Smokey FETCH, or Rocky SIT. An intelligent puppy will want to please his owners and it's up to the owner to make this a simple process.

Your Pomeranian's Documents

If purchasing your Pomeranian puppy or adult from a reputable breeder, you'll be given a series of documents.

Vaccination Record

Vaccinations prevent puppies from contracting dangerous canine diseases. The puppy should have received his first vaccination at least 10 days prior to leaving the breeder's premises. Most breeders start vaccinating at around six weeks of age. The vaccination record you receive from the breeder should be signed by an authorised veterinarian.

If you're unfamiliar with "puppy shots," don't fret. They can be called a number of names, including C3, C4, DHLPP or "five-in-one." These shots immunise against familiar dog diseases, such as distemper, hepatitis virus, parainfluenza, parvovirus and leptospirosis.

Microchip information

With today's technology, your Pomeranian should be microchipped. This allows him to be identified if he goes missing. Most reputable breeders microchip their puppies. If your breeder hasn't already taken care of this issue, it will benefit you to have it done yourself. The breeder will need to provide you with a form enabling you to transfer the microchip information to your name and address.

Worming record

A good breeder will have wormed your puppy every two weeks. Ask for details if not provided.

Puppy's diet information

Reputable Pomeranian puppy breeders should provide new owners with a "diet information sheet" that details what, and when, your Pomeranian has been eating. To prevent any tummy upsets, keep the puppy on this schedule for at least two weeks, and then gradually change the diet if you wish.

Sales contracts and warranty

All reputable Pomeranian breeders have a sales contract that protects both buyer and seller. You should receive a copy of this contract before buying your puppy. The contract will include warranty details and necessary requirements of all parties. While you're reading the contract, you should ensure you get answers to questions such as:

- Are you being given full ownership of the dog, or does the breeder retain partial ownership?
- Does the breeder require you to spay or neuter your Pomeranian?
- What's required to enable you to return your dog (if necessary)?
- What's the time limit for you to return your Pomeranian?
- You might be surprised by unusual items in your breeder's contract. This is why you must read through the contract thoroughly and ask any questions of the breeder prior to signing the contract.

Kennel Club registration papers

Ensure you're aware of your puppy's registration status prior to purchase. Pet puppies are usually sold with limited registration. This means your Pomeranian can't participate in shows or be used for breeding. If you intend showing or breeding your Pomeranian, main Kennel Club registration papers are required.

Champion Dochlaggie Delightful Desire. Photo by Ariel Xuran Li

The Correct Way to Lift and Hold Your Pomeranian

Lifting and holding your Pom might not look like a complicated thing to do, but there are lots of pet owners who do it the wrong way. There's a safe way to lift and hold a small dog.

Understanding the right way to lift and hold your beloved pet is safe for him/her and it's safe for you as well. The trick is to always support his rear and chest because that equally distributes his weight and won't give you any back pain.

Learn the best way to lift and carry your small dog. This will prevent you dropping him accidentally and causing him an injury.

Tips on Lifting Your Pom

Prior to lifting my dog, I'll give him a verbal command that indicates he's about to be lifted from the ground. Think about it…If a person walked over to you, lifted you up and carried you off - with zero warning, I bet you wouldn't like that at all.

So, for that very reason, I have taught my dogs the verbal warning, "Up." You can select any word you want, but ensure it's only used for that purpose or it will get your dog confused. Then he knows that whenever he hears that word, you're about to pick him up.

Squat down and put your dominant arm behind your pet's hind legs. Put your other hand around his chest. As you start lifting, his back and front legs will fold together a little, so the body rests in your arms.

As you slowly stand and lift, bring the body in towards your chest. This gives him more support while ensuring he's secured with your arms. This also eliminates excessive stress on your lower back area.

What You Should NOT Do

1. Lots of people assume it's fine to lift dogs up by the scruff of the neck simply because they see mother dogs do it to their puppies. The problem is that it's very uncomfortable and possibly even painful for the dog. The mother only ever picks her pups up like that when they're extremely young. Once the puppy matures a bit, that behaviour ceases.
2. Never, ever pick up your dog by the collar. This is extremely dangerous. Lifting a dog by the collar will cut off the air supply briefly and it may also cause his trachea permanent damage.
3. Do not lift your dog by his tail. Tails aren't handles and, if you pull it, you can seriously damage its muscles and nerves. If it's serious, he may not be able to wag it anymore. Experts believe he may no longer be able to go to the bathroom. Lastly, but not least, you may partly or completely break the tail and if you have ever seen a dog with a broken tail, it's sad as he can't wag it, and that's how he tells you he's happy to see you because he loves you.
4. Never lift your dog by his legs. There are numerous things that are wrong if you lift your dog this way. You can cause him pain and strain on his ligaments and

muscles. There's also a very high possibility that you'll drop him…for two reasons. The first is that you'll lose your grip. The second reason is that he's in discomfort and pain and he may decide to wriggle out of your grasp.

How to Correctly Hold Your Pomeranian

Don't put your hands between his front legs and push his elbows outwards. The right way is to wrap your hands around the legs of the dog and provide support in the right position, while holding his body close to yours for extra security.

Do not let your Pom's back legs dangle unsecured because he finds it extremely uncomfortable. He will also wriggle and maybe even scratch as he tries to escape your clutches, and fall to the ground as a result, possibly hurting himself. If you secure his rear and front, you'll reduce any shoulder and back pressure.

Part 4 - Feeding

Feeding Your Pomeranian

How much food should be in each meal and how often do you feed him?

How often you feed your dog will largely depend on how old he is. Tiny puppies can easily suffer from hypoglycaemia (low blood sugar), so he'll need to eat plenty of small meals. Numerous breeders recommend a process of free feeding until puppy is 6 months old.

Tiny dogs need more calories for each kilogram of weight than big dogs require. This means choosing foods full of energy and essential nutrients. Read labels on different dog foods.

While you don't need to be a licenced nutritionist, if you learn some of the basics, you'll be able to make smart choices. Dry foods that are designed for tiny puppies and dogs are good choices.

A good test of the correct diet is the dog's physical appearance, energy levels, and the dog's stool (colour, odour and firmness) are excellent indicators of the suitability of most dog foods).

Low-quality dog foods frequently contain a high percentage of indigestible "fillers." These will trigger loose stools.

Your adult Pomeranian's weight will ideally stay the same and his body should be well-balanced. You'll be able to feel his ribs with the tips of your fingers, just beneath a very thin layer of fat.

An adult Pomeranian requires a minimum ratio of 2% to 3% of his perfect body weight in food, over the course of 1 to 2 meals.

Throughout the winter months, ensure your Pomeranian is exposed to sunlight for a few minutes each day because it's essential for his well-being. Lack of sunlight in a dog results in loss of pigmentation and what is often referred to as a "winter nose."

Please ensure all meals are minced or chopped as fine as possible because Pomeranians can easily choke on largish pieces of meat. Dogs should never be given cooked bones.

Feeding a Pomeranian puppy

Think about the amount of energy a Pomeranian puppy uses in relation to his tiny size and ability to quickly utilise the food eaten. A small puppy must produce more than enough energy to run around and play. His diet should also include enough nutrients to allow for growth. He must be fed a quality diet, or his health and growth will suffer. The correct way to feed a Pomeranian puppy is to offer him a small amount of quality food often.

The best person to ask for advice on feeding your new Pomeranian is your breeder. Most breeders will give you a diet sheet for your puppy. He'll probably have years of experience feeding Pomeranians and, unlike your veterinarian, won't have any interest in selling you a certain brand of dog food.

Unless you have time to study and research canine nutrition, it's better to feed your Puppy a quality, commercial canned puppy food instead of meat, because all puppies need to have the right calcium to phosphorous balance. This kind of diet provides most of the nutrients a puppy requires. Look for a quality dry food that's suitable for toy dog breeds and purchase the "puppy variety" of that food.

Your new puppy will initially require 3 to 4 meals a day. Gradually change this until, at six months, he's having only two meals daily. Twice daily feeding is also recommended for adult Pomeranians.

If your dog is fed a good kibble, it's believed that supplements, in the way of meat and vegetables, are not necessary. I, personally, wouldn't like to be fed the same diet, day in day out, year after year.

Dry puppy food should always be available to puppies. In addition, a meal consisting of one to two heaped dessertspoons of canned puppy food, with a dessertspoon of puppy milk poured over it, should be given to your puppy 3 to 4 times daily. During the colder months, puppy meals are warmed prior to serving.

Until 12 months of age (when he becomes an adult), your

Pomeranian puppy will greatly benefit from the addition of puppy milk and yoghurt or grated cheese every day to help build strong bones and teeth.

Most commercial dog foods will show the amount that should be included in each meal, whether it's on a can or bag. These suggestions are just that: suggestions. Use or ignore according to your own knowledge and experience.

The amount of food your puppy gets will depend on how big he is, his metabolism, the environment, and how active he is. If you feed him too much, he can become a little tubby and excess weight can also cause bone abnormalities and other problems related to his health.

If he seems to be gaining too much weight, slowly reduce the amount of food he's eating. However, if his ribs are sticking out, you need to increase the amount he eats. Pet dogs in many breeds are commonly larger than show dogs because it's typical for a pet owner to give his dog extra food. If you don't give your puppy enough food, he may succumb to hypoglycaemia. If you don't know what he should look like or weigh normally, talk to your vet or breeder.

To give you a rough guide to follow, your puppy should eat a minimum of 3% to 5% of his ideal weight, in wet food, over the course of 3 to 4 meals. That's the correct amount for Pomeranians. Other dogs may have different percentages. Pom puppies may need up to 10% of their body weight each day while they're growing.

Photo by Shadow's Farm Photography

Recommended feeding options for Pomeranian Puppies:

- A high-quality canned puppy food.
- High quality dry puppy food (often called puppy kibble). A Pomeranian puppy is best fed a dry food which comes in small pieces).
- Feed your puppy dairy products daily. For example: puppy milk, yoghurt and cheese.
- Minced raw chicken carcass. (This is the minced chicken that contains small ground up chicken bones.)

How often should I feed my Pom Puppy?

- Premium quality dry puppy food should be always available.
- Water must be always available.
- Canned puppy food or minced raw chicken carcass together with puppy milk (or cheese or yoghurt) is offered to puppy three times per day.

How much should you feed your Pom?

- 1 or 2 tablespoons of canned puppy food with a little cheese or milk on top, three times per day.
- 1 or 2 tablespoons of dry food in a small shallow dish should be available 24/7.

Increase these amounts a little each month until puppy is about six months old. This is just a guide as puppies are individuals. A very active or bigger pup will require more food. Use common sense. If puppy is clearly still hungry and isn't fat, increase the amount you feed him.

- Avoid feeding him red meat.
- Avoid giving him calcium supplements.
- Increase the amount of calcium in pup's diet the safe way by feeding more dairy.

Pomeranian pups often require increased calcium while teething.

Signs of calcium deficiency include:

- One or both ears standing awkwardly or flopping over.
- The tail standing upwards instead of lying flat on puppy's back.

Signs of extreme calcium deficiency include:

- Spreading toes.
- Flat pasterns and east-west fronts.
- Limping, or occasionally refusing to walk on one back leg.

Avoid patella surgery on Pomeranian pups under 12 months.

During the teething period, increase calcium in your puppy's diet by increasing the amount of dairy he consumes.

Phosphorous and calcium

Phosphorous and calcium work well together to maintain the structure and growth of your dog's skeletal system. If your Pomeranian is deficient or has too much of either mineral, he can have problems with his bone structure. This is especially true in young puppies.

In the long term, it's critical to good health that you feed your Pom the correct ratio of these two minerals. Problems with these minerals generally don't exist nowadays because it's easy to buy commercial pet food with a healthy balance of both substances.

Problems will usually occur if you feed your Pom too much of these minerals or feed an unbalanced homemade diet. Young, rapidly-growing puppies face this problem a lot more than older dogs.

Calcium deficiency

The correct ratio of phosphorous to calcium is vital. Calcium deficiency in dogs used to be a fairly normal problem. It was mainly due to feeding dogs a diet high in meat and organ meats that are low in calcium and high in phosphorous. If the dog wasn't fed calcium supplements, he could develop rickets (a skeletal abnormality) and many other ailments.

Learn How to Read Dog Food Labels

The very first component in your dog's food should be meat; Genuine meat, not a meat by-product. Don't be fooled by photos of choice cuts of meat on the bag or can.

Dogs are carnivores. They weren't designed to eat corn and wheat. Generally, if the first ingredient listed on the commercial dog food label is a corn, wheat, meat by-product, bone meal or anything other than a real specified type of meat, avoid this dog food.

By-products are the leftover animal parts and can include the eyes, hooves, skin, feathers and feet. In fact, by-products are any animal parts that aren't good enough for human consumption. If the food includes animal by-products, don't use it. Beware of wording such as "animal" and "meat" rather than "chicken," "beef" and "duck," etc.

The energy providers

While you might consider that food creates energy, this is only one of many functions:

Carbohydrates

Most ingredients in commercial dog foods are carbs and the two that are most digestible are sugars and starches. However, canines are only able to use nutrients that are found in cooked carbs, and the degree varies according to food type. The best to worst foods are the following:

1. Rice.
2. Corn and potatoes.
3. Oats, wheat and beans.

Dogs that are active can have difficulty maintaining a stable weight if they eat too many carbs. The number 2 and 3 options on the list are the toughest ones to digest and can also cause flatulence and diarrhoea. If your dog sounds (or smells) like this, never blame him. Simply adjust his diet so he's eating better quality carbs or a higher protein level.

It's essential for Poms to have specific enzymes to help digest carbs within soybeans and dairy products. However, if your dog isn't consuming these foods consistently, the activity of those enzymes may be low. If your aim is to feed soybeans and dairy foods to your Pomeranian, start low and gradually build to a higher level.

If you need extra persuasion, think of this: if the activity of the enzyme is low, colonic bacteria will ferment the carbs and your Pom will experience flatulence and diarrhoea.

Protein

- Proteins contain numerous amino acids and their job is to create the basic building blocks for antibodies, the coat, muscle and bone.
- The products containing the simplest to digest and highest quality proteins are eggs, milk, fish, beef and chicken.
- Older dogs require higher levels of proteins, followed by puppies and then adult dogs.

Keep these facts in mind:

Your Pom doesn't need much food so think about options that contain high-quality proteins.

Meat and many other protein sources, derived from animals, are dearer than protein options that come from plants. So, commercial manufacturers of such foods more often use only small amounts of protein from animals and they also opt for sources that are not wholesome, including animal by-products, bone and meat meals.

Many dog owners will add eggs or meat to the commercial dog foods, which is a wise move. However, your dog's entire diet shouldn't contain more than 10% of supplements.

Ensure egg whites are cooked before feeding them to your dog. If you use a variety of meats, you'll have the ideal sampling of essential amino acids. Plant proteins are harder to digest.

Fat

Fat helps improve taste, provides energy, and assists the

movement of fat-soluble vitamins. However, if your Pom consumes more than he should, he may experience obesity, diarrhoea and a reduction in his appetite for more nutritious foods.

If your Pom's diet is lacking in vital fatty acids, he may experience skin problems and reduced growth, as well as a possible reduction in his ability to reproduce.

To ensure your Pomeranian's diet contains a healthy balance of fats, you should include foods such as vegetable oils and egg yolks. His diet should also contain at least 5% dry food (i.e., nutrients minus water content).

The Non-energy Providers

Nutrients possess certain substances that keep your dog alive, despite them not directly providing fuel for his body. Fibre and water, as well as vitamins and minerals, are crucial elements of a healthy, well-balanced diet.

Water

The most important nutrient is water. Your Pom (and all canines, humans and other living "creatures") can miss out on virtually all other nutrients for a day, or even a week in some cases. However, we must all have water every single day. Water helps lubricate joints, helps control your Pom's body temperature, dissolves and helps to transport various other nutrients, ensures good blood flow and does hundreds of other things as well.

Your Pomeranian's body is primarily made from water so if he ends up dehydrated, he might become severely ill.

As a human, by the time you feel thirsty, you're already dehydrated so you grab a drink for yourself. If your Pomeranian is thirsty, he'll head straight to his water bowl to have a drink. It's critical that he always has access to water to prevent dehydration. The "water cooler" idea is great because it keeps filling his bowl as he drinks. Ensure it's always full.

- Use bottled or filtered water.
- Ensure his water container is always full.
- On a daily basis, you must wash the bowl and refill it with clean water.
- In warm weather, check your Pom's water bowl more often to see if it needs refilling.
- Also, during warm weather, add ice to his water bowl.

How Much Water Should Your Pomeranian Drink Daily?

Many Poms drink when they're thirsty because it's a natural instinct. However, there are others that don't drink enough OR drink too much water, and each of these have their inherent dangers.

If you're a new Pom parent, it's essential that you monitor how much water your dog is drinking each day. If he doesn't drink enough, dehydration can set in and that can cause kidney stones and, in the most serious cases, organ failure. If he drinks too much, it may be toxic. Monitoring his fluidic intake can tell you if he has any health problems to be concerned about.

This amount will vary according to his size, age, level of activity and the weather. A healthy guideline is one cup of water for a dog weighing 2.26 kgs or 2 cups for a dog weighing 4.53 kgs. However, Pom parents usually feed their puppies food that is very moist (raw or slightly cooked food). This means he gets some of the fluid from food so reduce the amount of water he needs. If you're only using dry dog food, add more water to compensate.

If your puppy is small in size, he'll need smaller amounts of water every two hours so this must be closely monitored.

Always have water for your Pom if you take him for a walk or out to play and give him frequent short breaks for a small drink.

If your Pom doesn't drink enough water, he:

- Can quickly become dehydrated.
- May have pancreatitis, parvovirus or leptospirosis.
- May have a different health problem.

If your Pom drinks too much water he:

- Might be doing so due to an infection in either his kidneys or bladder.
- He may also be drinking it while he's swimming and/or playing.
- May have other medical problems.

Water sources

If your Pom drinks from any water he can find, whether it's the water you have for him, a dirty puddle or an old container, then he probably has a health problem. Excessive thirst can strike a dog of any age and shouldn't be ignored.

If your Pomeranian isn't drinking enough water, praise him when he does drink from the water bowl you provide for him. If he doesn't go to a bowl for water, put it near him, whether it's in his bed or play pen area. Then he can easily have a drink. Some dogs dislike the taste of water because not all taps produce the same standard. If your drinking water isn't very good, consider using filters if it's economical. If that doesn't work, consider adding flavour to his water.

Is your Pom sufficiently hydrated?

Here's a trick you can use to see if your Pom is drinking enough water. Gently lift the skin on the rear of the neck. If it falls fast and easily back into place, he drinks enough water. If not, it will fall slowly into a tent-like shape. If this trick doesn't appeal, check his gums. If they're moist and feel slick, he's ok. If they feel sticky or dry, he needs more water.

Vitamins and minerals

Dogs need numerous vitamins including A, B1, B2, B12, D, E, choline, niacin, folic acid, pantothenic acid and pyridoxine.

They also need minerals for many reasons. They help build organs and tissues, as well as being important parts of enzymes and bodily fluids. If they have deficiencies or an abundance of minerals, many problems can occur including poor growth, anaemia, vomiting, fractures, convulsions, weakness, hypo-glycaemia (low blood sugars) and other issues.

Most dog foods contain the ideal percentages of vitamins so it's hardly necessary to add supplements. Giving him supplements, particularly calcium, isn't wise.

Fibre

Fibre (such as various gums, rice bran and beet pulp) can adversely affect the way other nutrients get absorbed. These include fats, proteins, carbs and other minerals and vitamins.

Fibre often increases the size of a Pom's stool volume and makes him go more often. If your Pomeranian's volume is large, check how much fibre there is in what he eats. You may be using a particular food containing more than the recommended amount of fibre, or it may be a cheaper food with plenty of peanut hulls so the manufacturer can save money. The ideal fibre amount in food should be 4% for dry food and 1% for wet food.

Switching from Puppy Food to Adult Dog Food

Pomeranian pups go through many changes during their first year. For correct growth and bone development, I'd recommend feeding a high-quality puppy food until your Pom's first birthday.

Around the 12-month mark, Pomeranians should be fed a diet more suited to that of an adult Pom. This type of food will be filled with the correct balance of vitamins and nutrients for adult dogs. One reason for the change is that adult dogs require less food and calories than growing puppies. The minerals and vitamins required by adult dogs differ as well.

It's wise to make the transition slowly so, by the time he's 52 weeks old, he's only eating adult dog food. If you don't complete the changeover by this time, there may be consequences. One is that a puppy's metabolism slows and so the additional calories he's consuming aren't being burned off and a result could be a little tubby Pom.

The best way to make the change go smoothly is to replace 1/8th cup of puppy food with adult dog food. Increase by a further 1/8 every few days until the whole amount is replaced.

If your puppy has an upset stomach, reduce the adult food and then make the change at a far slower rate.

Consider cooking for your adult Pomeranian. Home cooking will ensure he eats a variety of nourishing, healthy meals. Food can be cooked in advance and frozen in meal size portions for later use.

Adult dogs only require feeding twice a day instead of the three to four times daily that he was eating when younger. If stomach upsets occur, revert back to thrice daily for a short time.

Ensure you understand how much food the recommended daily allowance is when you change to adult dog food. Generally, it will be less than before.

Again, talk to your vet or breeder about the number of calories required as well.

During the change from puppy food to adult dog food, you may have to try different things to see what works best. If your puppy doesn't like adult dog food, add a small amount of canned puppy food, fat-free turkey or chicken broth. Praise him when he eats the new food combinations and, if nothing you try makes him eat, you can even pretend to eat it yourself, to show him that it's delicious.

Why Keeping Your Pomeranian Trim is Vital

Should your Pomeranian become overweight, the negative effects can be serious. The most significant result of excess weight is a reduction in your dog's life by as much as two years.

Being an overweight little dog also means they're less capable of enjoying themselves through pain-free physical exercise and play, due to associated joint and health issues.

Some specific issues that may develop from, and be exacerbated by, weight issues include:

- Arthritis, joint damage and joint pain.
- Type 2 diabetes.
- Heart disease.

- Reduced exercise endurance and stamina.
- Increased anaesthetic and surgical risks.
- Reduced liver function due to fatty liver.

Owners of overweight dogs will eventually end up visiting their veterinarian more frequently and, in actual fact, the excess weight will reduce your pet's lifespan.

If your tubby little Pomeranian has gotten that way due to over-eating, you have to carry out a bit of tough love. Try giving him smaller than normal portions of a food that's lower in calories. Commercially made diet foods contain approx. 15% fewer calories than standard dog foods. The protein content should still be moderate to high to prevent loss of muscle when he's on a diet.

It's possible that a dog may look fat but it's due to a medical issue such as hypothyroidism, early onset diabetes or heart disease.

These are many reasons for you to always have his health checked before you put him on a diet. Your vet might also be able to give you a healthy type of dog food made specifically for a diet.

Is My Pomeranian Fat?

Check your Pomeranian's ribs. Look at his rib cage. Look and touch his bones to learn what you need to know.

Looking – Stand over your Pomeranian. The easiest time for this is after his bath when the fur is wet and not in the way. Does his stomach curve inwards? Can you see the distinction between the lower and upper parts of his torso? If you can't, he has too much fat.

Touching – Using your fingers and pushing his fur aside, touch his ribs. If he's underweight, his bones will be against his skin and may even protrude in spots. If he's overweight, you'll feel a thick amount of fat between the bones and your fingers, if you can even find his ribs at all. If you can't touch his ribs, your dog is obese.

Tips on Handling a Fussy Eater

You have most likely been feeding your Pomeranian the same food each day for quite a while, so it's hardly surprising that he starts to get sick of it.

Dogs aren't omnivores; they're carnivores, meaning they're meat eaters. They were never designed to consume dry dog food. They may look different from wolves but, inside, they're the same.

I suggest you feed your Pom an appropriate, healthy home-cooked diet. Meals can be cooked and stored in your freezer until required. Your Pomeranian will also benefit from eating raw meat and chewing on raw bones.

Purchase the raw meat and freeze it into meal size portions. Avoid all commercially made dog snacks and treats and, instead, give your Pom a large raw bone to chew on, a few times each week.

Lots of dogs are fussy eaters. Wild animals will eat just about anything because they have no choice. In a residential home, the dogs have learned that some foods are delicious, and others are just edible. Even if you're strict and don't feed your dog foods designed for humans, it doesn't mean they can ignore your food because they can smell and see it.

There's a difference between a fussy and a picky eater. A picky eater can be tempted with a small piece of human food if he doesn't eat his own food. A fussy eater is one who has refused to eat certain foods anymore. It's important to rule out any health problems first. However, if your vet says he's fine, then there are ways to tempt him to eat.

Persuading a fussy eater:

Reduce the treats you give him. He'll be more likely to eat his meals if he doesn't fill up on snacks and treats.

Feed him smaller amounts more often, three or four times per day.

He needs exercise. Take him for a walk before his meal because it will make him extra hungry and then he'll eat whatever you give him.

Neuter or spay your puppy. It has a lot of benefits, including preventing him from becoming fussy about his food.

Feeding time should be positive. If you can associate mealtimes with positive experiences, he will be less fussy.

If he connects food and punishment, he'll want to avoid eating.

Use a quiet environment. Ensure the room is quiet when you feed him, and he does not have other dogs or children around to distract him.

Change his mealtimes. Feed him at different times of day to see what works best for him.

If everything else doesn't work, you can act silly. Before you put his bowl on the floor, hold it near your mouth and pretend to eat it, while making "yummy" sounds. Who cares if that seems silly? Nobody else is around and your pet can't share your secret.

What are the Best Treats for My Pomeranian?

Commercially available canine treats and cookies often consist of unhealthy, even harmful, ingredients. For the health of your Pomeranian, it's advisable to avoid feeding any doggie treats containing preservatives, refined flour, sugar and artificial colours.

Pom owners concerned about the safety of canine treats should refrain from feeding imported pet treats or products containing imported ingredients.

When shopping for these goodies, search for products containing wholesome, nutritious ingredients. The best, and healthiest, dog treats are homemade.

Boiled beef hearts, kidneys or livers, cut into small pieces and put in the freezer in zip lock bags are tasty and healthy home-made treats. They'll last in your freezer for a couple of months.

Another safe treat is small pieces of cheese.

Give your Pom large beef bones from your butcher. Be sure there aren't any sharp edges. If you're worried about hygiene, boil the bone for a few seconds to kill germs. Allowing your Pom to chew on these large beef bones will assist with teeth cleaning and improve gum health.

What Can Pomeranians Eat?

If you offered your Pomeranians just about any human food, do you think they would say no? Of course not! What they will do is grab it from you or empty their bowls in record time. So, it's up to you to know exactly what foods are safe and what foods may harm your Pomeranian and make sure everybody in the household knows this information as well.

Make a list of SAFE foods and a different list of UNSAFE foods. Use the lists below as a guide. They should be printed off and displayed where you feed your dogs as a means of checking whether the food given is safe for your Pomeranians to consume. You never know what may happen if foods are mixed up and your Pomeranian might even like a particular food you never knew.

List 1 – Feed your Pomeranian these foods anytime

Here's a long list of human foods you can safely share with your Pomeranians whenever you desire. It includes:

Turkey, chicken, fish, bison, hamburger meat, venison, crawfish, shrimp, pork, beef liver, lamb, asparagus, carrots, beets, asparagus, bell peppers, green beans, kale, quinoa, rice, pasta, broccoli, cauliflower, watermelon, strawberries, raspberries, mangoes, cucumber, lettuce, blueberries, eggs, kiwi fruit, plums, pineapple, lettuce, honeydew melon, cantaloupe, peanuts, peanut butter, cheese, honey, cottage cheese, apples, bananas, yams, potatoes, peas, flaxseeds, sunflower seeds, zucchini, nectarines, peaches, pears, blueberries, cashews, nectarines, apples and eggs.

After reading that long list of foods, you'll see it's not so bad because most of them are natural whole foods. People, and many animals, find these foods delicious so it's not hard to get a good balance to ensure that people maintain good health and help their animals also keep healthy.

List 2. Your Pomeranian should only consume these foods occasionally

The foods on this list are still healthy for Pomeranians but should not be eaten as often as those on list 1 for various reasons.

List 2 foods include:

Crackers, bread, waffles, popcorn, bacon, marshmallow, guava, coconut, bacon, potato chips and maple syrup.

Regard this list of foods as occasional dog treats or you can follow my expert opinion and never give them to your Pomeranian at all. However, it's up to each owner.

Which Human Foods Should My Pomeranian Not Eat?

On the opposite side of the coin, you have human foods your Pomeranian shouldn't eat and they sit in one of two categories.

List 3. These foods are usually meant to be avoided

It's ok for your Pomeranian to eat these foods sometimes but, be careful, especially if you notice any side effects after your Pomeranian has eaten these foods. The reason is that they may fall on the borderline between what's safe and what's unsafe. So, these are the "grey area" foods that you may be tempted to give your Pomeranian in small amounts or you may choose to never feed your Pomeranian.

List 3 foods include:

Meatloaf, processed cheese, macaroni and cheese, ice cream, pickles, almonds, wheat, corn, tacos, spam, sausages, margarine, ham, deli meats, infant formula, pistachios, almonds and hot dogs.

Foods you should NEVER feed your Pomeranian

Lists to help manage the types of human food you can always feed your Pomeranians, the ones they could eat sometimes, and the food that you may choose to give your Pomeranians occasionally.

This final list is human foods your Pomeranians must NEVER eat under any circumstances, because they can harm your Pomeranians at best and be deadly at worst.

List 4 foods include:

Macadamias, walnuts, pecans, grapes (including raw, jelly, jam and juices), currants, raisins, chives, leeks, shallots, garlic, onions, chocolate, coffee grounds, anything containing caffeine, cinnamon, wild mushrooms, cherries, seeds, fruit pits, tomato sauce, yeast dough, anything with xylitol, and all restaurant food.

Dangerous chemicals and additives in food

In human food and dog food, there are lots of chemicals and additives. Even when eating whole foods that are supposed to be all-natural, there will be traces of some chemicals because of the way modern agriculture works. Some of the chemicals used can harm Pomeranians. The list includes:

- Caffeine.
- MSG (Chinese "super salt").
- High levels of salt.
- Xylitol (a specific type of sugar).

When it comes to additives, human food may have some ingredients harmless to people but may be dangerous for dogs. Pomeranians are highly susceptible to food allergies. These typically exist because of the presence of food additives. Additives that should be avoided within human food include:

- BHT (butylated hydroxytoluene).
- BHA (butylated hydroxyanisole).
- Corn and wheat gluten.
- Propylene glycol.

- Ethoxyquin.
- Rendered fat.
- Food dyes (blue 2, red 40, yellow 5 and 6, 4-MIE).

The issue with these types of chemicals and ingredients is that they'll often exist in human food, particularly today with modern cuisine. Gaining a strong understanding of the chemicals and additives in your food will help your Pomeranian when he's enjoying your leftovers. It will also help you and your family by learning what bad and good ingredients are being consumed.

Do not allow others to feed your Pomeranian

When other family members and friends visit me, my Pomeranians are ecstatic. They get plenty of attention as they run around in such an excited manner. They know the best way to get attention is to beg for human food (whether it's snacks or table scraps), and they have become so adept at it during their years living in your home. However, you must not allow your visitors to be enticed into feeding them.

You can pre-empt trouble by asking all the visitors to practice restraint whenever they want to give your Pomeranians any human food. As an owner, you should be an expert when it comes to knowing what human foods are safe and not safe to feed your Pomeranian but you can't expect visitors to have the same degree of knowledge.

Therefore, the household rule for animal feeding needs to be one of two options:

1. Anybody not living in the house must check with you before feeding your Poms.
2. Nobody can feed your Pomeranians unless they live in the house.

Then it's your choice if you want to stick with one option or swap them, depending on who is visiting. These simple rules will keep your Pomeranians safe from harm.

Feeding Pomeranians Raw Food

The main reason why owners feed their Pomeranians raw foods is to replace highly processed canned foods and kibble with homemade, all-natural foods that will do your dog much better in the long run.

Use a variety of meat, uncooked bones, a small number of organs and small quantities of vegetables and fruits because this diet is healthier for your dog than a kibble diet. As a Pomeranian is a small, dog, breed modifications need to be made to most raw food diets to better suit a Pom.

Making changes in your Pom's diet, especially if you're introducing raw foods, is often an issue due to the onset of gastrointestinal problems. If you change the diet too fast, it may also cause diarrhoea.

The way a dog's body processes kibble is vastly different from raw foods. Kibble is recognised as a starch by your dog's metabolism. On the other hand, raw food is treated as if it's a protein and is kept in the stomach for an acid bath. If you combine dry foods with raw foods, your dog's digestive system can become confused and he may become gassy and belch a lot.

If your Pom has a healthy gut and you want to try out new food of any kind, it's ideal to trial it for a day as a "treat" and watch his stool for any changes over the ensuing days. Slowly after the initial first day (if there are no visible changes), increase the "new treats" and keep an eye on his stool.

After a couple of days without problems, replace one of his meals with the new food. Continue this for another couple of days and then (as long as there are no side effects) you can safely use only new foods.

If your pet has only ever eaten one type of kibble in his life, you may have to take weeks or perhaps months to change his diet so patience is required.

In the initial stages of feeding your beloved Pom raw food, you need to vary his diet to ensure he's getting a healthy balance of vital nutrients. Calcium and fat levels are critical to monitor. Any imbalances may cause health problems.

Other issues may occur if the food you use contains bacteria such as Listeria monocytogenes or Salmonella. Raw foods have a greater chance of containing bacteria than processed foods and kibble. The good news is that your dog's digestive system can handle bacteria better than humans as their system isn't as acidic or as long as the human digestive processes.

Talk to your Vet

Keep in mind that your vet may try to send you home with the brand of dog food he's currently selling. So, don't blindly take his advice. Do your own research and ask questions and get his help to find the ideal balance and see whether it does match his ideas or not.

Most vets won't suggest a raw food diet for puppies because the correct balance of phosphorus and calcium is hard to achieve. It may cause deformities and, if your dog has cancer, he certainly should not be on such a diet.

Puppies require a correct ratio of calcium and phosphorus and for that reason I recommend feeding Pom pups a commercial diet until 12 months of age.

Calcium and phosphorus should be maintained at a ratio of 1:1 for adult Poms. Bones are low in phosphorus while meat is high in it. Tripe is a great food for both minerals.

This doesn't automatically mean you need to give him 50% bones in his diet. It means you need to feed him the same amount of both minerals. This means his diet should be 90% meat and 10% phosphorus.

What to feed your Pomeranian

Raw is...uncooked fresh meat. Dogs are carnivorous. Raw feeding is feeding fresh wholesome food, not food out of a packet, and lots of raw meat.

Meat can be: turkey, chicken, duck, lamb, beef, rabbit, venison or offal (but sparingly for the offal).

Vegetables can be: carrots, cauliflower, green beans, okra, peas, pumpkin, squash, celery, sweet potato and parsley. You could also add a little fruit like apple, banana, pear, strawberries or blueberries.

Other foods can include: tinned fish, cheese, yoghurt, whole grain and pasta.

It's advised that you use raw meaty bones and meat that's human grade. Certain pet bone products, meat rolls, meat and mince may contain harmful preservatives. (e.g., sulphite preservatives, which can cause a deficiency of thiamine, a condition that can be fatal.) Sausage meats, sausages and manufactured cooked meats can also have sulphite preservatives as well.

Chicken feet and tripe may sound foul to you but dogs like any meat, regardless of what it is. It's cheaper to buy these types as well. Add these to the shopping list: and beef trachea, tails.

An example of an average Pomeranian meal

Mince steak with either home cooked, pureed veggies. e.g., potato, pumpkin, carrot, cauliflower, beans, broccoli or, if in a hurry, tinned pureed baby food veggies.

Give him bones to chew on. That helps increase his calcium intake as well as keeping him occupied for a while. Large meaty beef bones from your butcher are a great choice.

Whole chicken frames are another great tasty treat but should be fed under supervision. Under no circumstances should chicken wings, necks, tips or legs be fed in any shape or form; too many Pomeranian have lost their lives choking on these items.

I feed minced chicken frames (i.e., the mince contains finely ground bones as a source of calcium) to lactating Mums and their pups.

Raw bones can be placed in the freezer for a few minutes prior to feeding to your Pomeranian.

Do not ever feed your dog cooked bones because these can

cause serious harm if they splinter and get swallowed. They can block your dog's insides or cause cuts and abrasions as they go down.

You can feed your pet organ meats, but they should only comprise 10% of his diet. They are ok for one or two meals per week or as an addition to meals with other foods. Dogs love liver but too much in the diet can result in runny stools.

Include extra nutrients

The other aspect of your Pom's diet should be foods such as grains, fruit and vegetables. Overweight Poms will benefit from having the green vegetable percentage of their diet increased. Pureed cooked green beans are an ideal diet if they're carrying extra weight.

Pumpkin is a great vegetable to help regulate your dog's system. Vegetables can be prepared in advance and stored in meal-sized portions in your freezer to be used as required.

Always cook grains prior to feeding them to your dog. Wholegrains are best. Grains, however, are completely unnecessary since commercial pet foods are always grain-based diets. Many people believe their dogs require the addition of grains, but it's just not true. Some of the positive effects of feeding raw foods are related to eliminating grains from your dog's diet.

Apple Cider Vinegar: Add half a teaspoon of vinegar to meals each day.

Add either a fish oil supplement or flax seed oil to give him sufficient omega-3 fatty acids. Better still, add a tablespoon of tinned salmon 3 or 4 times a week to his diet and you will soon notice the startling improvements to your beloved pet's overall health and well-being. Never feed uncooked fish to your Pom.

Coconut Oil: can be added daily. Add a teaspoon mixed into the food.

Calcium: in the diet can be increased with the addition of a little plain yoghurt, cottage cheese, or dried, ground eggshells. Use ½ a teaspoon per pound of meat in your dog's meal.

Avoid feeding him raw egg whites because they have enzyme inhibitors that may cause digestive issues, particularly in young puppies and senior dogs.

Always process vegetables before adding them to your dog's food because it helps extract the most nutrients. Steam for a few minutes and puree them. The ideal choice are dark, leafy greens.

Never wash meat. While the temptation may be there, it just spreads around the existing bacteria. It can be splashed on surfaces around the sink, and that's a potential for more problems.

Always use safe food handling measures

All utensils used on your dog's raw food must be kept completely separate from all other utensils. Use hot soapy water when cleaning them properly or place them in your dishwasher. Disinfect all surfaces that the food may have touched.

After touching all types of dog foods, particularly raw foods, you must thoroughly wash your hands in warm soapy water for a minimum of 20 seconds. Clean underneath your nails as well.

Part 5 - Grooming

Grooming Your Pomeranian

A Pomeranian is a long-coated breed of dog that requires regular grooming during his lifetime. Teach your Pomeranian puppy that grooming is lots of fun. The optimum time to begin grooming a young Pomeranian is following exercise and after his evening meal.

Train your dog to lay quietly on each side, as well as on his back for brushing and toenail trimming. Helping the puppy to understand he should be comfortable on his back is a particularly important part of training for grooming.

The Pomeranian shouldn't be allowed to get up if he's struggling to get away.

Once he's fully relaxed and soothed by the owner's voice, then he can be allowed to get back on his feet and be rewarded with a treat. Quite often a puppy will prefer to remain on his back once he understands there's no danger and will enjoy the extra attention.

Pomeranians should be groomed on a weekly basis, as their coats require regular attention. Make grooming part of a routine with your dog, and you will both come to enjoy this special bonding time.

Trimming hair around the Pomeranian's anus for cleanliness is recommended.

Bathing your Pomeranian

When playing or petting your Pomeranian puppy, do you sometimes notice a rather unpleasant odour? If so, then it's time to give him a wash. However, you might have overlooked the question of whether he's old enough to be bathed.

The general rule is that a puppy should not be bathed if he's under eight weeks old. The reason is that he is unable to properly regulate his temperature and could catch a cold. After he hits the eight-week mark, bathe him once every month during the winter months, and more often during summer.

Bathing will not soften a correct Pomeranian coat. Dirt, grime and talcum powder can damage a dog's coat. Clean hair grows; dirty hair will break off.

1. Choose a Location

Before you can wash your Pomeranian puppy, you need to select the best place to do it. The kitchen or bathroom sink is the most popular choice. Because a Pom is so small, filling a whole bath isn't worthwhile. You won't want to chase your wet pom around the bath, and bending over the tub can be tiring.

2. Get out all your supplies

Before turning on any taps, you must get out everything required to wash your Pomeranian puppy. You need the right shampoo and conditioner as some won't do a good job and certain products could cause damage to your Pom's coat.

Pomeranians are known for their dry coats, so you need to use a shampoo that nourishes and moisturises the skin. I recommend conditioners and shampoos that contain healthy ingredients such as aloe vera and oatmeal. If possible, never use shampoos for human or artificial ingredients.

3. Brushing your Pomeranian

It's essential to brush your Pomeranian's coat thoroughly before you put him in the water. His coat will often tangle and mat and, once his coat is saturated, it's virtually impossible to get his hair untangled again. Brushing is also good for improving the blood flow to his hair follicles and removing dead hair.

4. Preparing his bath

Before filling the sink with enough water, it's a wise idea to put a rubber mat on the bottom of the sink. That will stop your puppy slipping. Also place a filter in the drain to prevent dog hair from clogging it.

Fill the sink with enough water that it touches your Pomeranian puppy's elbows. The water needs to be warm, not hot. Use your elbow to test it and adjust the warmth if needed. Put the towels, conditioner and shampoo near the sink so it's easy to grab them when needed. Ensure your dog can't knock a handle and make the water extra hot without you being aware of it.

5. Bathing your Pomeranian

Don't call your puppy right before you want to give him a wash. Pick him up and wet his feet first. Then gently place him in the water, while talking in a soothing voice. Lift him up and softly wet his paws. Then slowly ease him into the water.

Next is to wash his face, carefully his ears. Clean your Pomeranian puppy's face with a sponge. Squeeze some of the shampoo in and rub it into your Pomeranian's coat, beginning at his neck and slowly and thoroughly work your way down.

Then you need to rinse the shampoo off him completely. Then it's time to put the conditioner on him and gently wash him to get rid of it.

Lift your Pomeranian out of the water and wrap him in a soft, clean towel. He will shake all the water off, so be ready to get a little wet.

Caring for Your Pomeranian Puppy After a Wash

After taking your Pom pup out of the sink, here are several tasks to do.

The number one task is to properly dry your puppy. If you don't dry him sufficiently, he can catch a cold and/or fungus may begin to grow,

You may choose to dry your puppy with a towel, but it's going to take a long time to ensure his coat is 100% dry. So, it's better to pat him as dry as you can and then use a blow dryer for the final drying effort.

You don't need the added expense of a dog dryer if you have a human one. However, you must be careful if you use a human dryer and don't turn it straight off from the top setting. Gradually lower the temperature and ensure you keep it as far as possible from your Pomeranian puppy, so you don't burn him accidentally.

Blow him with the dryer while simultaneously brushing with your pin brush. Stand dryers are very useful and are a necessity for anyone doing a lot of dog grooming.

The best results are obtained from working on one small section at a time. Start by drying the underneath, and then move to the ears, top and front of the ruff. The tail area is next, finishing on the side and back areas.

Careless owners have been known to place their wet dog in a crate and then use the dryer on him. Never do it! Numerous dogs have died due to negligence on the part of their owner. The dog can't get away from the heat within the crate. It's very dangerous.

Apart from making sure your Pom is dry, you also need to look after his ears. If any moisture is left, it can cause an infection. Inspect his ears and use a special ear cleaner to help remove all debris and dirt. Then thoroughly clean his ears with cotton wool.

Some owners of Pomeranians like putting cotton balls in the ears of their dogs prior to giving them a wash. However, it's unnecessary if you don't wet his ears and clean and dry them properly after you're done.

If you observe your Pom pup shaking his head or scratching his ears a lot, it may be because you haven't dried all the wetness from his ears. If you notice an odour and/or a redness, your puppy quite likely has a yeast or bacterial infection. Don't attempt to fix the problem yourself. You would be much wiser to take him to the vet.

After a bath, a Pomeranian puppy would normally tremble and shake for a little while. The very first bath is an extremely stressful experience for nearly all puppies. If your Pomeranian won't stop shaking, it's essential that you speak to the vet for advice.

How do you wash a very young Pomeranian puppy?

As I previously mentioned, the age of your puppy will govern when he should be bathed. However, even if he's less than two months old, there might be times when he needs a wash.

One example is when he's being weaned. Pom puppies generally get food all over their coat and face. There might be times when your Pom puppy gets something hazardous on his coat. Puppies have an innate curiosity and get into all sorts of mischief. In such scenarios, you must give your Pomeranian puppy a good wash as a matter of urgency, ensuring you're extra gentle if it's only his first wash.

A full bath is too big for one small puppy because they don't yet have the ability to properly regulate their body temperature. That's why all the puppies snuggle up with their mother and each other as much as possible.

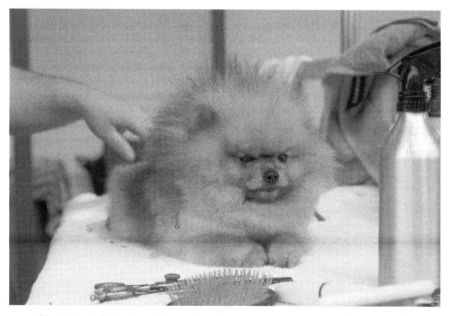

Champion Dochlaggie Dark N Dangerous. Photo by Ariel Xuran Li

The best alternative is to wipe your Pom puppy with a wet cloth until you have achieved your goal of getting his coat clean. Ensure the cloth is soaked in lukewarm water and that he's thoroughly dried at the end.

Wet wipes are also useful because they're easy to carry when you're not at home, and they help keep your pet Pom clean and presentable at all times. Always choose the wipes that don't have alcohol or fragrances and are pet friendly.

How many times per month can you wash a Pomeranian?

How often you need to wash your dog will depend largely on his type of skin. Dog breeds with coats that are oily need washes more often to control how they smell and get rid of that oily residue.

The skin of a Pomeranian is dry. Because of this, they don't need to be bathed often. They do need grooming products suitable for dogs that do have dry skin. If you wash your Pomeranian puppy too often, the body's natural oils will get stripped from their coat, making it much drier and increasing the chances of it flaking.

Specialists usually suggest bathing a Pomeranian puppy at least once per month. However, if your dog isn't dirty, you can get away with washing him 2-3 months during the winter months.

During the period of the puppy uglies (when the coats of Pomeranian puppies change), you may consider washing your puppy every two or three weeks. The reason is that he'll be shedding his hair like crazy and when you wash him, you open his hair follicles and using a dog dryer removes dead fur.

Pomeranians are among a small number of breeds that are exceptionally clean, but they still need baths sometimes to keep their majestic coats in perfect condition. That's why you must understand how to do it and how often you must ensure your Pomeranian is washed, dried and clean whenever necessary.

Brushing your Pomeranian

When they're young, Pom puppies only have shorter fur. It's very soft and, although it grows, it won't get too long because inside his first year, it all falls out.

Older puppies, from around 4 – 6 months of age, move into the "puppy uglies" phase (so named because the fur often looks quite patchy), where their puppy fur will fall out and be replaced by a new adult fur coat.

At one year, Pomeranians should have a thick double coat. The Pomeranian's coat is comprised of two layers. He has a dense undercoat that's woolly and holds the outer hairs off the body.

Then there's the outer coat which is coarse and long and is known as guard hairs.

It's simple to brush the outer coat so your dog looks great. However, you must also brush the undercoat to prevent it from becoming matted.

How often should you brush?

Ideally, you would brush your Pom each day, either as a form of relaxation or while watching TV. However, most people's lives aren't always ideal. You can still get great results if you brush your dog every second day.

Every dog sheds hair and it must go somewhere. It may become entangled in the outer coat and cause a clump of matted hair. It may blow down your hall. It can get onto furniture, bedding, clothes or even you. When you brush your dog, it catches a lot of the shed hair. For that reason, it's wise to groom every day, if possible.

Line brushing

Best results are obtained by using a brushing method called line brushing. Laying your Pomeranian on his side, work in rows down each side of the body, then repeat on the chest area, rump area and underneath him. Brush each layer of hair from the skin outwards.

Brushing steps

I apply the following 3 steps prior to bathing or trimming my Pomeranian. It helps to ensure there are no snags or tangles and every hair is separated:

Step 1 is completely brushing your Pomeranian using the line brushing technique. Using a pin brush, start from the shoulders and separate the coat in a line down to the skin from shoulder to base of the tail. Brushing one layer at a time, brush from the skin out. Pay attention to the areas that matt, tangle and knot easily, behind the ears, under the front legs and the groin area.

Step 2 is repeating the first step using a soft slicker brush.

Step 3 is repeating step 1 using a metal comb to completely comb through the Pomeranian's coat.

Brushing helps your Pomeranian's coat in 7 ways

1. Assessing and preventing tangles and mats.

These words are often used interchangeably. Tangles are knots that form in his hair.

Mats are thicker knots of weaved hair that's very close to his skin. These problems can occur and grow rapidly; they can be hard to remove unless you cut off some of his fur, and the process can cause your Pomeranian pain when his hairs get pulled in and his skin is pinched. You need to create a regular routine whereby you brush his coat to stop these issues from happening and, while you brush, check for small mats and tangles.

2. Body oil gets distributed.

A dog's natural body oil seeps out of his pores and can quickly build up. When you brush his coat, that helps to distribute the oil more evenly. It dissipates the smell that can exist when oil just sits there on his skin. It also gives his fur that healthy shine.

3. Brushing removes hairs that have been shed.

Pomeranians shed their hair all the time. There are usually two main seasonal sheds and most of the loose hair falls out from his undercoat. If you don't pull out dead hairs, they can stop the circulation of air, attract accumulated body oil (which will make him smell bad) and they'll twist with live hairs and cause mats to grow.

4. Improved health for skin and coat.

When you brush your Pomeranian's skin, it's like a massage and it improves the flow of blood and stimulates hair follicles which lead to better fur growth.

5. Tiny debris gets removed.

Brushing gets rid of microscopic debris and bits of food that get collected by his coat.

6. Golden opportunity to use a leave-in protective spray.

While brushing, it's the perfect time to use a conditioning spritz. A good quality spray will ensure his coat is moisturised properly, adds extra shine, stops mats and split ends and repels contact irritants and allergens, and any urine "splash back."

7. A well-groomed, tidy Pomeranian.

Brushing helps your Pomeranian look presentable all the time and helps him feel better about himself. A healthy dog is a happy dog.

Handling Mats In Your Dog's Coat

Mats are common. If your dog's coat is scratched, chewed, dirty or ignored, it's likely that mats will form. The first areas to mat will generally be those with fine, soft hair such as below and behind the ears, between his back legs and under his armpits. Rubbing talcum powder through the soft hair behind the ears can help prevent this area from matting.

If your dog only has isolated matting, either cut or brush the affected areas. Brushing should be your first choice, or your dog could end up looking moth-eaten. Cutting is a last resort.

Eliminating mats

When you find a large mat on your dog's coat, it's best to get rid of it in a couple of sections. As you brush out the mats, remind yourself that if you had done more regular grooming, you could have stopped the mats from forming.

To start with, use a slicker brush and lightly brush the mat's outer edge, slowly going in deeper. Never brush the mat out of the hair. Brush the hair out of the mat.

If you don't do grooming right through to your dog's skin, he'll most likely have large sections of matted hair. This is called felting. Never attempt to comb out mats if your dog is felted. It will cause too much pain and you really need a professional groomer to give him a proper shave. His skin could be damaged and may be irritated or raw in places. You'll have to sign a release form before a groomer will do this job for you.

Cutting out mats

If your dog's coat has a mat only connected by a couple of hairs, it's easy to cut it out. If there's a large mat secured by lots of hair and it's close to your dog's skin, it's possible you'll cut him while attempting to cut that mat. To prevent this from happening, wriggle a comb between the skin and the mat to act as a protective skin shield. Once you have removed the knotted fur, use thinning shears to smooth out a bad line.

You can also try cutting the mat into several smaller mats and then work on each of the small mats. When cutting out a mat, always cut down into a mat; never cut across a mat.

Make a few downwards cuts into the mat, then brush the area with your pin brush to remove loose hair. Often the rest of the mat can then be gently pulled apart with your fingers. If not, repeat the process, making downward cuts into the mat, brushing the loose hair out, and then attempt to pull the mat gently apart with your fingers.

Repeat until your Pomeranian is mat free. A mat breaking tool can cut and comb simultaneously.

Important Pomeranian Hair Care Tips

The importance of brushing

You need to brush his coat regularly and ensure you're using the correct grooming tools for Pomeranians.

Pomeranian grooming kit

To ensure you can maintain the best-looking coat of your Pomeranian, it's vital that you have the right tools. A good quality comb, a pin brush and a slicker brush should be the vital tools in your Pomeranian grooming kit.

Pomeranian bathing

Bathing a Pomeranian is a necessary regular task for optimum coat condition.

Correct coat drying

Take care when drying your Pom's coat: Make sure you take plenty of care as you dry your Pomeranian after he has been bathed (or got wet in the rain) because incorrect coat drying can affect the coat's condition. Conditioner should be applied after you shampoo so there's no need to spray in a leave-in conditioner, unless the coat is severely matted.

Apply a leave-in conditioner

If you don't protect your Pomeranian's fur coat, it can easily become damaged, sometimes permanently. In order to retain its natural beauty, choose a good quality leave-in conditioner (one you spray on and it doesn't get washed out) as it can offer a range of benefits:

- Protection from contact friction as this can cause split ends, frizz, dullness and dryness.
- Repels debris and dirt, outdoor allergens and splashes of urine.
- Protection from the sun's UV rays as they can discolour and dry fur over time, particularly dark to medium colours.
- Prevents tangles.
- Improves the texture of his fur, making it shiny and soft to touch.
- Makes the hair stronger, thereby reducing the possibility of split ends.

Some products also have a pleasing smell, which is an added bonus. Every time you brush his coat, this leave-in conditioner needs to be used afterwards. Most formulas only require a light spritz. Don't go overboard or his fur may seem weighted down.

Use the best shampoo for Pomeranians

The particular shampoo and conditioner for use on your Pomeranian will make a mammoth difference to how healthy and appealing his coat will look.

If you select products with one or more of the following: artificial fragrances, parabens (chemical preservatives, sulphates (harsh detergents), and/or a pH that's higher or lower than 6.5 to 7.5, then your Pomeranian can experience: itchiness, rashes, irritations, dryness, and/or a coat that's dry and dull.

Some of the additives are also connected with health problems ranging from allergic reactions and asthma up to various forms of cancer.

Instead, choose shampoo that: is all-natural, is free of additives, contains natural fragrances, has plant-based cleansers, and is the right pH for dogs (6.5 to 7.5). Don't skip the use of a conditioner you wash out. It's an essential ingredient for good Pomeranian coat care, making it look and feel soft and healthy.

When you shampoo your Pomeranian, the hair cuticles will open. The right conditioner helps to smooth them down once more.

Pomeranian spot cleaning

If your Pomeranian gets any dirt, stains, food, pollens or even urine splashes on his coat, it needs to be cleaned immediately or it can leave permanent marks or discolour his fur, especially if it's light in colour.

Because you only bath a Pomeranian once or twice per month, spot cleaning and wiping him down will maintain a beautiful looking and smelling coat. You get the added benefit of getting rid of irritants and allergens that may exist.

Don't ignore Pomeranian tear stains and face stains

Although this is only about the face, it's included because a Pomeranian's overall look can easily be changed if his face is unkempt. Pomeranian eye stains are usually brown or red around, or under, his eyes.

Omega fatty acids

If a Pomeranian's coat quality is poor, increasing his intake of Omega fatty acids will usually help. It improves the health of the Pomeranian's coat and skin, helps him grow longer, thicker fur, improves the texture and makes his coat shine.

A Pomeranian diet can include Omega fatty acids that mostly

come from seafood (mainly fish), nuts, certain plants, seeds, canola oil and soybeans. The best choice to keep your Pomeranian's coat healthy is the long-chain omega-3 fatty acids DHA and EPA. These are both derived from fish and, if possible, use wild fish instead of fish that has been farmed. You can introduce additional fish to your dog's diet (cold-water fish such as salmon, pollock and mackerel are the ideal choices) in three ways. Prepare home-cooked meals, add fresh fish into his kibble, or add a small amount of fish oil to his meals because most dogs adore its taste and smell.

Pomeranian Trimming

This tip to help your Pomeranian's coat be fluffy, thick, healthy and stunning to look at has a warning to remember.

Pomeranian trimming isn't necessary in all cases. When a Pomeranian's coat is natural, it's often perfect without needing to be touched. The majority of Pomeranians that do have trimmed coats compete in conformation show rings because it's a requirement. So, if you like the look of a trimmed coat, then read on.

A Pomeranian's coat won't grow perfectly on its own. It needs the touch of a caring owner. This is the same in people. Imagine letting your hair grow for a year with no attention. What a sight!

A certain amount of asymmetry is expected and is normal. When his guard hairs become long, they don't do what they're supposed to; namely stand outwards from his body with a thick, full look. Instead, the weight makes it look flat as it weighs his coat down. If a trim is carried out correctly, it will tidy up everything necessary. His fur will be trimmed and layered so it looks more rounded and the ends are symmetrical.

Unfortunately, there are a lot of cases of bad grooming where his owner delivers him to a groomer and asks for a quick trim. When collected, the poor animal has been shaved to the extreme, and his previously great looks have vanished, often never to return, depending on the exact nature of the close shave. As fur struggles to reappear, it's likely to be patchy and it can take a lot of time and effort to restore your Pomeranian's look back to being a healthy one again.

If you use a grooming service, ensure it's somebody you have complete faith in and that your instructions are interpreted accurately. A "tidy trim" is just that, NOT a bald dog that has to tolerate that unpleasant feeling for a long time. Precise instructions and maybe photos of examples will help the groomer understand your needs, especially in the beginning.

Correct Pomeranian Diet

We have kept the most important coat care tip for last. Feed your Pomeranian dog wholesome food. Avoid cheap, processed dog food and, if possible, feed him a correct, well-balanced diet of raw and home-cooked dog food. Many people treat their dogs better than their human family members in some ways. This applies to the food choices as well. After all, if your Pomeranian isn't healthy on the inside, his coat won't be healthy on the outside.

Your vet can always give you information on the right foods to keep your Pom healthy and happy if you aren't quite sure.

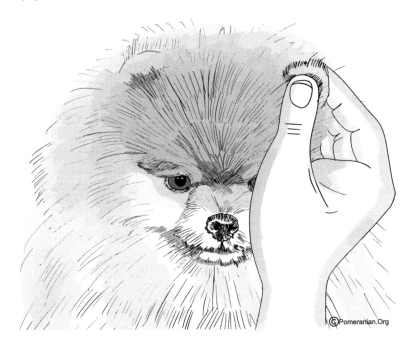

©Pomeranian.Org

Pomeranian trimming guidelines

Learning how to correctly trim a show Pomeranian takes time and a great deal of practice. Trimming is done firstly for neatness and, in the show ring, to enhance a Pomeranian's attributes and to minimise any faults.

When done the right way, trimming can provide a stylish look and outline. However, you can't compare a Pom to a clipped hedge or a trimmed bichon or poodle. Trimming certainly has its value. If a Pomeranian hasn't been trimmed, he virtually has zero chance in any show ring. A properly trimmed Pom won't look artificial; he'll be well-groomed and neat in appearance.

Great care must be taken when trimming any of the sables for the show ring. So much beauty can easily be lost if the colour in the coat tips is heavily trimmed.

Prior to commencing a full show trim, watch your Pomeranian running around and observe his faults and attributes. Think of ways to make the faults less obvious and, most importantly, ways to make the most of his attributes. Only trim a little at a time. Put your Pomeranian down on the floor and again watch him as he runs around. Checking the areas where more or less hair would be an advantage. There isn't a trimming chart for Pomeranians. They shouldn't be trimmed the same way as a Poodle.

Ears

The objective is to make the ears look tiny. Position the ear leather between your finger and thumb. Find the end of the ear leather with your fingertips. Use your fingers to protect the ear leather.

Brush the entire coat on the front and back of the ears upwards and trim this hair to the tips of the ears. Always keep the length of the inside cuts shorter than the outside cuts.

Try not to make the cuts to the tips of the ears too long. Trimming an excessive amount of hair from the ears will merely create the illusion of a Pomeranian with very large ears.

Properly trimmed, the Pomeranian's ears and ruff will present the image of tiny ears poking out from a halo of hair encircling the head.

Feet

Toenails need to be trimmed short before you start trimming the feet. Begin trimming excess hair from between the pads. Show Pomeranians should display cleanly trimmed feet and pads when moving away from the Judge.

Place the Pom on his back. Then, using small straight scissors, trim the hair between the pads and just the underside of the foot.

Stand the Pom again and, using small straight scissors, trim around the dog's feet, removing any hair protruding beyond his toes.

Trim the hair shorter near the toenail, leaving the hair longer near the top of the foot.

Blend this hair directly into the lower- leg coat. It can be neatened with thinning shears.

Legs

Commencing with the front legs, use an imaginary line straight down each side of the Pom as a guide. Using straight scissors, trim any excess hair sticking out from this line. Then switch to the side and brush the hair upwards with the slicker. Again, trim away excess hair.

You're striving for straight legs with the appearance of no toes. Excessive hair on the front of the legs, in the knee region, should be trimmed; otherwise, your Pomeranian may possibly appear to have "knobby knees." Trim the hair on the back of the hocks. Place the Pom on the table and the front of the back legs are trimmed in a similar manner to the front legs.

Trimming the tail

Commence tail trimming by finding the base of the tail with your thumb.

When trimming the tail area, be aware that no amount of trimming will disguise a poor tail set. In fact, too much trimming can make a poor tail set look lower than it actually is. Hair should be trimmed around the anus in a circle shape.

Trimming any untidy hairs on the body of your Pomeranian

Retain the required outline foremost in your thoughts. Use the tips of the ears as your guide to the height of the ruff. Trim the top of the ruff level with the ear tips with thinning shears.

Brush hair downwards and raise a layer at a time with your pin brush, then trim any straggly hairs in a semi-circle with your thinning shears. Repeat layer by layer.

Brush the hair outwards and into ridges on the sides of his body. Trim any excess along each side of the body, using either thinning or straight shears. Laying your Pomeranian on his back, the underneath can also be trimmed in a similar manner.

Always be working towards your goal of a circle effect. During trimming, take a short break and have someone move the Pomeranian so you can evaluate what's required to keep the desired shape.

Nail Trimming

Nail trimming isn't a pleasurable grooming task; however, it's one that can't be neglected. Your Pomeranian will quickly go down on his pastern if nails are left long. Lengthy toenails may force a Pomeranian's toes forward and this could have an impact on his stance and gait.

To achieve the desired cat's-paw look, your Pomeranian must have very short toenails. He should be comfortable having his nails trimmed from an early age as it will be a major part of his grooming regimen throughout his lifetime.

To clip nails, hold your Pomeranian firmly. Talk calmly while clipping. Hold the foot in one hand and shorten the toenail by taking one quick clip. If you're going to trim your Pom's nails, you must have the right tools.

There are many different nail clippers available. Your choice will vary depending on the type of nails your Pom has.

The quick is a blood vessel that flows through the middle of each toenail. If the nail is a dark colour and the quick can't easily be seen, make numerous cuts, starting at the claw's tip, until you can see the grey or pink oval on the nail's surface. Always use trimmers that are sharp and clean. The rear claws are usually shorter and need less cutting than the front ones. To finish off, use a file to smooth the surface.

Always have the trimmer blade facing you and not your dog so you don't cut into the quick. If you do cut it, your dog will suffer pain and bleeding, so take good care. If you do cause bleeding, it will usually stop after a couple of minutes. Styptic powder or pencils can be used to stop the bleeding faster.

Before clipping toenails, identify the "quick" in each toenail. The quick is easy to see on light coloured toenails, but very difficult to locate on dark coloured toenails. If trimming dark coloured toenails, simply take the nail back a tiny sliver at a time.

This blood vessel will grow down near the end of the toenail if nails aren't trimmed. With regular trimming, the quick will recede, making the task much easier.

The best time to clip toenails is just after the Pomeranian's bath, as the warm water will soften the nails. If using a grinder, trim nails before bathing.

Most Pomeranians hate having toenails clipped and an alternative method of trimming toenails is to use a small grinder.

Care must be taken when using this method. Please wrap your Pomeranian tightly in a blanket or towel to prevent his coat being caught in the grinder.

While you're trimming toenails, don't overlook any dewclaws. The inner side of your Pom's paw is where the dew claw is located, and it's connected to his leg by loose skin. The dewclaw never touches the ground but may grow extremely long and possibly grow into the toe-pad. You can bend it away from your dog's leg so you can use a guillotine trimmer on the tip.

If your Pomeranian has dewclaws, these extra toenails will require checking and clipping frequently. If left unclipped, dewclaws can easily grow in a circle and pierce your Pomeranian's skin.

Once you finish trimming, use a metal file to smooth all rough edges. The colour of his nails will depend on the colour of his adjacent skin. Light coloured toenails are simpler to trim than darker ones because you can see the quick much more easily. You should cut your Pom's nails to within 2 mm of his quick.

Tear Stains

All Pomeranians have a degree of tearing around their eyes. It's very common, particularly with lighter coloured dogs. The orange colour has an iron ingredient that the Pom secretes in his saliva, tears and urine. This is why he may have orange on his lips or anywhere else he licks regularly.

To reduce this issue, follow these steps:

- Human eye drops can be used to flush your dog's tear ducts. A couple of drops twice a day in each eye may stop ugly eye staining.
- Use a damp makeup pad to wash away the stains each day. (Use sterile water to moisten the pad or eye drops). Never use tissues around your dog's eye area. Tissues are made from wood and may cause severe eye irritation.
- Get antibiotics from the vet to prevent staining.

Many breeders also recommend:

- Only providing distilled water for your dog to drink.
- The use of moisturising eye drops.
- Giving your dog vitamin C.
- A small amount of coconut oil added daily to your dog's food as it's thought to also help with this issue.
- 1 teaspoon of apple cider vinegar added to your dog's food daily may also be helpful. Some dogs won't eat their meal with the vinegar added, so start slowly by only adding a few drops and increasing slowly to one teaspoon of apple cider vinegar daily.
- As a first step, however, your veterinarian should check for an eyelid or lash problem that could be irritating his eyes or blocking his tear ducts. Sometimes surgery can fix the problem.

Pomeranian Grooming Chart

Grooming Task	Schedule	Why is this required?	Outcome if not done
Wipe under eyes.	Daily.	Remove "sleep" from under eyes. Prevent eye stains.	Tears stains and possible infection.
Brush Pomeranian's teeth.	Daily.	Prevent dental issues.	Bad breath. Dirty teeth, dental decay, gum infections and tooth loss.
Check Pom's bottom area.	Daily.	Faeces often becomes stuck to fur.	Soiled & irritated Pom's bottom.
Brush your Pom's coat.	2 to 3 times weekly.	To remove loose coat and prevent mats.	Coat mats may develop.
Pomeranian bath.	Every 2 to 3 weeks.	Maintain skin and coat health.	Bad body odour and poor coat health.
Apply nose balm (if required).	2 to 3 times weekly.	Prevent dry, chapped noses.	Dry noses can start cracking.
Apply paw wax (if required).	2 to 3 times weekly.	Protect paws.	Dryness and cracking.
Trim toenails.	Every 2 to 3 weeks.	Keep nails short.	Ingrown toenails, broken nails and poor gait.
Coat trimming.	Every 4 to 6 weeks.	To maintain desired coat length and shape.	Longer coat can develop mats and tangles.

Pomeranian Shedding

Contrary to popular belief, Pomeranians don't shed much fur. The shedding can be easily managed with most long-coated breeds because it's seasonal and, in the case of female dogs, hormonal shedding (after a season or after weaning a litter).

In contrast to Pomeranians and other long-coated dog breeds, smooth haired dogs are heavy shedders and they usually do it every day.

Pomeranians shed in one of three ways:

1. The "puppy uglies" is the name for the period when Poms lose their puppy fur and grow their adult coat.
2. Seasonal shedding is experienced by most adult Pomeranians.
3. Total shedding may occur after a female weans a litter, due to hormonal changes.

Puppy shedding

Your puppy will be 4 to 6 months old when he starts to shed his baby fur. All puppies are different, of course, and the entire process will take around five months before all the puppy fur is gone and he has his adult double coat.

The colour of your Pom's fur can significantly change during this period. As an example, a heavy sable Pomeranian pup may end up with an orange adult coat or a white Pom puppy can go through the puppy shedding stage to end up as a cream-coloured Pom.

While the puppy fur is being shed, your Pom can look quite funny. This is because, at different times during the process, he'll have missing patches of fur. Don't be concerned because this is normal and won't last long.

Once your puppy is 10 months old, his adult fur should be really starting to grow. By the time he hits the 12 – to – 15 - month point, his adult coat will have fully developed. You'll feel the coat's difference. A puppy has soft fur which is replaced with a coat consisting of harsh guard hairs and the soft undercoat.

Adult Pomeranian shedding

Some Pomeranians will do a complete shed once again during the 12 – to – 18 - month period. There does appear to be a greater chance of this occurring if your puppy turns12 months old during the summer. After 18 months, your Pomeranian may do light seasonal sheds.

There are several variables that govern when your Pom will shed. The climate you live in and the environment the puppy grows up in are both key factors. Light changes are also a factor and shedding may occur twice a year.

You can expect most adult Pomeranians to do some seasonal shedding. It will be a heavier shed with females who haven't been desexed. They'll often experience shedding after each season. Adult desexed Poms of both sexes will undergo some light seasonal shedding.

During the shedding process, how much fur will your Pom lose?

If adults lose too much fur, to the point where there are patches missing, this isn't regarded as normal. Adult Poms rarely lose that much fur except if they're females (as mentioned in the third shedding option below).

If patches appear, there may be a medical reason and you should contact your vet. The reasons why this occurs include thyroid troubles, allergies, mange and many more. Your vet will run a large barrage of tests and examinations to determine the actual cause and then the right treatment can begin.

The third type of Pomeranian shedding is the total shed after an adult female has whelped a litter of babies. Mothers typically do a total shed when the litter is six to eight weeks of age.

A time period of at least six months is invariably required following a litter for a Pomeranian mother to return to her former full-coated beauty. Don't be concerned about her complete shed as this is normal, owing to hormonal changes.

Removing shed hair is vital

Pomeranian owners should be prepared to brush the coat daily with a pin and slicker brush to remove dead hair during coat shedding. The quicker you remove the dead coat, the faster the new hair will grow in its place. Brushing daily will also reduce the need to remove your Pom's dead coat from your furniture and clothing.

Remember, if a dead coat isn't removed promptly, it can become matted and that often leads to skin problems, yeast infections and other canine ailments. If a mat occurs, it requires lots of work to extricate it without cutting it off. Dog conditioner may be useful as it helps loosen the mat, and the tip of a grooming comb can be ideal to get it out. If the mat can't be removed by these methods, you'll have to cut the fur to prevent the matt from growing in size.

The shedding of dog fur is a natural, healthy renewal process. However, you can do certain things to control the shedding and avoid having hair spread all around your home.

1. The best brushes to use when your Pom is shedding are a large, soft slicker brush and a good quality pin brush. Add a Teflon-coated comb and you have what you need.
2. Plan a schedule for grooming. Some owners enjoy dog grooming after dinner, while they relax in front of the TV.
3. If you have nice weather, groom outside if you can. Warm, dry weather is ideal. Doing the grooming outside helps reduce mess.
4. If your pet has been a member of your family for more than a year and you haven't tried using a tape lint roller on your carpet, you'll be amazed at what you'll find. Regular vacuum cleaners aren't powerful enough to grab all dog hair. Get a vacuum that's designed for pet owners and the better models have special filters that can catch allergens that may affect your pet and your human family as well.
5. Don't forget parts of your Pom's coat. When he sheds, many owners mainly work on their dog's back because it's the biggest area. However, fur can fall from any part

of his body, including his tail. So, the best way to deal with a heavy shed is to start brushing the underneath area first - e.g., the tummy area, then move to the chest area, hairs on the legs, ruff, pants, tail and, lastly, move onto his back.

6. Bathe your dog every week and shampoo and condition his fur well. Blow as much dead hair out with a dryer, while you're brushing.

Shaving a Pomeranian

Taking your Pomeranian to a groomer is often a risky venture, especially if you haven't used that person's services before. You need to give clear instructions on what you want to be done and, just as importantly, what you don't want done.

Shaving or clipping the coat very short on a double-coated dog, like the Pomeranian, may cause damage to the hair follicles. Most coats that have been clipped will start growing back almost immediately. However, it's possible that the clipped hair may never grow back, or it could take a very long time to do so. The older your dog gets, the greater the chances are that there won't be any growth or that it will be very slow.

If this happens, your dog will have a patchy, scruffy appearance. Shaving or clipping your Pomeranian's coat very short may alter the coat for the rest of his life. This problem is usually referred to as post-clipping alopecia.

Clipping the coat during the resting phase is thought to be a cause of post-clipping alopecia which may be an advanced indicator of hypothyroidism or other problems associated with your Pom's metabolism.

The coat on a Pomeranian dog is fur. Humans have fur on our arms and legs and hair on our head. The difference between fur and hair is that fur only grows to a certain length while hair keeps on growing.

Fur goes through a resting period, called the telogen phase, during which the hair follicles are dormant. The growing phase is called the anagen phase. In the Pomeranian and other Nordic dog breeds, it's believed that this is a short phase. Hair will grow to predefined lengths, thanks to the dog's DNA. Then it stops growing and goes into the telogen resting period. The length of the two coat phases can vary according to the amount of stress your dog is experiencing.

It seems pointless to buy a long-coated dog, such as a Pomeranian if you're just going to clip his coat. If you really want to do that, perhaps you should think more about the breed of dog you want, before making the purchase. Also, consider the amount of overall grooming involved if it's not something you want to do. Maybe you would prefer a dog that doesn't need as much grooming.

Pomeranians have a double layer coat. The undercoat has short, fluffy soft hairs and acts as an insulation and helps support the much longer outer layer. In other words, the dog stays cool in summer and warm in winter.

The stronger, longer guard hairs help to insulate your dog against the heat from the sun. Evolution blessed the Pomeranian breed in this manner. If you clip the coat very short, you eliminate the dog's natural cooling and heating ability, so you cause more harm than good.

There's a considerable contrast between dogs and people. Dogs don't get cool through their skin. Their paw pads sweat, and their major cooling method is panting. Owners also foolishly believe that shaving their dog will stop him shedding. Poms and other double-coat breeds will still shed after they have been shaved.

To sum it all up: Shaving or close clipping any double-coated dog can severely hinder their ability to keep themselves warm and cool. It also eliminates natural protection of their skin.

The ideal way to make your Pomeranian comfortable and cool is to give him regular baths and brush his coat. Shaving should only be done if the dog's hair is badly matted.

Pomeranian Puppy Uglies

Your Pomeranian's coat will go through numerous changes over the years. Owners new to this breed often don't realise the fluffy, puppy coat generally starts to fall out when the Pomeranian is around four months of age. Puppy's legs get tall and gangly and his coat becomes short and wispy. It's common for some areas of the puppy's body to grow faster than others and your pup may appear a little odd looking for a few weeks.

This period is actually referred to as the Pomeranian puppy "uglies" or puppy transition. Most puppies have to go through this awkward phase of puppy adolescence. It will be more obvious in some than in others. In most Pomeranians, it will be a moderate to severe phase that can worry owners who may not be aware that it's normal for this breed.

Looking after your Pom's coat during the "Puppy Uglies" phase

Regularly brush his coat to get rid of the remnants of the older, dead coat. The faster the dead coat is eliminated, the quicker the new coat can begin to grow to replace the dead puppy coat.

Maintain his regular bathing schedule but make sure you brush him properly and that all of the dead coat has been removed before you begin. If this isn't done correctly, the coat can become severely matted.

6-month-old Dochlaggie Debonair going through the "puppy uglies"

Dental Care Tips for Pomeranians

Part of loving any Pom is ensuring good dental hygiene is always maintained. While you can give your dog treats and toys that are designed to help clean his teeth, that's not the sole answer. This is especially relevant in small dog breeds such as Pomeranians, whose teeth are tiny.

If your dog's teeth aren't being brushed regularly, there are numerous problems that may occur:

A build-up of tartar and plaque

Small scraps of food and saliva mix to create a sticky substance that coats the teeth. This can't be eliminated solely by chewing food.

Gingivitis

This is a major problem. If you don't use a high-quality dog toothpaste and brush his gums and teeth regularly, bacteria will grow beneath the gums. After a short time, inflammation will occur, and the gums may even bleed. All these problems can cause cavities and lost teeth. Some may need to be extracted.

Infection

Certain infections can travel through your Pom's body, affecting his brain, heart, kidneys and liver.

Infections within the sinuses

Infection can enter the jawbone and pus pockets may get into the nasal cavities, thereby causing nasal discharge and chronic sneezing.

Difficulty eating

If your Pom manages to survive these problems as well as the loss of teeth, eating will become difficult when he's a senior. Without teeth, he'll find it tough to maintain a healthy weight range.

How to brush a Pomeranian's teeth

A major reason why Pomeranian puppies struggle when having

their teeth brushed is because it's an intrusive, terrifying new activity. Before you even think of trying it, you should use your fingers to make him comfortable.

Canine specialists recommend that you choose something your Pom puppy finds tasty and dip your fingers in it. Then you can let him lick your fingers as you gently touch his teeth. That will help him become more at ease when you eventually do use a toothbrush and toothpaste.

Do this activity for a short period (usually only a few days) and you'll watch your Pomeranian puppy get so excited whenever you touch his mouth.

Learn the best way to open your Pom's mouth

Brushing is an activity that your puppy needs to enjoy, or the daily ritual will quickly become a nightmare. You must NEVER attempt to pry his mouth open with a degree of force. The trick is that you put your thumb beneath his jaw. This action keeps his mouth shut and enables you to lift his lips until you see his teeth and gums.

Using your fingers on the other hand, lightly rub his gums and teeth for just a few seconds before letting him go. Always have a yummy treat for him to reward his good behaviour and repeat this activity as often as you can, to help your Pomeranian gradually build a tolerance to this activity.

Choose the ideal time for brushing his teeth

The next decision to make is when to brush your Pomeranian's teeth. Poms love predictability in their lives. Establish a time that's also suitable for you and stick with it. If you brush his teeth at a specific time every day, he won't put up a fuss.

Brushing your Pomeranian's teeth shouldn't feel like a chore, something you want to cross off your daily list as fast as you can. You need to make it an enjoyable experience for you and your canine companion. Because of this, it's necessary to choose a consistent time when you won't be busy, in a rush to finish other things, or exhausted. Remember there are two schedules to consider. The second one is your Pomeranian's schedule. For example: brushing his teeth would be much harder if he's excited about going to have his daily walk, or if he's hungry. Consider the available option times and stick with it.

Select the ideal toothpaste and toothbrush

Some owners choose a toothbrush that's the right size for human children, as a way to clean their Pomeranian's teeth. I recommend using a dog toothbrush for breeds that are small. As soon as your Pomeranian is at ease with the actual toothbrushing procedure, you should then consider progressing to a battery-powered human toothbrush for superior results.

When it comes to toothpastes, NEVER use human products because they all have fluorides as ingredients and if your Pom has even a tiny amount, it can prove fatal.

Natural toothpaste is another dangerous product because some have an ingredient called xylitol, and this can cause low blood sugar within minutes, thereby proving fatal to Pomeranians.

Doggie toothpastes with tempting flavours are readily available.

Gradually get your Pomeranian used to the paste and brush

If you have already achieved everything set out in this guide, your puppy will be ok when your fingers touch his mouth area. The next stage is to help him become comfortable with the toothpaste. Then comes the toothbrush and the finishing line grows much closer.

Put something tasty on the brush to start with (maybe cheese or a sardine). Then call your Pom to you and allow him to smell and explore the brush.

It's not time to brush yet. The goal is to get him to associate the brush and tasty treats as the same thing. After he's used to the brush, it's time to start with the paste. Put a little on one of your fingers and let your Pomeranian puppy sniff and lick it as he gets used to it. At this stage do not attempt to brush your puppy's teeth.

It's Time to Brush His Teeth

After your Pomeranian is used to the feel of brush, you can begin brushing. Get everything you need as well as your Pomeranian and find a position that's comfortable for you both. One example would be to put him on your bed while you kneel on the floor. On the other hand, you might cuddle him if you think that would be an easier way for you to brush his teeth.

Next, you'll need to put your thumb beneath his jaw and gently lift his top lip. First you should brush his canine teeth in circular movements. Then move further back. After completing both sides, you move to his front teeth (aka incisors).

When you first start doing this, it will only take 10-20 seconds to completely brush his teeth. Slowly you'll increase the time until you reach two minutes. Your phone is best for accurate time tracking.

It's common for your Pomeranian to be a bit fidgety during the teeth cleaning sessions. If, however, he's too anxious or uncomfortable, stop brushing and go back and work more on improving his tolerance level. If he struggles a lot while you're using a brush, you can buy a finger toothbrush or, alternatively, wrap a little gauze around one of your fingers and use that like a toothbrush.

Reward your Pomeranian

After you have finished all your Pomeranian's teeth and he has behaved, let him go, praise him for such good behaviour, and give him a treat. End every brushing session in a positive manner so he learns that it's an activity to enjoy.

Part 6 – Health

Pomeranian Health Concerns

All dogs may experience health issues common to their breeds, including crossbreed dogs. Genetics and environment play a big part in the health of your Pomeranian and the following issues are the most typical:

Luxating patellas

Though the term "luxating patella" may sound confusing, it simply means a kneecap that has slipped out of place. Luxating patellas are common in Pomeranians and their knees are graded by the Orthopaedic Foundation for Animals (OFA).

Early diagnosis is helpful in slowing the progress, but treatment depends on the severity of the condition. If your puppy has a higher grade early in life, he'll be more likely to need surgery, which can be expensive. A surgical procedure to remake the groove, as well as tightening any tissues that may have become stretched, may help your Pom.

A young dog who has either a grade 1 or 2, as well as any

with a grade of 3 or 4, is generally a viable candidate. While operating may not fix his leg 100%, it should allow him to walk and run with little to no pain. An orthopaedic surgeon is an ideal person to treat your dog's condition.

If you give your dog supplements, they may help in the low grade 1 level but won't do a lot for the higher grades.

Hypothyroidism

A low-level thyroid, or hypothyroidism, is sometimes seen in Pomeranians.

Pomeranian coat loss

Pomeranians sometimes experience a coat problem called black skin disease. This coat loss may also be referred to as BSD or Alopecia X. Pomeranian puppies with beautiful, full, fluffy coats may develop early-onset BSD. Pomeranian puppies with these types of coats often lack the harsh guard hairs and feel like "cotton" to touch.

These Poms often don't shed their puppy coat and go through the ugly stage like most Pomeranian puppies. Coat loss usually occurs at around 14 to 16 months and these cases are referred to as the early onset version of black skin disease.

Late-onset black skin disease usually occurs at around three to four years of age, but cases have been documented where the Pomeranian has developed Alopecia X as late as nine years of age. Because Alopecia X is thought to be genetic, you should ask your breeder for information regarding this condition.

Collapsing trachea

A Pomeranian that makes a honking or cough-like noise (much like a cat regurgitating a hairball) may have a collapsed trachea. An x-ray can diagnose the issue, and medication can reduce the symptoms. A collapsed trachea can be deadly and immediate veterinarian treatment is required.

In minor cases where the trachea may collapse, these steps can be taken to help alleviate the problem:

- Use a harness instead of a collar.
- Help him lose weight.
- Keep him away from irritants including cigarette smoke.
- Give him vitamin C and glucosamine to help strengthen his cartilage.
- Avoid putting him in scenarios where he may cough, pant heavily, get stressed or become overheated.

Any coughing should be investigated, and it could also indicate worms, heart disease or hairballs. Pomeranian puppies have been known to die from hairballs. Fur can be ingested by the puppy while feeding from his mother.

Heart problems

Pomeranians can experience heart problems. Issues ranging from extremely minor to life-threatening are common in all dogs. Like humans, heart disease in dogs is associated with genetic factors and poor lifestyle which includes poor diet, obesity and lack of exercise.

Again, any reputable Pomeranian breeder should have a plethora of information on a puppy's lineage to help determine if heart issues run in the family.

Hypoglycaemia

Hypoglycaemia in young, very small, active Pomeranian puppies isn't unusual. Discuss any potential problems regarding hypoglycaemia and your new Pomeranian puppy, with the breeder prior to collecting him.

Hypoglycaemia is very low blood sugar. Glucose is the form of sugar found within the bloodstream. It's created during digestion of foods and it can be stored within the liver in a storage form called glycogen.

Most cases of low blood sugar (hypoglycaemia) in puppies are the result of insufficient or low-quality food. Excessive exercise or even over-handling a new puppy may possibly cause his body to require more sugar than is accessible. A young puppy with hypoglycaemia will certainly be lacking energy. Glucose is the fuel the body burns for energy. Devoid of glucose sugars, the puppy will be lethargic. In serious cases, the puppy might even have a seizure and, in extreme cases, can become comatose and die.

Glucose is essential for the brain tissue and muscles to function. The dangers of hypoglycaemia depend on the severity. Hypoglycaemia, because of insufficient food, excessive exercise or too much handling, is easily remedied.

If, however, the cause is a liver disease preventing the storage of glucose as glycogen, or intestinal disease interfering with the absorption of food, hypoglycaemia might be chronic, and even life-threatening. If your puppy is lethargic and fatigued as a result of low blood sugar, immediately give him some glucose. Karo syrup and honey are excellent sugar options and should be immediately given to your puppy. Please contact your veterinarian without delay.

Seizures

Idiopathic epilepsy (that which has an unknown cause) can appear in the Pomeranian breed. Sometimes, the epilepsy is caused by head trauma, liver disease or kidney problems, but it can have other causes as well. Most epileptic Pomeranians exhibit symptoms between three and seven years old.

Perthes disease

Perthes Disease occasionally occurs in Pomeranians, generally before they're a year old (4-11 months). The condition is caused by a loss of blood supply to the hip joint and results in extreme pain and lameness. The reduced blood supply could be the result of injury, abnormal sex hormone activity or genetics.

Eye issues

The inward rolling of the eyelid on a Pomeranian will cause his eyelashes to rub on the eye's surface. The resulting discomfort makes him squint and/or become sensitive to the sun and other bright lights.

Fortunately, this type of eye issue can be corrected with surgery (recommended for Pomeranians over 1 year). Occasionally, as the puppy grows, this condition may self-correct. If a Pomeranian with this problem isn't treated with surgery, corneal ulceration and/or scarring can occur.

NOTE: Veterinarians trained to do Canine Eye Registry Foundation (CERF) testing can also look at a Pomeranian's eyes for genetic problems. CERF has a database to give buyers of Pomeranians information on the parents (and possibly other relatives) of all registered Pomeranian pups.

Open fontanels

Open fontanels are an opening in the top of the puppy's skull, similar to an open fontanel in a newborn human baby. They're not a rare occurrence in small dog breeds. Fortunately, most of the smaller sized open fontanels seen in Pomeranian puppies will cause the dog no problems and most will close before a puppy reaches 12 months.

Gonad descent abnormalities

Male Pomeranians may experience the abnormal descent of their male parts (one or both). If this is the case, castration is the usual route taken. Ignoring this issue (which is thought to be inherited) can put the pup at a higher risk of testicular cancer.

Retained deciduous (puppy) teeth

When Pomeranian puppies are born, they have no teeth at all. By the time Pomeranian puppies get to about six weeks old, they grow deciduous teeth, usually called puppy teeth. Pomeranian puppies have 28 teeth that are temporary and begin to erupt at 3-4 weeks. By the time they're 6-8 months, they'll have 42 teeth that are permanent.

When these teeth start falling out, the incisors come out first, then the premolars and canine teeth. The canine teeth are a lot bigger and the top and bottom canines are at the back of the mouth. Both bottom and top incisors are found in the Pom's middle section.

The deciduous teeth start coming out when the puppy is between three and seven months of age. Each of the roots from these teeth will get absorbed by the adult teeth. However, there are times when this doesn't happen the right way.

Occasionally the permanent teeth don't push out the deciduous teeth. If your puppy has both teeth at the same time, it's known as retained deciduous teeth.

In a Pomeranian, this will generally happen with the upper and lower canine baby teeth being retained. They should lose each puppy tooth prior to the adult tooth coming through but toy breeds are notorious for keeping their baby teeth and end up with a "double row of teeth."

I begin checking the mouth of every puppy on a weekly basis from the age of 4 months, so I can assess whether any puppy teeth still exist and how well the new adult teeth line up.

Consider risks connected with the retention of puppy teeth

If your Pom has puppy and permanent teeth, the mouth gets

quite crowded. This can even displace permanent teeth, so they grow at a bad angle. This abnormality may cause the jaw not to grow normally. The baby teeth may rub against the roof of the Pom's mouth, causing pain and injury. Infections, or an abscess, can occur as a result.

Talk to your vet if you suspect there are retained teeth. Removing the retained teeth and de-sexing your puppy are procedures that can both be done at the same time.

Photo by Ariel Xuran Li

Choosing Your Pomeranian's Veterinarian

Below are helpful tips for making the best decision:

1. Conduct research on vets before bringing your Pomeranian puppy home, or as soon as you can afterwards. Don't wait for a problem to arise.
2. Search for a veterinarian by word-of-mouth. Talk to colleagues, family members, friends and, if applicable, your puppy's breeder, obedience class instructor or groomer.
3. Check out any animal hospitals in the area and ask them for recommendations for veterinarians.

4. Look for vets that specialise in smaller dog breeds. Some aren't as comfortable with tiny pups as others.
5. Look for a vet who has experience with Pomeranians. Those who do will know what to look for when it comes to medical conditions common to the breed.
6. Find a vet that's fairly close to your residence in case you have an emergency. Who wants to drive for hours if time is of the essence?
7. Find a vet with office hours and emergency hours that fit your lifestyle. The greatest vet in the world can't help you if you can't get to his office.
8. Find a veterinarian who's helpful and friendly. He'll be more likely to work with you if problems should arise.
9. Visit prospective vet offices before making your final choice. Are they clean? Staffed with caring professionals? Listen to your instincts? if you feel there are "red flags," go with your gut and find another option. There are plenty of vets in the world!
10. Find out how to make appointments. Do you have to call? Can you "walk in?" Do they have a website? Can you make appointments via the Internet?
11. Make sure you ask about their fees. This could save you from a future shock if your Pomeranian has a health issue. Though most vets in your area will probably have similar fee schedules, you don't want to go to the most expensive veterinarian to get the best health help for your Pomeranian if it's not necessary. There are plenty of vets that do excellent work at reasonable fees.
12. Ask vets if they offer other services such as boarding or grooming. Then take a tour of those facilities.
13. Ask if a prospective veterinarian is a specialist in a specific area, such as surgery or cardiology. Of course, finding the right vet is only half the battle. Because this relationship will become a partnership, you need to become a smart, considerate customer. This means learning what's normal for your Pomeranian, and what constitutes an emergency.

You'll need to visit your vet on a regular basis, so always keep appointments. Doing so will ensure you get the best treatment possible for your pet. It will also make you appear to be a conscientious client and avid pet lover to the office staff. They do notice and they do appreciate caring pet owners.

When in the vet's office, keep your Pomeranian on a harness or in his crate at all times. This is for the protection of your pet and the other animals in the room. For dogs, a visit to the vet can be a tangle of emotions – excitement, stress and tension. Keep him in your arms (or in his crate) and don't allow him to roam.

Finally, remember that vets are people, too. They have lives. Don't inundate yours with "emergency" questions that aren't real emergencies.

What to do in case of an honest-to-goodness medical emergency

The unthinkable has occurred, and you need emergency medical attention for your Pomeranian. Instead of floundering and wasting time, follow two simple steps:

1. Call your veterinarian and see if he or she is available.
2. If your vet isn't able to see you, ask for a referral to an animal hospital or emergency vet service nearby.

Tips on Your Pom's First Vet Check-Up

Don't let your first vet visit be an emergency

Once you have brought your new Pomeranian home and he has settled in, it's time to check his overall health. This is where your vet comes in. If he's your first dog, you'll need to locate a vet nearby. If you own other dogs currently or have done so in the past, you'll already have a good vet when needed.

Don't ignore a visit until your Pomeranian has a health problem. You may be unable to get a vet appointment, especially if you're not already a customer. Building a good relationship with your vet is important for both you and your Pom.

An annual check-up

Dogs need to have a complete check-up at least once every year. Dogs age faster than people so regular care is vital. Once a dog is seven years old, check-ups should be more frequent. Don't put it off because, once it's done, the vet has a guide for checking your dog's health from then on.

The vet will check your puppy's health in various ways including:

- Weight.
- Heartbeat.
- Knees.
- Teeth, ears and eyes.
- Possibly palpating the internal organs softly to see if there are any tumours or enlargements.
- Possibly running urine and/or blood tests to verify there are no internal problems.

It's important to ask about fees for the various tests. Obviously, the money isn't as important as your Pom being healthy, but it could be a factor in some cases.

Intestinal infections

There are two intestinal parasites that are very common but aren't worms. They're single-celled organisms called protozoa. They're usually picked up through the environment so it's hard to avoid them.

The protozoan intestinal infection known as "coccidiosis" can cause intense diarrhoea (leading to dehydration if not treated) in Pomeranian puppies.

Symptoms of coccidiosis include rank-smelling faeces and stools containing mucous and blood. A faecal exam can determine whether coccidiosis is present.

Giardia is another type that's commonly found in dogs and puppies. Often there are no symptoms, but the main symptom is a light-colour loose stool. A stool sample is required to make a diagnosis and the vet can prescribe medication to treat the problem.

Understanding Vaccinations

Until recently, vets believed that they should give as many vaccinations as possible. However, today's information tells people that puppies should only be given the vaccinations they need, and at the appropriate time.

So, what is needed?

This depends a lot on your country of residence. Here in Australia, we're free of rabies, so the rabies vaccination isn't included in the core group of vaccinations.

Two main vaccination categories:

Core vaccines: All dogs need to have hepatitis, parvovirus and distemper. Dogs outside of Australia also need the rabies shot.

Noncore vaccines: Only some dogs need these shots and the non-core vaccines include: kennel cough, coronavirus, Lyme disease and leptospirosis.

Your vet will know what vaccines your pets need from the non-core group. Lifestyle, environment and location are all deciding factors. Boarding kennels require vaccination for kennel cough.

Vaccinations - when and what?

Your puppy first gets antibodies from his mother's milk within his first 24 hours of life. At that point, vaccinations don't help. Once a couple of weeks have gone by, that early protection gradually fades and so the puppy is then vulnerable to diseases and his system can now benefit from vaccinations and produce an immunity to many diseases.

Puppies don't all lose immunity provided by colostrum from their mother at the same speed and age, so it makes giving vaccinations a little hard to carry out at times. To make it easier to manage, the vet should give a series of vaccinations commencing when the puppy is six weeks old. Future vaccinations can be properly timed for maximum protection.

During a short period from 6 to 16 weeks, there's uncertainty regarding a puppy's immune status. You need to ensure your puppy does not go anywhere that other dogs could congregate. Parvovirus can exist in the environment around six months.

Dealing with Fleas

Most Pomeranians and other dog breeds will have fleas one or more times during their lives. Even if you have no idea how your dog got fleas, you should remember it's a possible reason why your pet scratches so much. Your dog may get fleas while playing in a dog park, visiting your local pet store and many other possibilities because a flea can jump up to six feet at a time and they can also jump from dog to dog.

Symptoms of fleas

Fleas are incredibly small but when they bite, it can cause your dog to be intensely itchy. Many dogs have an allergy to the saliva of the fleas so when it touches your dog's skin, as he enjoys a blood feast, the intensity of the itchiness increases immensely.

Your Pom will try to scratch all areas that feel itchy. He'll use his paws where possible but, in some cases, he'll rub himself against the floor, a wall, bedding or other places, to stop that annoying sensation. If his paws itch, he will chew them to stop the itchy sensation.

Fleas reproduce extremely fast. This means that if your Pom has a few fleas to start with, he will quickly become infested with them. If he's allergic, one bite may create such a deep itchy sensation that he will gnaw at the affected area, causing some loss of fur as he tries to burrow deep down. His paws are the most common place for fleas to congregate.

While fleas jump, they don't have wings and, therefore, do not have the ability to fly. This means you will never see swarms of fleas circling your poor Pomeranian. Have a close look at parts of your pet's body where he can't scratch (for example, the back and tail) and you'll notice the tiniest black or brown dots that resemble finely ground pepper specks. Wipe some of them off with a white paper towel you have moistened. Then fold it and squeeze and you'll usually see little speckles of blood.

Fleas are nearly impossible to kill

Fleas are incredibly resilient and almost impossible to eradicate completely. They prefer a moist, temperate climate but may go dormant for as long as a year, until ideal conditions for reproduction and survival exist once more. In their dormant state, they can be inside or outside, in wall and floor joints, carpet, bedding, furniture, indoor plants, yards and gardens.

Your car is not safe from being infested either. If your Pomeranian has fleas and spends time in your car, some may go dormant by jumping off his body and hiding in the car. He may have anywhere from 100 to 4000 fleas on his coat at any time. Fleas have four life cycles which means your Pom could host a thriving flea civilisation and most of the fleas won't be noticed by you.

A Pom's fleas will exist in one of four cycles:

1. Adults that take their food from your Pom's blood and these are responsible for most of the itchy sensations.
2. Eggs. One female flea can lay anything up to 50 eggs each day, but the majority fall from the dog's body and settle into carpets, bedding and other similar places.
3. Larvae. Larvae emerge from the eggs when hatched. At some point between 5-20 days, they start spinning miniscule cocoons.
4. Pupae. When fleas are in the cocoons, they're called Pupae. They may be in the cocoons for days up until one whole year, and they only come out as mature fleas once the ideal conditions exist.

If you see ONE flea, there will be at least another 100 in their various developmental stages.

How do you eliminate fleas?

Talk to your veterinarian for the best method of attacking any flea problems. Ask for advice on a product that will kill all the fleas on your beloved Pomeranian in their four cycles, and advice on protecting other pets you may own.

If your Pomeranian and other pets are treated with one of the modern flea insecticide treatments, the fleas in your home and garden will eventually die. Unfortunately, the flea can live for up to six months without feeding from a host animal.

Your vet may suggest that you bomb your home. This will send a light mist into corners and crevices where normal cleaning efforts can't reach. Select a product that protects your home for six months once used and ensure it's a product that's completely dry within an hour.

If you decide to use a pest exterminator, ask questions first. What chemicals will they be using? What effects can such chemicals have on your pets? Always verify credentials and claims of the company you plan to utilise.

Kill fleas in the car and garden

You have numerous options if you're willing to do this yourself. You may also opt to pay a professional to carry out the job instead.

Choose from among the non-toxic options because they are much safer than ordinary pesticides. For example, Diatomaceous Earth dries out the areas so fleas leave because it's not a place in which they can survive. This is a food grade quality, and this means it's supposedly safe for animal and human consumption, while killing fleas and certain other worms. It also means your dog can go outside and play without risking his health.

Choose your Pomeranian's protection wisely. Despite using any flea destruction method, fleas can still infest dogs sometimes. Choose the best products to keep your beloved pet safe. Monitor your pet's reactions to products as dogs may have unpleasant reactions to specific preventatives.

Fleas are an essential part of the reproduction and life cycle of certain worms so ensure that, apart from the flea treatment, your Pomeranian and all other pets will require worming.

Worms

There are several different worms that can cause health trouble for dogs. It's essential that you know them all so you can safely protect your beloved pet.

Tapeworms

Tapeworms are flat and have parts that spread across your Pom's body. The head has muscular grooves, or suckers, that let the worm connect to the intestines of your canine friend.

A mature tapeworm growing in your dog may be up to 50 cms in length. In puppies, tapeworms can cause anaemia, inhibit growth and cause blockages in the intestines.

The most common method for getting tapeworms is by swallowing one or more fleas because they have tapeworm eggs. A less common method is coming into proximity with lizards and/or rodents that have tapeworms.

Dried parts of tapeworms may be around the anus of your Pomeranian and are usually about the size of a single rice grain. They cause itchiness and your dog may drag his butt on the ground to get rid of the itchy feeling. Whole worms can often be seen in your dog's droppings.

If you think your dog may does have tapeworms, talk to your vet about the issue. Once diagnosed, he can be prescribed with products to remedy the problem.

Hookworms

These worms are incredibly nasty. Hookworms may exist on your Pomeranian for one of three reasons:

1. Hookworms may exist from the moment a puppy is born.
2. A puppy may attract hookworms while drinking his mother's milk.
3. The final cause is that a Pomeranian could swallow hookworm larvae. They're microscopically small and may exist on grass blades, in dog bowls for food, and many other places.

After your Pomeranian is infected by these nasty worms, symptoms may appear but they can also copy other medical problems. Examples include: diarrhoea (generally bloody or black in colour), loss of appetite, vomiting, weakness, slowed growth, emaciation and his mouth may have mucous membranes that are pale and clouded.

Prevention:

There are a couple of ways you can prevent your Pom from getting hookworms.

1. Hygiene is a crucial factor in preventing hookworms. Never leave his faeces in your yard.
2. People need to wash their hands regularly, especially if playing with pets and then doing other things. Ensure your pet is clean and regularly groomed.
3. Hookworms can travel from dog to dog to environment and then to another dog. Because of this, avoid parks that aren't clean.

4. If you give him home cooked food, cook the meat really well.
5. When you clean your home's hard surfaces, use bleach as this destroys the larvae of the hookworms.
6. The single most vital method for protecting your Pom from hookworms is to have regular vet check-ups. This is in addition to getting help for any health issues that can occur at any time. Your vet can treat hookworms easily once it's correctly diagnosed.

Roundworms

The most common type of parasite that occurs in dogs is roundworms. They're four inches in length and looked like strands of cooked spaghetti, being a white colour.

Roundworms exist in a dog's intestine, where they remain alive by eating food that hasn't been fully digested.

If a dam has roundworms, they may be passed onto their puppies who are born with this type of worm. A puppy may also get roundworms from drinking his mother's milk.

The mother may not be diagnosed for roundworms but can still pass it onto her newly born puppies. This is because she could have undeveloped larvae. Dogs may swallow these worms if they're chewing on rodents and consuming soil containing the worms.

There are usually no visible symptoms of roundworms in the initial stages. So, it's critical that you have a regular de-worming action plan. Your vet will give you a plan to which you must adhere.

If your Pomeranian is hit with roundworms, he may vomit. When doing so, you'll notice roundworms because they're round instead of, like the tapeworms, segmented. His stomach may be swollen, he may have pneumonia and, as the worms move through his body, some symptoms can vary in intensity.

Regular check-ups should be top of the list. If your Pom starts chewing on rodents, soil or carpet rugs will help blocking roundworms from entering your dog's body.

Medication can kill worms. It forces the worms to release their grip and then they get pushed down and expelled from the dog's body during bowel movements. There are multiple methods to kill the parasites.

Heartworms

Heartworms are of similar sizes to tapeworms and roundworms. Heartworms can kill dogs if not treated soon enough. This worm resides in the Pomeranian's right ventricle of his heart as well as blood vessels near it. An infected mosquito may bite a dog and that causes the dog to become affected himself.

It's astonishing that the tiny mosquito can have a powerful impact on your Pomeranian. The larvae enter the dog's body and begins to grow. It takes approx. three months for heartworms to get into the heart, where it's time to roam. He'll grow up to about 35 cms and, within six months, the females will be ready to reproduce more of these worms.

It's often too late to do anything by the time the dog has seen the vet. Early symptoms may occur sometimes and they include:

1. Weakness.
2. Fatigue.
3. Coughing.
4. Loss of weight.
5. Breathing difficulties.
6. Vomiting.

Later stages of heartworms include:

1. Fainting.
2. Trouble coping with exercises such as walking, etc.

Medication is the way to treat heartworms if diagnosed early enough. Talk to your veterinarian about your concerns.

Ring Worms

Despite the name, the ringworm isn't a worm at all. Its name is Dermophytes, which is a fungus. The name literally means *"plants that live on the skin."* Previously, ringworms were regarded as worms, due to lesions on the skin that are circular in shape.

The fungi exist on your Pomeranian's skin surface and follicles and it retains its life by consuming fur and dead tissues. There are three fungi types that may cause ringworm. However, the dominant one on dogs is named Microsporum canis.

Ringworms are spread from a different infected animal or even a human. It can move back and forth between dogs and cats in the same way that it can move from dogs, to and from, people. It's highly contagious and you and your pet can have it or infect the other creature with it. It can be spread during grooming and petting of the dogs and it's also spread by cats, cows, horses, pigs and goats.

The spores from this fungus may live in the right environment for days, weeks, months and, after all this, even years. Ringworms can be contracted and spread by your pet's bedding, carpets, and grooming tools

The necessary incubation period runs from 10-12 days. So, you won't see any issues unless you check yourself first and then, after the incubating period, lesions may appear. You may get infected if you're touching soil that's already infected. If there are enough nutrients in the soil, the fungus may thrive for months. However, a simple way to kill the spores is by mixing 500 ml of bleach and four litres of water.

Dogs who are very healthy overall often are resistant to ringworm. Young dogs and puppies are in a higher risk category because they have a weak immune system. Many carriers exhibit no visible symptoms but can still infect people and animals.

Symptoms of ringworms

The main symptom of ringworms on the coat and skin is a lesion. The lesion will grow and may develop in odd shapes.

Hair shafts get broken off and, that's why your Pom has patches of fur that are almost gone. Popular ringworm places on your dog's body include: paws, tail, belly, ears and face. These lesions are scaly and may get itchy and cause a swelling and reddish tinge.

It's impossible to diagnose ringworms simply by looking at your dog. Tests will need to be carried out by your vet.

If you don't do anything to treat your pet, the disease will usually fix itself in 2 to 4 months and the symptoms will also settle. However, most people prefer to take better care of their pets. This is also vital because your dog could be contagious as well and the risks of infecting others increases.

Methods of treatment include:

Taking anti-fungal drugs BUT there's also a risk for the animals because they may have horrible side effects. Only try medications prescribed by your vet.

Dips and shampoos. Lime sulphur dips can be useful and should only be carried out by your vet or by doing it yourself but be wary of the risks. Lime sulphur has a powerful smell, can cause your dog's coat to have areas of yellow (temporarily) and can also stain your clothing so protect yourself as much as possible when doing it.

De-worming of puppies

It's necessary to create a deworming schedule so you can mark off the days to do it. Your puppy must be dewormed when he's two, four, six and 8 weeks old and then at 3 months and four months of age.

Pomeranian Allergies

When it comes to dog allergies, there are four major groups:

1. Contact allergy. This occurs when your pet Pomeranian comes into contact with something to which he's allergic. Such elements include: carpet cleaner, shampoo, the material his dinner bowl is made from, and laundry detergent (used to wash his bedding).
2. Allergic to food. This is a food category but Poms and many toy breeds are often actually allergic to a food

additive. Additives include: colouring, flavours, preservatives and various other chemicals that make up the ingredients list of certain dog foods.

3. Environmental allergy. Your dog may inhale something that causes an allergic reaction. It may be pollen, weeds, grasses and other things in the air. Although at a higher level outside, they can also be a problem inside the home. Normal transference can cause it, but your dog may bring pollen and other environmental elements into your home as well.

4. Stings. Wasps, bees and various other insects that can sting may cause your dog to react badly. This form of allergy occurs less often than the others. Minor stings can be treated with Benadryl and, for the pain, baking soda. However, some Pomeranians may have an extreme reaction and go into anaphylactic shock.

Pomeranian allergy symptoms

Signs of allergic reactions can be manifested in a lot of ways. The major symptoms include:

Itching. All allergy issues can make your pet suffer from moderate to severe bouts of itching. This alone may cause other problems.

Irritated skin. This may appear either as big spots or a rash made of itchy bumps. They are often called "hot spots." Skin can be red or pink and hair may thin out as a result of the problem or caused by scratching. If your Pom licks, scratches or chews on the irritated area, the skin can be cut and break open, allowing infections to enter as well.

Hair loss. A dog's healthy coat relies on having healthy skin. Long-lasting allergies can cause the coat's hair to thin out.

Changes in bowel movements. If a dog has food allergies, his gastrointestinal tract may be disrupted and that can cause runny or loose stools.

Upset stomach. Like the runny stools, an upset stomach may cause a reaction in the dog due to something he has eaten. This is regardless of whether he does or doesn't vomit.

Watery eyes/discharge. This symptom usually happens with inhaled or contact allergies. There may be a thick, yet watery, discharge and the thickness can vary from dog to dog. Some Poms may experience a thick discharge, often building up overnight as he sleeps. When he wakes up, his eyes are crusty.

Red, bloodshot eyes. Apart from the water eyes, they can look irritated and red. Ongoing bloodshot eyes is a typical allergy symptom, although the problem may sometimes be caused by the eye getting scratched or something getting into it, like wind blowing dust, etc.

Nasal discharge. This symptom isn't as common in Poms as many other symptoms, but it can occur in those with seasonal allergies.

Breathing issues. This includes wheezing and being short of breath. Days when there's high pollen levels in the air can aggravate this symptom. Although this is generally a seasonal problem, if enough pollutants are brought into the home, then it may be a chronic problem unhindered by the season.

Diagnosing allergies

When your pet has ongoing allergies, it's vital to have an experienced vet conduct certain tests to determine the triggers for your Pom's allergies. Many dogs are allergic to more than one thing so once you know what his triggers are, you can take steps to minimise or stop your dog getting exposed.

Skin allergy and blood tests can be conducted. However, it's crucial to remember that tests aren't always as accurate as they should be. Tests are only done to search for the most common dog triggers, not for every possible dog allergen.

How to diagnose food allergies at home

If you really think your Pomeranian is allergic to something in the food he eats, you need to check ingredients for everything you put in his mouth and this also includes all treats. Bright colouring is often guilty. Look at his whole diet, not just the suspect foods.

The goal of this method is to let the symptoms disappear and let him rest before testing him to determine the reaction. This is his new regime.

For two weeks, his meals should be white chicken meat (no bones or skin) and choose between sweet potato and white rice. The meals should have no seasoning.

After these two weeks, the symptoms should have been eliminated. Now it's time to add one extra food to the mix. Feed your dog the same food, with the extra food added and do this for two weeks. Monitor him to see if he reacts. If not, add another food every two weeks and follow this same process.

A majority of Pom owners find healthy food does their pets the world of good. This proves that it's chemical additives that cause the problems.

Some owners may decide to keep their dog on this diet to avoid future possible allergies. If so, then dogs should also be given healthy, crunchy treats so their teeth remain strong, healthy and clean.

How to treat allergies

Your vet can treat your beloved Pom's allergies in numerous ways that will also identify the allergy causes. Treatment options (depending on the type of allergies(s) include:

- Topical treatments. Generally used if your dog's skin reacts badly to the allergen.
- Eye drops.
- Antihistamines. Owners should never give their dogs any of these products at home without prior professional advice regarding the correct dosing.
- Antibiotics. These will be used if skin sores have opened, and an infection has occurred.
- Corticosteroids. Used just for a short time when the dog has moderate to severe swelling and itchiness.

Tips on controlling allergies at home

For inhaled / airborne allergies:

Owners can do a lot to clean their home and make it a safe,

healthy environment for their Pom. There are ways to help reduce, or eliminate, allergens and these include:

1. If the air is a high pollen day, take your pet for his walk in the late afternoon or early in the evening. Mornings are the worst time for pollutants in the air. You may decide not to walk but to do other fun things at home that your pet enjoys.
2. Wash your pet's paws after your walk and before allowing him back inside. In the warmer weather, a garden hose is handy. On days that are cooler, carry him to your laundry sink and use canine wipes to clean his paws and lower legs.
3. Vacuum your home regularly with a machine using a HEPA filter. It traps particles in the air and floor. You can also do the curtains and furniture.
4. Running ceiling fans is better than leaving windows open because you get a better flow of air.
5. Use your air conditioner and ensure the filters are HEPA-certified. This means even tiny microbes that linger in the air will get removed.

Treatment for contact allergies

All clothes and bedding for humans and animals must be washed in a hypoallergenic detergent. This list also includes pillowcases, blankets, washable pillows and blankets.

Check all your dog's stuffed toys. Test by removing them, one at a time, and watch to see if the other dogs play with them (if you have more than one). Sometimes the reaction caused by removing the "allergy" toy eases the stress.

Take note of any certain stuffed toys that you may suspect are causing the allergy; we know of a Pom that had troubling allergy symptoms for months and as soon as a certain stuffed toy was removed, his issues cleared right up.

Don't use plastic for your pet's water and food. He may be allergic Some Poms can have an allergy to the materials and others may get their face stained. The best dog food bowls are made from stainless steel, closely followed by ceramic bowls.

Look at all the grooming products you use for your dog. Sometimes cheap priced conditioners, shampoos and leave-in products can cause skin reactions and allergies.

Your dog may be sensitive to chemicals used on your lawn at home. If this is the case, his skin will react only on his tummy (if it's long grass), legs and paws. If this is what you suspect, don't let him on your lawn at all and other lawns that could have weed killers or other chemicals on them.

Pomeranian Reverse Sneezing

Whenever your Pomeranian greets a guest, he's always excited and, because of this, he has breathing trouble. This is known as reverse sneezing or a Pomeranian sneeze attack.

A quick fix for stopping this is to prevent the Pom from breathing through his nose. Gently hold his nostrils so he's forced to use his mouth to breathe. Generally speaking, you can stop any spasms by either: gently massaging his throat or closing his nostrils until he swallows.

Lots of Pomeranians have a problem called paroxysmal respiration. This is better known as reverse sneezing.

The way it works is like this: he quickly draws air in via his nostrils; whereas, in a normal sneeze, the air is quickly pushed out via his nose. Why your Pomeranian snorts is because he's attempting to inhale while, simultaneously, sneezing.

Reverse sneezing in Pomeranians occurs when your dog suddenly and forcefully inhales through his nose. That makes him snort repeatedly and the sound he makes resembles a choking sound. It looks and sounds likes he's trying to inhale a sneeze; that's where the nickname, "Pomeranian reverse sneeze," comes from.

He might do this if his palate and/or larynx are, somehow, irritated and muscle spasms can occur in his pharynx. While your Pom is reverse sneezing, he's also gasping inwardly, making hacking, snorting or honking sounds. The main cause of these problems is over-excitement.

Other causes of a reverse sneezing Pomeranian include: pulling too hard on his leash; as he runs; after lapping up lots of water; or after having something to eat.

Whenever you take your dog for a walk, never use a collar because a harness is much safer. A typical Pomeranian episode of reverse sneezing only lasts for a few seconds. However, there are some that experience it for a few minutes, more than once each day.

Reasons for Pomeranian sneeze attacks

Nobody knows the specific cause of a Pomeranian honking cough or reverse sneezing. Any time your Pomeranian has irritations in the back part of his throat, his sinuses, or nose, he'll start reverse sneezing. These episodes can range from extremely mild through to the more serious, but they're nothing for you to be concerned about.

These are potential causes of reverse sneezing:

- Getting too excited.
- Eating and drinking too fast.
- Perfumes.
- Pulling too hard on his leash.
- Foreign substances in his throat.
- Post-nasal drip or nasal inflammation.
- Household chemicals or cleaners.

Is my Pom in danger during a sneeze attack?

Most Pomeranians will experience a reverse sneezing episode and still go on to lead a healthy, happy life as the sneezing is not harmful and a lot of the time, there's no need for any treatment.

If these attacks occur quite often, your vet will prescribe antihistamines to hopefully stop the sneezing. If it occurs immediately after his inoculation for the kennel cough, it's advisable to give him antibiotics.

Never list Pomeranian reverse sneezing in the same category as far more serious Pomeranian breathing issues including heart disease or a collapsed trachea. If you ever see symptoms that make no sense to you (such as: snorting, gagging, honking or wheezing), do the smart thing and seek professional help and advice from your vet. It's better to be safe than sorry.

How to treat Pomeranian sneezing

The majority of cases of reverse sneezing don't need to be treated. If your Pomeranian has an episode of reverse sneezing, lightly stroke his neck as you calm him down. After he exhales through the nose, that's the end of the problem. It's extremely rare for canines to face complications or risks during those attacks. Most reverse sneezing episodes are finished inside 60 seconds, although there are cases where it lasts longer than ever.

Generally speaking, the occasional Pomeranian reverse sneeze episode is nothing to be alarmed about. It's only when it lasts for more than a few seconds or seems like it's causing your Pom undue distress that you should speak to your vet.

The vet is the expert in all things canine, so entrusting your Pomeranian to him for assessment and possible treatment is the most caring thing you can do.

Photo by Ariel Xuran Li

Winter Care

If you live somewhere that has very cold weather at times, you must learn how best to protect your pet Pomeranian against the harsh climate. The Winter weather can bring icy cold temperatures, snow and icy rain, and the air is often much drier. Your Pom's paws, skin and coat can be adversely affected, he may have difficulty controlling his body temperature and he may have other issues as well.

Winter is the season where your Pomeranian really needs extra care. Regardless of whether it's snowing, the air is still at its driest during this season. Moisture in the air is known as the humidity factor. When the weather is cold, it's difficult for the air to retain any moisture. Even inside your home, don't believe that's ideal because cold air meets with warm air and dries it out even further. Therefore, your Pom can't avoid damage that the season's harsh elements can cause unless you help.

Without your extra care and proper "winterisation," there are two main problems that can happen:

1. His skin may become chapped and very dry. If so, you'll notice he scratches more than normal and he may have irritated, red skin (hotspots). These symptoms warn you that his coat will soon become thinner.
2. Your dog's coat will have lots of static and the result of this is split ends that, if not properly trimmed back, can travel up to the root. Hair loss will happen and his fur will thin out as well.

It's vital that you use the best products at the correct times. A good quality leave-in conditioner should be used all year round but it's even more necessary in Winter. Spray his coat with plenty of the product so it coats his hairs and forms a protective shield to protect his fur from damage that Winter can cause. Your home will be less humid so don't assume he doesn't need the extra care just because he stays inside.

Protecting your Pomeranian's paws

Skin can be healthy one second and dry the next so in Winter, you must inspect his skin every day and then take protective action if you find any damage or skin that's drier than normal. Here are some great tips to help you:

- Use a good quality paw balm. If your Pom still has trouble on the cold ground or finds it hard not to slip, put booties on him and see if that helps. Paws are made from skin and can easily dry out when he's outside in the harsh climate. They can dry out more than his body skin.
- One major issue he may face is salt and chemicals that melt ice and are used on the ground in Winter. Even if you never use these products, local councils often do and cars travel on these surfaces and then into your local area, where the tyres leave residue on the roads and paths. Paws can be damaged or burnt by the chemicals and your Pom's nail pads may get hurt too.
- You may use booties when outside but it's still essential to use paw wax on a weekly basis to help stop your Pom's paws from cracking, drying out or being harmed in other ways. The wax can heal existing damage, stop cracking and moisturise at the same time. If your Pomeranian's paws are so sore that he can't walk properly or if there's any deep cracks, bleeding or other issues, see your vet as a matter of urgency so he can help fix the problems and maybe stop an infection.
- When choosing boots/shoes, they need to be resistant to the weather, easy for your Pom to walk in and tough to handle whatever they're used for. If they have the Velcro closures around the ankles, they're a great choice.

Nose protection for your Pom

Winter can be harsh on your dog's nose. Even before you suspect any problems, it may be crusty and cracked. Because he's always licking his nose, the dry, cold wind can quickly cause it to chap. However, it's easy to protect it. Use a good nose balm (or paw balm) or a nose chap stick. You only need to dab it three or four times to ensure it's protected from the cold air.

Controlling your home's humidity

Keep the humidity level in your home at a medium level and that will help with the health of your Pomeranian's coat and skin. It's also useful if your pet gets a dry cough. If you want to buy a humidifier, ensure it's the right capacity. Most units work to cover one or two rooms maximum. If your Pom is really badly affected by humidity, put one near where he sleeps. It's essential to regularly clean humidifiers to avoid bacteria. You can also opt for one or more of these home remedies instead of a store-bought gadget:

- Put metal bowls filled with water on top of heaters or heat registers.
- Leave the bathroom door open while showering and after you finish.
- Get a big Ziplock bag and poke 20 holes in it. Then insert a big wet sponge and you can place it anywhere you want - on bench tops, cabinets, wherever appropriate. Set up 5-10 of them and spread them out through the house.
- Get some houseplants as they release moisture whenever you water them.

Venturing outside with your Pomeranian during Winter

Naturally you can't keep your Pom inside the house all Winter. He will need to go outside sometimes. He'll need to go to the bathroom (unless you have him pee pad trained.) You should also try to maintain a regular schedule as much as you can. Dogs often eat less in the Summer and more in Winter. If you reduce exercise, his health could deteriorate. Exercising, particularly walking, is necessary because it keeps muscles and the heart healthy. That applies equally to you as well as your dog. If a dog can't get exercise, he's likely to get moody, bored and frustrated. If you both dress warmly, you can go for one or two walks a day (unless there's impossible bad conditions outside).

Dogs that fall into the toy breed category have more trouble maintaining their core body temperature than the bigger breeds.

So, it's critical that your Pom is kept warm during the Winter months. Whenever it's under 32F (also depending on wind chill factor), he should wear a thick warm jumper. If it's snowing, put him in a water-proof jacket.

Some Pomeranians hate the snow and expect their path to be free of snow when you go for a walk. He'll even bring you his booties before you get to put his leash on. However, other Poms love the snow more than anything else. If yours loves it, let him play while you watch him closely and only for 20 minutes because after that, even with protective clothing, he may get hypothermia.

Some dogs are so excited when they can play in the snow that their bodies heat up rapidly, and then they have a sudden point when the coldness hits, hence why you must always supervise your beloved pet. Once he's back in the house, use a soft, highly absorbent towel and gently pat (not rub) him dry. Then you may want to put a t-shirt on him to help him warm up again.

Winter changes

One aspect of Winter care for your Pomeranian is to learn what's considered "normal" and what signs indicate a problem. Here are a few things to keep in mind:

- It's normal for him to eat more in Winter and exercise less. You'll strive to take him for walks daily but there will be some days where the weather is too harsh. Hence the slight weight gain. If there's a large gain or loss in weight, talk to your vet.
- Your Pom may be more restless (cabin fever) as humans also can be at this time of year. Even if you're content staying inside, your dog might be frustrated because he wants to get out and run and play, and now he can't burn off that extra energy. If you only do one walk but usually do two per day, he'll feel the difference.
- Help your pet by playing with him and creating some fun activities for inside the house. Teach him new commands and new tricks or play old ones. Lay down a path of objects and you carry a basket and get him to

pick up all objects and give them to you. Use an excited voice as that will make him wag his tail and have more fun. Play hide and seek. Give him an ice cube to chase around the kitchen floor with. They're ideal for puppies who are teething and fun for all dogs, especially if they're bored.

- Some Pomeranians may feel like their routine is upset when the sunlight is minimal and there are less daylight hours. He'll want to go to bed early. You can extend the day by doing some grooming after dark as it makes him feel like things still happen despite the sun disappearing.
- Older Poms may suffer from arthritis and the associated aches and pains. Reassess his bed to see if it needs to be changed to an orthopaedic bed to make him more comfortable. Talk to your vet if this is something to consider.

Summer Care

If the place in which you live experiences hot Summer months or maybe you have hot weather all the time, you'll need to know extra steps necessary to care for your Pom during these warm times.

Most owners use fans and/or air conditioning to stay cool in Summer so they don't think about whether their dog needs extra help to stay cool, particularly in the spaces he normally spends his time, namely his bed area, rest area and wherever he plays.

Spend some time on a particularly hot day to check whether his space does get bombarded with heat that could make him uncomfortable. It may be necessary to close curtains or blinds or move his space to a different area.

Air conditioning can also cause problems in Summer. Pomeranians don't cope well when cold air blows directly on them. Ensure he gets the benefit of the cool breeze but isn't bombarded with a direct burst of cold air.

Ensure your Pomeranian is safe and cool during Summer

A cooling mat is very useful if you don't have air conditioning, or as a backup if it's not on or not working. It's useful to cool him down after he has been playing outside. A good quality cooling mat contains a pressure-active gel pad which is ideal because it means there are no potentially dangerous power cords. The gel absorbs heat from your Pom's body and is a safe method for keeping him cool when it's hot. The mats are portable so you can use it anywhere in the home and even outside if the need arises.

There are lots of things to consider when taking your Pomeranian outside:

1. Exercise. It's important for your Pom to keep up with his exercise routine or he can get frustrated and misbehave because he can't release his pent-up energy. However, you need to take steps to protect him at the same time.

This toy breed is best having two walks each day so, during Summer, do it in the early morning and late in the evening, when the weather isn't as hot and fierce, thus avoiding some of the potential problems. However, you may decide to lengthen the morning walk and shorten the evening walk due to the hotter conditions.

2. In your back yard. You may love spending hours in your back yard, whether it's swimming, gardening or having barbeques. The good news is that, with care and planning, your Pomeranian can keep you company and enjoy some outside time as well. Make sure there's plenty of shade for him, water and a way to get cool. A children's plastic pool is ideal for him to splash about in with complete safety, as long as you don't leave him on his own in the water. Another fun option is the use of an oscillating sprinkler which combines cooling down and fun.

3. Paw protection. It's critical that you keep your Pom's paws protected in Summer where the concrete and asphalt surfaces may be 30 degrees hotter than normal. Despite the fact that paws are made up of a thick skin, it doesn't mean they're impervious to heat, and it only takes seconds to incur first degree burns.

To prevent this from occurring, apply a high-quality paw wax. It only takes 10 seconds to be absorbed and will form a protection layer between his paws and hot surfaces. Apply this two or three times each week. You may opt to use doggie shoes and some dogs find them more comfortable to wear.

4. Always carry water. Regardless of where you're going, always bring water for both your Pomeranian and yourself. Dogs drink a lot more water when it's hot and by giving them more water more frequently, you can help prevent dehydration. If you're going for a long walk, stop every 20 minutes or so and have a short rest and some water. You can buy canine water coolers that have room to insert ice cubes to keep the water cold and a lid that doubles as a drinking bowl.

5. Protect his nose. As with humans, a dog's nose is very vulnerable to sunburn. After the top layer gets damaged, it will start peeling. If you don't take action to heal it, cracks can start to appear, and more serious problems may happen. Dabbing a balm or snout butter on his nose 15 mins before venturing into the hot sun can keep his leather healthy and provide the necessary protection.

6. Protect your Pomeranian's belly. Toy dogs are closer to the ground than larger dog breeds which means their stomach is extra sensitive and more prone to sunburn due to light reflected off the ground. It's wise to rub some canine sunblock on his groin and stomach areas if you plan on being out for more than 30 minutes in Summer.

If you're going to a lake, the beach or some other place that has both sand and/or water that may reflect the UV rays, you need to use protection for your Pom's belly, nose and paws. Always better to be safe than sorry.

7. Prevention of coat and skin dryness. The harsh Summer sun may cause multiple problems. The sun has a gradual burning effect and may even change your Pom's fur colour. A brown or black fur colour may gain a reddish tinge.

The sun may cause itchiness and/or peeling as the skin dries out. To prevent such problems, use a good quality leave-in conditioner. The light spray helps prevent any harm and if you select the right product, it will also work as a deodoriser, making your pet smell clean and fresh. You don't need to use much. Spray, and then brush his coat downwards so the conditioner is distributed properly.

8. Use a bandana. A canine cooling bandana is a terrific method for keeping your beloved Pom cool and comfortable when it's hot, regardless of whether he's inside or outside.

Choose one that's suitable for toy breeds or it will be too heavy on his neck. Another option is to get a "regular" bandana. Put it in cold water and secure it to your Pom's neck, like a collar, with space for you to slip in two fingers between his neck and the bandana.

Travelling in the car with your Pomeranian during Summer

Here are some safety precautions to keep in mind if you take your Pom in the car with you on a hot day:

- Each time you take your Pom in the car, first start the engine and then turn on the air conditioning (AC) to start cooling it down. Cars get extremely hot when parked in the hot sun. Open the windows as well because the hot air will be pushed out. Then shut them so the cooler air can circulate.
- Touch your Pom's car seat and ensure it's not too hot. (For example, the steering wheel gets too hot to touch in Summer).
- While you may love the cold air vent blowing directly on you, toy breeds are very sensitive to changes in the temperature so his vent can't blow directly on him.
- If your beloved Pomeranian gets car sick, open his window a small amount in addition to the AC running as it tends to settle that nauseous feeling. (This works equally well for people).
- Depending on how high his seat is, you may need car shades so his eyes aren't being subjected to direct bright

sunlight. That can cause discomfort and increase car sickness.

Swimming pool precautions for your Pom

The first thing to understand is that dogs are not all excellent swimmers.

Dog swimming safety tips:

1. Never throw your dog into any body of water. While he will instinctively dog paddle as best as he can to get to land again, it's not the best way to teach him how much fun he can have while swimming. It may even scare him.
2. Always supervise him when he's swimming, even if he appears to be having fun. Dogs can easily grow tired and find it difficult to get out of the water.
3. Most swimming pools contain lots of chlorine to ensure the water is clean. This can irritate your Pom so ensure you always rinse him thoroughly after he has a swim in the pool.

Heat stress and possible stroke

You can take every possible precaution to ensure your Pomeranian's health is good during Summer but it's impossible to know how he will react in all situations. If he suffers from heat stress, you need to immediately cool him down before it becomes heat stroke, which may be fatal. You must learn all the symptoms and signs of heat stress in your Pomeranian and what to do the moment you notice any sign or symptom.

Heat stress occurs when your dog's internal temperature hits 103°F. Heat stroke occurs at 106°F or more. It's extremely dangerous and could cause failure of multiple organs.

More Than You Ever Wanted to Know About Rectal Sacs

Rectal sacs (also called "rectal glands") are the two smallish glands that sit inside your dog's bottom. The substance that's excreted into these sacs can only be described as smelling vile.

They're oily, thick and stinky, and have a distinct "fishy" smell. Most wild animals can voluntarily empty the sacs in self-defence or for scent marking.

However, domesticated animals such as dogs no longer have this ability. Normal defecation and walking around are the two ways the sacs get emptied, but there are times when animals can't get them empty and they get impacted and very uncomfortable.

If your dog has impacted sacs, he may scoot his butt along the ground to try and empty them. Some dogs chase their tails and others lick that area. Some animals just feel uncomfortable, shiver, find it hard to walk, keep their tail down and can hide.

You can be kind and empty your dog's rectal sacs. Use a tissue or rag and squeeze both sides of the sacs. If the resulting secretions are pasty, then this method isn't enough to completely empty the sacs.

Another way is to wear rubber gloves and hold the back end of your dog under the tap with warm running water. Squeeze both sides of the rectal area until the sacs are empty and clean.

What if scooting continues?

If scooting continues for a few days after you have cleaned him out, you need to check him again. In some cases, it can take a couple of turns at helping empty his sacs. If he keeps scooting but his sacs are empty, other problems may exist, such as tapeworms, itchy skin or lower back pain. You'll need to consult your vet and get him checked out.

What happens if you can't empty an impacted sac?

An abscess may form and it can rupture through the dog's skin. It's messy, painful and smelly and is sometimes misdiagnosed as rectal bleeding. If your dog has an abscess, get him to the vet urgently as antibiotics will be necessary as well as treatment for the abscess.

How often do rectal sacs need to be emptied?

It's impossible to say because animals are different. Your dog will let you know if his sacs are full. If you see him scooting, it's time to help empty them again.

What if it seems like my dog's sacs need to be emptied all the time?

Having the vet empty them all the time can prove costly so get him to teach you how to do it properly yourself. It depends on whether you're more comfortable doing it or paying the vet to do so. The latter is the more common choice. You can also change his diet to a high-fibre diet that creates bulkier stools that help empty the rectal sacs as the food passes by them.

Rectal sacculectomy

If the sacs need emptying every few weeks, you may decide to have them surgically removed. This procedure isn't straightforward because there are lots of nerves in that area that control continence and any change to the muscles can affect faecal continence.

Also, if your dog has chronic sac problems, his anatomy will be a bit distorted. If the gland isn't fully removed, draining tracts may form. However, even with the complications, it's still regarded as a fairly minor procedure by experienced veterinary surgeons.

Lots of owners will never even be aware of rectal sacs if no problems happen. If you ever have questions about the health of your dog, talk to the vet.

Pomeranians In Heat

If your Pomeranian is female and not desexed, you'll need to understand her heat cycle. Although the discharge isn't as pronounced as bigger breeds, there will be some physical and behavioural changes due to fluctuating hormones.

You want your pet Pom spayed before her initial cycle as this could happen when she's a mere six months of age.

However, the normal range of ages is roughly six – nine months. In rarer cases, she may be late in blossoming and can be one year old before it happens.

Sometimes your Pom exhibits signs before her cycle. These signs can happen from one day to one week prior to the heat kicking in. If you have no idea what to look for, it's easy to miss them:

- A full or slightly swollen vulva.
- Enlarged mammary glands.
- You would be likely to know your Pom has a flat, pink belly. However, when she's in heat, teats will begin to pop up in the upper part of her chest.

Once your Pom is completely in heat, the signs are very obvious:

- A vulva can swell up to three times its regular size.
- Teats are clearly visible.
- A discharge. In toy breeds, it's usually a pink/red colour and then it becomes completely pink after roughly one week's time. It may turn a very pale pink roughly 10 days into her cycle and this is usually where the Pom's ability to be impregnated is at its highest point. When her bleeding has ceased, she can still remain in heat for up to a week so you need to take precautions to avoid a pregnancy that's not planned.

There can be behavioural changes:

- She may start humping because it's a strong urge and then she'll hump inanimate objects or other dogs.
- Your Pom may lick all over herself at times. This is known as self-grooming.
- Your dog may demonstrate nesting-type behaviours. This may include: gathering toys and food and other things she finds and putting them away in a safe area.
- Your Pom may crave extra attention or may have the desire to be alone in isolation.

How long does it last?

You can't say with certainty that dogs go through heat cycles twice annually because the actual cycle length can vary enormously. On average, it will last for three weeks.

However, it may last between two and four weeks and still be regarded as normal. The heat cycle occurs between 5.5 and 8 months so it can happen twice or three times per year.

If your Pom's first cycle is in January and her second one is in July, the next one after that would be the following January if the cycles occurred every six months. That means she has two cycles each year. When calculating the time between cycles, you start from the first day of the cycle until the first day of the second cycle.

It's strongly advised to avoid breeding a female younger than two years of age. However, the AKC will accept litters from female Poms that are between 8 months and 12 years of age.

The vital thing to be aware of is that a female Pom will emit a specific scent that male dogs quickly take notice of…and not only those dogs in close proximity. It's believed that males who are not neutered will sniff out the female's unique scent from as far away as 4.82 kms.

Because of this, it's crucial to protect your female Pom from male dogs. Never have a play date with an un-neutered male dog. You should avoid all dog parks and any other places where male dogs may be found.

Each time your Pom girl urinates, there will be a small amount of blood that's also excreted and that contains a heavy scent that can linger for longer. Remember this whenever you take your dog outside to attend to her toilet needs.

A male dog could be wandering the area anticipating your dog's next visit. Never underestimate the urges and desires of a dog who hasn't been neutered, regardless of size or breed. If you're outside with your dog and a male dog approaches, pick her up and take her back into your home or car.

You should have a fenced-in safe, back yard for your dog to play in and be exercised. If she is taken anywhere else, always have her on a leash and harness.

Red flags – finding lumps during, or after, the end of a heat cycle

If you see lumps appear on your Pom's nipple area during a cycle or after it has finished (in the dog's mammary area around her teats), it's a strong indication of the existence of mammary gland hyperplasia. This is where there's too much growth of mammary epithelial cells. These cells are benign cancers. In breast cancer, the cells are actually malignant.

There's only one way to decide if the lumps are cancerous or non-cancerous and that's to operate and remove all lumps so they can be examined. As an example, your Pom may have five lumps removed and tested. One may be malignant and the other four are benign.

50% of tumours in Pomeranians are diagnosed as malignant so it's critical that you pay attention to any lumps that may appear on your Pomeranian's nipples at any time, especially after a cycle because that's when they're the most obvious.

Neutering Facts

Whether you have purchased a Pomeranian from a reputable breeder, or you have adopted your adorable canine, the most critical decision to make is when to neuter your family member.

Over the years, numerous myths have surfaced related to the reproductive needs of Pomeranians. The main myths are that males become sissies, while spayed females become fat.

Male Pomeranians, especially those that possess a submissive personality, tend to be much better pets. They roam less, and don't mark their territory (including all furniture) as often. If you neuter your dog before he becomes an adult, his desire to force his dominant personality over family members becomes less frequent.

Your Pom will be healthier overall and, because he's neutered, his risk of testicular cancer is zero.

Many owners heavily rely on the neutering process to fix

problems with their dog's behaviour. However, they must train their dog to behave, just the same, regardless of whether he's in public or at home, so they can't be lazy.

Females are more likely to become better pets if they're not having a heat cycle regularly every 6 - 9 months. Such cycles bring hormonal changes that can lead to changes in personalities. Females that experiencing oestrus need to be quarantined to help avoid pregnancies. As females grow older, their heat cycles may cause their reproductive systems to have mammary and uterine cancers.

Some female Pomeranians get fake pregnancies that are annoying to handle, as well as infections in their uterus that may prove fatal. Despite changes in hormones being caused by sterilization, and being overweight, female and male dogs don't usually get fat just because they have been neutered or spayed.

Like other mammals, the weight they gain is from too little exercise, too much food, or if they have been programmed to be overweight.

Any gain in weight following surgical sterilisation can be linked back to the changes in hormones. However, the problem will be intensified if you keep feeding your dog a diet that's high in energy while he does not need as much energy because he has achieved his correct adult size. If there's extra energy in his food, it turns into an excessive amount of fat on his body.

Neutering a Pomeranian provides a range of positive benefits, all aimed at improving his overall health. He is protected from several potentially fatal maladies, and it also helps the Pom live a longer life. His behaviour usually improves quite a lot. Like with anything, complications may happen, but are rare. If you're not planning to breed your Pom, the best thing to do is neuter him.

Pomeranian Spaying Aftercare

When you have had your Pom spayed, she will require extra care until such time as she has completely recovered. It's vital that you severely restrict all her normal activities due to possible harm.

Don't Wash Your Pomeranian Before She Is Completely Healed

There's at least one serious issue your vet would have told you about, and that's bacteria. If you wash your Pom after the surgery, the incision site could come into contact with bacteria and you must certainly avoid this at all costs.

Check Your Pom's Incision Area Regularly

When checking her incision area, there are a number of specifics to look for: bad smell, inflammation, infection, or anything else that may seem somewhat unusual.

Think back to what her incision looked like on day 1 post-surgery. (Take photos if it helps). It needs to look healthy and not have any discharge, swelling or redness.

If you have no idea how you should be checking her area, do it like this. Roll her over and expose her tummy. If you can see swelling, bruising or a few red areas, that's what you would expect to see.

However, there should NOT be any major changes in her tummy. If these symptoms exist, urgently take her to the vet and ring to advise him you're coming so he's prepared.

After surgery, your Pom must always wear a cone

It's critical that your Pomeranian not scratch herself. Her incision will be so itchy that the only way to stop her from doing it is to make her wear a cone at all times. You can't allow her to hurt the area on, and around, the incision. In the beginning she'll absolutely hate it and it will also be very uncomfortable and restrictive. However, after a few days of use, she will quickly get accustomed to wearing it.

Nevertheless, it's imperative that you're always directly watching her, even while you may be doing other household chores. Making sure she doesn't destroy the cone is essential to her continuing good health. When you're not closely observing your Pom's activities, you would be surprised at the speed in which she chews her sutures.

Spaying after-care means restricting your Pomeranian's behaviour

Regardless of the age of your Pomeranian, proper care after she has been spayed is about looking after her health, even if she can't do all the fun things that are normal for a brief period. Don't let her play, run or go for a walk post-surgery because stretching or too much movement may slow the recovery period, open the incision and possibly cause swelling.

If she walks on grass, her incision may pick up an infection and, because you can't wash her, it may rapidly become worse.

If your Pomeranian has loads of energy and you have no idea how to let her expend it, choose a small room in your home and allow her to walk as much as she wants. Doing it like this means you're still protecting your pet from potential infections during the recovery period (which is usually 14 days for most dogs).

Think about the quantity and types of food your Pomeranian consumes, Paying close attention to your dog's diet is especially important when she's recovering from surgery. Dogs who are recovering from surgery generally have a decreased metabolism.

So, you must ensure she gets plenty of nourishment until she has fully recovered. Depending on her age, you may need to reduce or increase their calorie intake, a decision your vet can help you with.

Potential risks and complications

Fortunately for us, risks and complications that may occur during, or after, spaying are rare. The procedures are quite common and, over time, have been perfected so any experienced vet that knows all the ins and outs and can easily supervise the surgery.

Despite the rarities, it's still possible for risks and complications to occur so this is a list of what may go wrong after surgery (in no particular order).

- Infection.
- Urine Leakage.
- A re-opening of the incision.
- Post-surgery trauma.
- Anaesthetic complications.
- Excessive loss of blood (animals that may be pregnant, in heat or a pyometra) during the surgical procedure.
- Part of the ovary or uterus removed.

In the rare chance that anything on this list happens, the vet will contact you urgently. If you see there's an infection after you have taken your dog home, you'll need to take her back for more tests.

Caring for Your Senior Pomeranian

As dogs age, they're more likely to face health problems, including those related to genetic and lifestyle issues. The good news, though, is that with today's advanced medicines, a diagnosis usually takes place sooner, which means prevention and intervention can extend your senior Pomeranian's life.

Older dogs tend to experience health problems over time, rather than suddenly. Be on the lookout for anything that appears to be an issue, no matter how small. In almost every case, early detection offers the best outcome.

Nutrition for senior Pomeranians

As your Pomeranian ages, his metabolism slows. Exercise becomes more trying and fewer calories are expended. Thus, special diets should be used for pets over five years old. You can create these in tandem with your veterinarian's suggestions.

Older dogs will also need more fibre than younger Poms, for the same reason as older humans. However, they also need enough vitamins, minerals, fat and protein. Some owners decide to stick with their Pomeranian's typical foods, offering it in smaller portions. Other owners choose special food specifically created for senior dogs.

These types of food have:

- A basic protein content of around 18 per cent (14 per cent for Poms suffering from kidney disorders),
- A basic fat level of 10 to12 per cent.
- A basic fibre level of 3 to 5 per cent.
- They also may contain additives such as vitamins.

You'll find food suitable for older Pomeranians in cans or bags in commercial stores or through your veterinarian.

If your dog gets a bit fussy, just warm the food slightly to increase the taste and smell and he'll most likely munch away!

How to handle problems with senses

As with people, older dogs can have issues with cognitive functions and senses growing weaker. However, dogs are more capable of handling such changes than most older humans.

Loss of sight

As he grows older, the black pupils start becoming a little hazy. It's normal for a dog, and only minimally affects his sight.

A dog eye specialist can operate and take out the affected lens. An artificial lens can be inserted. This is the same way that people have their eyesight improved.

Your vet needs to ascertain two major elements before operating:

- Is your Pomeranian healthy enough to handle eye surgery and the recovery process?
- Is your dog's retina still working properly?

After your Pom has the cataract procedure done, he'll need lots of love and care, but it's certainly worth it for you and your dog. If he goes blind, his life will change dramatically, as will yours.

Unfortunately, there are sometimes problems with eyesight that can't be cured. You might not even realise he's slowly losing his vision until he's virtually blind.

To assist your older Pomeranian in getting around safely, there are a few precautions you'll need to take immediate action on, so he can lead as "normal" a life as possible if he does go blind.

Actions include:

- Not moving furniture unless necessary.
- Closing off hazardous areas such as your pool, staircases and anything else where he may stumble, fall and hurt himself.
- Use smells and sounds around your home to help him work out where he is. Examples include ticking clocks, radio or CDs, perfumed face towels or other fabrics, and smelly shoes that always get put in the same place.
- Create paths he can touch. For example, use gravel paths outside or carpet runners inside.

As with people, most blind dogs can go on to lead long, relatively normal lives.

Loss of hearing

Older dogs often succumb to hearing loss. Dogs can usually hear very high-pitched noises but, as they age, this can change. If your dog doesn't react when you call or whistle for him, try using a lower voice.

Hearing aids are not an option for dogs. So, it's up to you to retrain him to communicate in different ways. Hand signals can be understood quite easily. If he's outside and you call him to come inside, he may not respond, so train him to come in when you turn the porch light on and off a few times. It's important to pat your dog a lot so he doesn't think you have stopped talking to him.

Loss of cognitive functions

If your old Pom seems to be pacing up and down, wandering around aimlessly or standing in a corner and wondering what to do, he may have an issue with cognitive dysfunction. In other words, his thought processes aren't as sharp as they used to be.

Your vet may prescribe various medications to help. However, the process can take weeks or even months and, even then, there's no guarantee it will work. Dogs vary in how they react to medications. Owners of dogs that have had remarkable results are extremely happy, with their dogs being back to "normal."

There are other ways you can help. Provide small challenges to make your dog think more, teach him new tricks or games. If he still loves the games he played in his younger days, you can keep doing them as well. However, don't do too much because he'll tire easily.

Fewer activities that require a lot of energy are ideal. For example, hide some treats and get your pet to look for them. Car trips are fun because they're not draining him of precious energy, and he gets to see new sights. Having you for company is what all dogs crave. Studies have proven results that doing these things will help avoid a reduction in mental capacity.

Older dogs have more health issues

Humans suffer from more health problems as we get older. The same thing applies to your Pomeranian pet. Lots of parts can be affected including bones, joints, kidneys, heart, brain and various other organs.

Cancer is more likely to occur in older dogs as well. Your dog needs more preventive actions to avoid such problems.

Have the vet do a full examination twice every year. Older dogs will need more things checked. For example, blood tests are essential because they can reveal all sorts of real and potential problems such as anaemia, clots, high white blood cells, infections, deficiencies in vitamins and minerals and so on. Tests can determine if your dog has diabetes, liver or kidney failure and other major health concerns.

Here are more typical ailments affecting older dogs:

Arthritis: Poms remain cheerful for most of their lives. However, you shouldn't push older dogs as hard as young dogs when it comes to physical activities. Use a doggy ramp or steps to help him get on and off furniture instead of making him jump and cause injuries.

Older dogs should still get some physical exercise but when it comes time for a rest, ensure his bed is soft and comfortable. Short walks will most likely be all he can handle. Your vet may prescribe certain medications to improve the arthritic joints and ease the symptoms as well as rejuvenate cartilage and increase the collagen production.

Body odour: The smell of an older dog is generally more powerful than that of a younger one. The most common causes are ear infections, teeth issues, and kidney disease.

Body temperature: As dogs age, they become more susceptible to cold and heat. If he's too hot and is panting, or if he's shivering from the cold, do what you can to help him feel comfortable.

Dry skin: As they grow older, dogs lose a lot of the moisture in their skin, thus making it itchier. Brush him regularly and you'll stimulate the production of oil and more moisture will be created. When washing your Pom, use a moisturising conditioner.

Issues with his teeth: Older Poms often have problems with their teeth including licking lips, doggy breath, a dislike for chewing and avoiding your hands touching his mouth. However, these issues tell you that a visit to the vet is needed. He can pull out any loose teeth, give your dog's remaining teeth a clean and check to detect other issues.

Problems with digestion: Diarrhoea and vomiting both cause dehydration and an energy drain in older dogs and this can happen quite fast. Liver or kidney troubles may be the cause. As he's older now, you shouldn't delay in getting him to your vet.

Immune system issues: Older Pomeranians have a weaker immune system. Titre testing is the favoured option to regular vaccinations for older dogs. If he spends all his time at home, you may not need either, but ask your vet.

Cushing's syndrome: (there's too much cortisol in his system) is another serious health problem. It can cause your dog to have a pot belly as well as other symptoms including: diarrhoea, weight loss, a runny nose, coughing, changes in his appetite, a distended abdomen, extra thirst and more frequent urination.

Older pets are prone to numerous other health issues including diabetes, cancer, kidney disease, heart disease, and liver disease.

Most ailments can be treated and cured, providing you take action as soon as possible. The "wait and see" approach isn't wise as aged dogs become ill faster than young dogs. Always contact your vet if you observe any unusual symptoms. It's better to be safe than sorry.

Letting Go and Saying Goodbye

A time will come when you'll need to decide the best way to let a canine member of your family pass on to the great Kennel in the sky. The time when it will most likely occur is when your dog has reached a senior age and is suffering from a serious diagnosed medical condition that can't be treated or eased with medication.

In a situation like this, you should always get a second opinion, regardless of the length of time you have dealt with your current vet, or how much you might trust him. Then you'll know for sure that what you have been told is 100% correct.

It's possible that another vet or dog specialist could propose an alternative treatment plan and/or diagnosis. Euthanasia is never a decision to be taken lightly and, in the end, it needs to be based on the level of pain your dog is enduring. Pets rely on us to look after their every need, and that includes not letting them suffer.

Once you arrive at the point where a decision must be made, it's important to remember that part of truly loving your four-legged family member is ensuring his needs are considered ahead of yours. If he's suffering most of the time, you can choose to feel the intense emotions that saying goodbye will release but it's necessary so you can allow your close friend to receive the gift of not suffering any longer. It's the most caring, unselfish thing for you to do.

If you're ever in this position, my thoughts are with you and I sincerely hope this information helps you manage this sad, but sometimes necessary, situation.

Questions When Choosing Pet Insurance for Your Dog

As Veterinary science becomes more advanced, it means vet bills also increase. Some owners find the cost of owning a pet is financially stressful. Insuring your pet can help to offset some, or all, of the expenses of diagnosing, managing and treating your dog whenever he has an illness or injury.

Pet insurance is not for all pet owners. If you're thinking about it for your pet, you should talk to your vet and do your own research to work out the various options available to you. Here are a few basics to consider:

An insurance provider must fully, and clearly explain all details (including exclusions and limitations) of coverage options for general care, emergency treatment and any conditions that may require long term extensive care.

Ask if premiums will increase if you make a claim or as your pet ages. Is there a discount if you own more than one pet?

All fees, including deductibles, co-pays, add-ons and other expenses, must be explained fully and clearly to you so you know what you're up for to begin with.

Ask the insurer how they handle pre-existing conditions and what their definition of such conditions are (i.e., conditions or illnesses your pet has had in the past or currently has).

Does the provider offer add-on options for particular types of coverage? This may include your pet's dental care or travel insurance, etc.

Are there specific breeds or types of pets they don't insure? Is there a maximum number of pets in their "high risk" category that you're able to insure?

You should be permitted to select your own vet to care for your pet.

Generally speaking, pet insurance plans work by you paying all costs up front and then receiving all applicable reimbursements from the provider. If this will be a problem for you financially, ask your vet whether he has any flexibility in payment options if you face that situation.

Emergency First Aid Tips for Your Dog

Life is always full of surprises, both good and bad. Your Pomeranian may become very ill or be injured at home, but the risks are higher when outside, whether it's while walking, in a park or if you're out hiking.

You should always be prepared for emergencies. Store your vet and emergency numbers in your mobile phone and wallet/purse so you can call them while enroute so they can be there ready to give assistance immediately.

Get a pet first aid manual that covers everything you should do in the event of something happening to your beloved dog. You should also have a dog first aid kit in your home and another one in your car with all the necessary requirements. Make sure it's clearly marked because it will have different items compared to a human first aid kit (which you should also have in your car).

You should also buy Rescue Remedy, a flower essence formula that can calm your pet instantly in case of any stressful situation or to help him overcome behavioural or emotional issues. i.e., scared of loud noises such as fireworks or backfiring cars, excessive barking or separation anxiety.

Such homeopathic remedies are effective and act fast. Here are some others you may wish to stock:

Pet Essences are homeopathic and completely natural. They're made from the Essences of various flowers. You can buy concoctions for different canine issues (as well as remedies if you have other pets).

Pet Essences Diarrhoea, Colitis and Vomiting are digestive remedies to ease acute digestive issues. Although diarrhoea and vomiting are rare, when they do happen, these Essences can help ensure your pet's comfort whilst enroute to the vet.

Pet Essences Pain Relief helps with anxiety caused by injury or sickness and calms your pet so the vet can work on him much easier.

Pet Essences Emergency helps with traumas including bruises and bumps and more serious traumas.

Here are tips every dog owner must know about in the event of emergency situations:

Bleeding

Muzzle your dog if he's stressed. If it's only minor, (e.g., a toenail) a styptic pencil can fix it. If the wound is a lot more serious, cover it with gauze, a clean cloth or even a folded newspaper and then apply firm pressure to stop your pet from bleeding. Maintain pressure for three minutes or until you know the clots can stop the blood on their own.

Choking

If your dog is pawing at his mouth, finding trouble breathing or you hear choking noises while he's coughing or breathing, he may be choking. Examine his mouth to look for foreign objects. If you see something, gently remove it with tweezers or pliers or put a spoon in and flick it out. Be very careful or you may push it further down his throat and make the problem much worse.

You can try a modified version of the Heimlich manoeuvre. Put him onto his side, put your hands on his ribs and apply quick, firm pressure a few times. Your aim is to push a big burst of the air out and that should also expel any objects that are preventing him from breathing. If you can't get it quickly, ring the vet and tell him to expect you immediately.

Sprains or Fractures

Your Pomeranian may bite if he has a sprain or fracture, especially if you touch or move him. Put his muzzle on to protect yourself from such bites. Put him on a blanket on a flat surface and try to splint his leg (if possible) so he's easier to transport. The blanket can be used as a sort of sling to carry him. Then get him to the vet if you can.

Poisoning

Many foods that are harmful for people to eat are also bad for pets. In addition to those foods, extra foods that are harmless to people are toxic to pets. This list includes: macadamia nuts, raisins and chocolate. Drugs such as aspirin, ibuprofen and acetaminophen are also dangerous. Never give your pet a human drug unless you have asked your vet.

If you know, or even suspect, your pet has consumed a toxic substance, ring the emergency vet clinic, your vet, or the Animal Poison Control Centre hotline. Do not try to make your pet vomit without being told to do so. If he has already done so, collect some of it for examination and take it with you to the vet.

If a toxic substance (such as cleaning products) has gotten onto your dog's skin or into his eyes, wash with lots of water and a mild soap if necessary. Don't use soap in the eyes and, if they're affected, flush them with cold water.

Seizures

If your dog has a seizure, keep him calm. Do not restrain him or put your hands near his mouth. However, move him away from all furniture and other objects or he may hit them and hurt himself. Time how long the seizure goes for and watch him closely so you can tell the vet exactly what happened in great detail. Ring the vet as soon as possible and ask what to do.

Points to remember

Emergency treatment is no substitute for the care of a good vet but there are times when it's necessary and, in fact, it may very well save your pet's life, even whilst on the way to your vet's office or emergency animal clinic.

Any injured or sick pet may be in pain, be confused and scared. This makes him unpredictable. If he's sore, he may bite, even if he has never bitten you before. Treat him with kindness and gentleness but avoid his mouth and, if necessary, use a muzzle for safety and as a precaution.

How Long Do Pomeranians Live?

Most small dogs, such as Pomeranians, generally mature earlier than larger dog breeds. The good news is that they also tend to have longer lives. The average lifespan of a Pomeranian dog is 10 to14 years.

Some Poms can and do live longer than that. However, there are some things that are deadly for a Pomeranian dog and all care must be taken to avoid them to ensure a long lifespan for your dog.

Pomeranian Life Span Facts

- Average Pomeranian life span is 10 to 14 years.
- Keeping your Pomeranian trim and fit will help your Pom dog live a long and happy life.
- Number one cause of death in Pomeranians dogs is trauma.
- Toy dog breeders mature earlier and also live longer than bigger dog breeds.
- Genes can affect the average Pomeranian lifespan.

Major Causes of Pomeranian Dog Fatalities

Pomeranian Puppies: The number one cause of deaths in almost all toy breeds, including Poms, is trauma.

Pomeranian Adults: The four major causes of death in Pomeranian adults are:

- Trauma: This is the second main cause of adult Pomeranian dog fatalities and the main cause in Pom puppies. Trauma can include being trodden on accidentally, being dropped, being hit by a car or being in a car that has an accident.

- Gastrointestinal: Problems here include intestinal blockage, inflammatory bowel disease, pancreatitis, lymphangiectasis, exocrine pancreatic insufficiency and various other problems associated with the loss of protein.
- Infection: Issues of this type include fungal infections, viral diseases (distemper and parvovirus), bacterial infections (such as leptospirosis) and protozoal diseases (such as leishmaniasis and babesiosis).
- Ticks: Ensure tick prevention methods are current. Check your Pom every day in areas that are prone to ticks.

Tips on increasing your Pomeranian's Life Span

The single most important way of guaranteeing (as well as you can) that your Pom lives a healthy, happy, long life is to make sure his environment is as pet friendly as possible.

The Following Points Will Help Increase Your Pomeranian's Life Expectancy:

- Keep your dog's weight in a healthy range. Trim and fit Pomeranians live longer lives than their fatter, unfit counterparts. Feed him well-balanced, home cooked meals and avoid commercial pet foods where possible.
- Feeding your Pomeranian fresh food instead of manufactured foods with added colours, fillers and preservatives will make a massive difference to his health in the long term.
- Clean living. Pets will have shorter lives if they live in homes where there are smokers present. Passive smoke is just as dangerous to animals as it is to people.
- The ideal balance of activities. Don't give your Pom puppy too much exercise as his growth plates will be

affected. On the flip side, if your Pomeranian is lazy and doesn't bother to move, he'll start losing lean muscle. If he's already a healthy size, he'll gain extra, unwanted weight as he gets older. You want to ensure your pet is as healthy as possible. One or two very short walks adding up to a maximum combined 20 minutes in total is the ideal amount of walking to be done. Add a few sessions of playtime (playing fetch or catch) and he'll be a healthy, happy pet.

- Neutering or spaying your Pomeranian will help increase his lifespan too. An unchanged dog is at greater risk of cancer and other diseases related to their reproductive organs. Vaccinations and the follow up boosters must be kept up until your dog turns five years old.
- Infection is the second main cause of fatalities and vaccines can prevent many of these problems. After 5 years, unless a vaccination certificate is required for a boarding kennel, I wouldn't vaccinate because of the high risk of vaccine-induced autoimmune diseases.
- Proper dental care is also essential. Your Pomeranian's teeth need regular brushing. Lots of dogs become sick or even die from infections in their mouths and teeth or if a tooth infection spreads through the Pom's body. Dogs that lose teeth because they have been neglected will find it more difficult to eat enough food to get sufficient nutrition.

Because trauma is the number one killer of Pomeranian puppies and the number two killer of adult Pomeranians, you must:

- Handle your Pom carefully.
- Ensure everyone in the house is always watching where your pom is sitting or lying down before moving in case they tread on him.
- Use the right car seats.

- Always use a leash and harness when you take your Pomeranian outside.
- Be careful when other people open doors in case your pom tries to escape by getting off his leash.

Part 7 – Training

When Should You Commence Pomeranian Puppy Training?

Most owners think Pomeranians and other small dogs have no need for obedience training. However, this is a fallacy. If your Pomeranian isn't well-trained, he can be yappy, bossy and misbehave whenever he's near strangers.

When is the ideal time to begin training your Pom pup? You need to start training from the time he enters his new home. If you leave it until he's mature, you will need to break him of all bad habits he has accrued during his early months with you.

Pomeranians are not difficult to train. They learn commands quickly, they're clever, and you can use food to motivate them to do whatever you want. However, they can also be very stubborn and, unless they regard you as their pack leader, they may simply ignore your orders completely. You must be firm and confident before you can achieve your training goals.

What Is Needed to Train a Pomeranian Puppy?

1. Location and Time

Pomeranian puppies have a very short attention span and can get distracted so easily. What this means is that you need to choose a place that is quiet, free of other people and animals, and has nothing that can distract your Pom pup. Otherwise, you won't have a chance of making him focus on what you have to teach him.

You also need to find a good time for training. It should not be viewed as a chore. YOU must be in the mood. This means not tired, exhausted, or angry. If your Pomeranian puppy is tired or sleepy, there's not much point training during that time.

Pomeranians are usually receptive when they feel a bit hungry so before breakfast or dinner time should be ideal times. So, the time needs to be ideal for both of you.

2. The Right Rewards

Another special trick for Pomeranian puppy training is to identify special treats he loves eating. Choose a treat that's so delicious your Pomeranian will do exactly what you want so you'll give him another one. It's important that this becomes your training treat and isn't used for anything else. Then you'll have his attention as he does what you command, in return for these special treats.

A vital part of training is to give your Pomeranian his reward on the spot. Then he will mentally associate the action and the reward. If you wait even 5-10 seconds, your Pom will become confused. So always have a treat in your hand, whenever you train him.

Any time you find your Pom puppy doing something he shouldn't, redirect his attention. For example, if he's chewing your shoes, give him a good chew toy because that converts bad Pomeranian behaviour into good behaviour.

You must make sure your Pomeranian gets plenty of exercise every day. If not, he'll soon grow bored and, because he has pent-up energy, he's bound to misbehave. It's something you would do in his shoes. To prevent it, give him lots of different toys and mental stimulation so he'll be an obedient, happy puppy.

It's easier to train Pomeranian puppies than adults because puppies have open minds when it comes to new experiences and "bad" habits have not settled in.

That's the biggest reason for beginning his training as soon as possible once he's home. However, be patient with your Pomeranian puppy behaviour, never behave harshly, and you should enjoy a long, happy life together.

How to Give Treats When Training – Yes, It Matters!

Am I serious? Am I saying there's a specific way to offer a dog a treat? If you're training your dog to do things on demand, then, yes! There's the right and wrong way to feed your dog a treat.

Hold a treat in your clenched fist, with a small part exposed so your dog can see it but can't get to it. Instead of standing a foot away, put your fist right up in his face, inches from his nose and eyes. This prevents your dog from coming forward, which you don't want to occur, especially if you're training him to obey "down" and "sit" commands. If he attempts to move forward, maintain the hand position, and you can even move closer to his nose to control how far forward he can move.

As soon as your Pom puppy has obeyed you, let him have a nibble on the treat still hidden in your hand. If you have chosen a very appealing treat, you'll now have an invisible string connecting your hand to your dog's nose, letting you manoeuvre him into whatever position you want. In a way, it's like having power steering but with your dog instead of your car. You also have full control over when you choose to reward him.

Never throw the treat. Your dog will stand up so he can grab it. You never want your puppy to believe he can break the "down" or "sit" commands.

When you hide the treat within your fist, it also stops your dog from grabbing your fingers. Sure, your dog will slobber and lick your hand until it's drenched and feels horrible, but forget about that for the moment. You can easily wash your hands any time you wish. If your dog is "grabby," tighten your fist and say "gentle!" or "easy!" and place the fist behind your back for a minute. Refuse to offer any part of the treat until your dog takes it softly. Your Pom will quickly learn that grabbing doesn't work.

Some owners prefer to cut treats into tiny pieces which can be harder to handle and locate if the pieces are scattered in your pocket. I prefer using a single bigger treat because it's easier to handle, whether it's in your pocket or hand.

Your dog will surprise you with the speed at which he learns what you're trying to teach him.

Socialising Your Pomeranian Puppy

Puppies go through an extremely significant socialisation process between eight and 16 weeks of age. Throughout this particular time frame, puppies mature incredibly quickly. Dogs must be exposed to the outside world as puppies or they can mature into fearful adult dogs.

Puppies raised in remote locations, such as a garage, generally experience minimal contact with humans. If puppies don't leave their restricted, isolated quarters, they may never encounter external stimuli such as cars, children, and loud noises.

Pets that receive virtually no human handling between the ages of eight and 16 weeks of age frequently remain fearful and anxious when subjected to new situations. Obtaining a puppy younger than eight weeks of age can additionally lead to further difficulties and complications.

Puppies leaving their mother and litter mates under eight weeks of age are deprived of essential interactions that occur between dams and puppies. The key to guaranteeing your new puppy matures into a well-adjusted Pomeranian is to ensure he's exposed to most situations prior to 16 weeks of age.

Your new puppy won't have had all his vaccinations. However, you could perhaps take him to a family or neighbour's home to provide him with extra stimuli. Don't attempt this until your new puppy has been in your home for at least a week and he's eating and sleeping well.

Stimuli can be provided during the first week by gradually getting him accustomed to new sounds. Activities can include sitting him on your knee while watching television. Socialising your Pomeranian puppy will be considerably simpler if your household has other family members and pets.

Whenever you have visitors, ask them to give your puppy a treat. Have them tell your puppy to sit and reward him for sitting with a treat. Puppy will quickly learn that sitting for visitors will result in a treat and that visitors are fun. This important lesson will also teach him not to bark at visitors or jump on them.

Puppy kindergarten classes offer great benefits to new puppy owners. At the same time puppy has his first vet check, ask about enrolling your new Pomeranian puppy in doggie kindergarten classes.

Selecting the ideal Pomeranian for your family situation is extremely important. Exposing him to pleasant activities and stimuli between eight and 16 weeks of age is necessary to develop a well-adjusted mature Pomeranian.

Pomeranian Exercise Requirements

The Pomeranian is small but has an amazing amount of energy. This adorable dog is a great companion, so he needs exercise each day to remain in good health.

Pomeranian exercises

If your puppy gets too much exercise, it may affect his growth. If a Pom of any age gets too much exercise, his body can be badly affected in many ways. He can become overheated. His body may suffer unnecessary wear and tear in many parts, including his hips and knees.

Use common sense. Watch your dog closely. If he's panting heavily or shows signs of excessive fatigue, give him a break or call an end to that particular exercise session.

Poms are regarded as indoor dogs. However, they should also enjoy outdoor activities.

Physical health

When you take your Pom for a brisk walk, or if you play with him and he runs around and expends energy, it also helps maintain his muscles. These exercises will improve blood flow and overall heart health.

Behaviour

Your Pomeranian enjoys cuddles immensely. However, he also loves walking and running around exploring new places in the outside world. These activities are an essential part of his emotional well-being. If he's left alone while you go to work, he should be able to go outdoors for a short time to play and burn off some of that bottled up energy when you get home.

Social skills

Whether you're going for walks with your dog or letting him play in the local dog park, these are ideal chances to teach him or fine tune his interactions with other people and dogs. Caution and common sense must be used when introducing your Pomeranian to larger dogs. Small dogs have been mauled to death by larger dogs at dog parks.

If you can slowly increase the number of meet-and-greets and the time spent in social activities, this can help him through any anxiety issues that may flare up when forced to socialise, especially if he's shy to begin with.

Pomeranian puppy and adult exercise requirements

A small dog, such as a Pomeranian, should have 15-20 minutes of regular exercise that boosts his heart rate moderately. If you intend going on a longer walk, carry your Pom part of the way or invest in a doggie stroller.

It's wise to arrange several elements of your walk ahead of time.

The route

In an ideal world, it's smart to only walk on roads with footpaths. Walking out onto the road as cars rapidly fly by can be extremely dangerous. You can't always predict how your dog will react to cars, especially if they toot horns or yell out. If your home area isn't good for walks, you should strongly consider driving to a park, so you can have a safe walk without any stress for you or your Pom.

Timing

You'll generally want to take your Pom for a walk when you don't have to rush. This should also be when your Pom is chomping at the bit to go for a walk. These two times don't always occur simultaneously, so a compromise may sometimes need to be made.

Some dogs never want to go for a walk in the early morning. These same dogs may be over-excited to be walked after dinner.

You need to enjoy the walk and that precious time alone with your Pom, so don't go when you're pushed for time or you have another commitment. This will spoil the enjoyment for you both, especially if you only get to walk for a short time.

A lot of dog owners prefer an evening walk after dinner. It's a great way to make your dog tired before his bedtime. However, the walk shouldn't be too close to bedtime. You and your Pom will need an hour or two to wind down after exercise, so the adrenaline isn't still pumping, making it harder to sleep.

How is house training affected by exercise?

Many owners make a big mistake while walking their dog. They let him stop along the way to do his business and sniff around at the same time. It's generally sensible to do this but it can affect the process of housebreaking your puppy.

When training your puppy to do his business, you should choose a particular place for him to do it. However, if you ignore your own rule and let him go potty anywhere along the walking track, he'll be thoroughly confused regarding where he can and can't do his business.

Obviously, you can't prevent your dog from having a bathroom break when the urge hits. But you can start your walks by taking him to the area you have chosen for his bathroom breaks. Give him 10 to 15 minutes to do his business and then start your walk.

If your Pom doesn't make potty stops during the walk, return to his bathroom area before you both go back into your home.

Safe exercise

Safety is paramount when it comes to a Pomeranian because he's so small. Brisk exercise is fine, but you must prevent him from dehydrating and overheating.

Here are some tips:

1. Pomeranians shouldn't be taken on long walks. The ideal for your Pomeranian is short walks of 15 mins and then a break in a doggie stroller or puppy backpack.

2. On very warm to hot days, the ideal times to exercise are before 10 am and after 2 pm. This is because that four-hour slot in the middle of the day is the hottest.

3. Check the surface of the road where you'll be walking. If there are lots of small pebbles, they can get between the paw pads and cause major problems. If the surface is very hot to touch, it can be unbearable to walk on. So, if either scenario happens, either take a safer route or think about delaying the walk until the day is cooler.

4. You should walk at a pace that's brisk for your Pomeranian's short legs, not one that suits you. A good pace is where your Pom walks at his ideal speed and you're walking slowly. His walk shouldn't be a stroll or a run. It should be moderate.

5. Take at least one break for 15 minutes. Spend this time sitting in the shade. Carry a collapsible bowl and a bottle of water so you can give your dog a small drink. Never allow him to drink a large amount of water because this is very dangerous and can cause a life-threatening problem called bloating.

6. Pomeranians love walking in cold weather, so don't let that discourage you from taking him for his daily essential walk to burn off energy.

Other activities

Walking each day isn't the only way to ensure your Pom is in optimal health. There are lots of other ways to have fun and get exercise as well. "Fetch" isn't a game reserved for the bigger dogs. Simply select the best discs, balls or toys for your dog and you can have hours of fun playing and giving him exercise at the same time.

Pomeranians are great at agility workouts. A Pom can sense if you're enthusiastic about something. Don't be afraid of being inventive. Set up an obstacle course for your dog. Make sure none of the tasks involves jumping down from anything high as that action can easily damage your Pom's knees.

Young puppies

Never allow your puppy to visit public places (especially the dog park) until he has been given all his puppy shots. It's also essential that you don't let him exert himself, particularly in the initial 12 months because over-exertion may affect his proper growth. However, it doesn't mean you allow your puppy to do nothing. You can find lots of regular exercises to do that are safe for him to enjoy.

Over-exercising

Over-exercising can contribute to many health problems and should be avoided, Great care should be taken when exercising Poms, especially with Pomeranian pups and senior Poms.

FAQs regarding a Pom's physical abilities and limitations

Can Pomeranians swim?

Yes, a Pom can be allowed to swim, as long as you follow proper guidelines. Some owners never even try it, but Pomeranians can swim and, even better, many love swimming. If your Pom doesn't like having a bath, you shouldn't assume he can't swim or enjoy the water in general. Swimming is different when comparing baths and swimming, as far as Poms are concerned.

Never let your pet swim in the ocean or in any type of deep water. It's best to take him into the shallow end of a swimming pool and stay with him. Don't make the sometimes-fatal decision to stop supervising him after he starts doing well in the pool. He must be watched at all times.

Pools have a large amount of chlorine so, after your dog's swim, he needs a thorough wash. If you don't, the chlorine will respond in the same way as bleach and make his fur's colour duller or, if it's light-coloured fur, it may create a green tint.

Can Pomeranians run?

Yes, but a Pom that's running isn't as fast as a person running.

This small breed would never be able to catch you if you went running. However, an adult Pomeranian in great health may love to run at his own pace for a short period of time. You shouldn't encourage a Pomeranian puppy to run because it may affect his growth plates.

Can your Pom go for a long walk?

Yes, he can, IF you follow the guidelines. A Pom can walk for 15 -20 minutes once or twice daily.

If you plan a long walk with your Pom, plan ahead:

1. Ensure your dog is in good health and isn't limping or breathing heavily.
2. Plan your route and check there are footpaths and safe walking areas.
3. Check the temperature. It should be between 55°F (12.7C) and 70°F (21C). If the weather is either hotter or colder than this, put little booties or shoes on his paws to protect them.
4. Ensure your Pom has a good drink before you leave home. For the purposes of training, also ensure he visits the bathroom area and uses it instead of waiting to find a spot while you're walking.
5. Carry lots of water and a snack with you. The water can be kept in a cooler with ice cubes). Also, have a folding waterproof travel bowl or a collapsible fabric combined water and food bowl.
6. Plan for a 10-15-minute break every 20-30 minutes. Find shade to rest in and offer your Pom a treat and water and encourage him to lie down or sit and rest.
7. If your dog is tired before you expect him to, or seems unable to keep going, have a rest in the shade and, if that's not enough, carry him the rest of the way.

Can a Pomeranian go hiking?

Yes, your Pom can go hiking with you as long as the route isn't too difficult, and you follow all safety guidelines explained in the "long walks" section. If you think you'll need to carry your dog if the path is too hard to manoeuvre, don't do it because you and your Pomeranian may both suffer severe injuries if you slip or have a fall. It's best to avoid areas that are difficult to manage.

Five Walking Tips

1. Act like a tree. If your dog tends to pull, immediately stop walking! Once he has put some slack on the leash, you can start walking again. If your dog pulls most times when you take him for a walk, perhaps you need a front-hook harness or a head halter.

2. Never let your dog get close to another dog before you ask the owner for permission. Although your dog may be friendly, not all dogs have the same friendly, quiet demeanour. Don't take offence if you're refused permission or attempt to make their dog meet yours. The other dog may be unwell or healing after surgery. His owner may be training him or he may have had a bad encounter with a different dog prior to today.

3. Always have a poop bag when you walk your dog. It's unpleasant to look at and even more so if you step in it. The waste that dogs produce can cause pollution in surface supplies of water and may contain pathogens such as giardia and E. coli. Always have your pack of poop bags when you go "walkies."

4. If your dog doesn't get sufficient exercise or mental stimulation, a common problem may occur. It's called leash reactivity. You can use treats and training as well as more frequent and longer walks. Running in the park, playing fetch and swimming are all great additional exercises to add to your dog's overall health plan.

5. Barking and lunging at cars, skateboarders, and bicycles as they pass by is a common habit in breeds that are good herders. As wheels go around and around, your dog may feel a predator/prey reaction because he's born with instincts that can cause a very strong urge to chase whatever passes by. It's important to redirect your dog the moment he sees a moving object. Create a further distraction by walking away from that object. Give your dog treats and encourage him to do simple tricks such as: down, sit, shake and make him follow you as you walk backwards.

Photo by Shadow's Farm Photography

Potty Training and Crate Training

Purchase your new Pomeranian puppy from a show Pomeranian breeder. Breeders often start potty training puppies at around four weeks of age. Pet shop puppies are usually sourced from commercial kennels. Puppies from these outlets generally have had nowhere to relieve themselves, other than their own living quarters, which is a habit quickly ingrained in the puppy and can be extremely challenging to conquer.

If you need to leave your puppy unattended for even a brief period of time, the puppy should be confined to his exercise pen or crate. Confine him to areas with tiles or another washable flooring so accidents don't spoil carpets or rugs.

Feed your puppy on a structured schedule and immediately following each feed, take him outside to his "potty spot." Don't play with the puppy until he eliminates. If the puppy isn't going to pee and defecate within 10 minutes, bring him back and crate him for 10-15 minutes.

Repeat this process until he finally has success. This is the time to praise puppy as though he has won a major award.

A puppy must have a routine. He needs to be taken to his potty spot frequently, at least every two hours, and immediately after he wakes up, during and after playing, and after eating or drinking.

Puppy should be praised and given a treat as soon as he has success.

Realise that a small Pomeranian puppy has a small bladder and that it may take several weeks of patience and consistency on your part to completely house train him. Keep puppy's potty place fresh by picking up faecal matter daily.

Potty training a mature Pomeranian

What happens if you decide you want to rescue a Pomeranian and you discover he's not house trained? In that case, it's time for some old-fashioned potty training.

Although some people believe it's tough to teach an older Pomeranian how to go to the bathroom outside, the opposite is actually true.

Why? Consider these facts:

- An older dog has more control over his body and can hold his bladder longer than a puppy.
- An older dog will likely respond to a consistent schedule quickly.

To begin your journey to a clean house and a happy, housetrained Pomeranian, take these measures into consideration:

- Take your Pomeranian to an area he can use to relieve himself before he enters your house for the very first time.
- After he goes to the bathroom, shower him with lots of praise.
- Bring your new dog into the house and allow him to explore.

- Anticipate times when he's likely to need to eliminate (e.g., after eating, every few hours and before bedtime), and promptly take him outside.
- Continue to praise your Pomeranian every time elimination happens, and he'll be happy to receive your adoration and cuddles.
- Should accidents occur (and they most certainly will), don't scold or punish your adult dog. Clean the mess quietly and keep training him.
- Be proactive; an older Pomeranian won't let you know when he needs to go to the bathroom, at least not at first. Eventually, he'll understand and respond accordingly.

Potty training problems

When I pick up my puppy, he pees

Puppies commonly become so excited that they pee themselves. It might be because they expect attention or receive too much attention.

If your little one does this, these tasks can help:

- Play with him outside.
- Take puppy to his designated spot so he can pee before you play.
- If he gets too excited, approach him from his side and begin playing slowly.
- If your puppy does urinate, don't pick him up immediately. Instead, kneel next to him, pat him slowly and calmly, then roll him into your lap. This stops the excited feeling of being picked up.

The moment I bring puppy inside, he poops or pees

- Make him focus on one task and give him ample time.
- Don't let him multi-task or roam the yard.
- Use a six-foot leash or a retractable one that goes out to six feet.
- Stand in the centre of his designated space and let him circle within it.
- He might sniff and look around but don't disturb.

Time matters

It would be great if your puppy did his business on cue. However, some need 15-20 minutes for their bowel muscles to relax before a movement.

If he pees, he might only half empty his bladder and need more time to expel the rest. Sit outside with a good book or your phone and give him time.

If he needs to pee the minute he comes in, have him sit in your lap because dogs normally won't pee on their owner.

However, there are three exceptions:

1. If he has a health problem making his bladder weak.
2. If he's highly stressed.
3. If his need to go is too strong to hold on.

Don't keep him in your lap more than 10 minutes before carrying him to his bathroom, where he'll probably pee easily.

My dog can't hold on for more than an hour

If he suddenly loses control of his bowels or bladder, this may indicate a health problem that must be checked first. Once the vet determines there's no health reason, you can look at other possibilities.

Apart from health problems, generally the solution is that he needs to strengthen his bowel or bladder muscles. Very young puppies won't have much control. As they grow, their muscles get stronger but how much stronger they will get will partly depend on what you do to help.

If you took your 8-week-old puppy out to the garden every two hours and stuck with that as he turned three and then four months of age, he'll get used to going every two hours. The answer is to increase the time between visits.

There must be a good balance between taking him outside and supervising him. Use the supervisory or confinement methods covered earlier. Your goal is to increase the time by 15 minutes and then keep increasing slowly as he gets better. If he's used to a three-hour interval and you try to get him to hold it for eight.

It's also critical that your beta dog(s) feel just as loved and important as your alpha. It's not negative not to be an alpha. You'll decrease the stress felt by all of your dogs if they know where they stand in the pack.

My dog does his business while I sleep without waking me

This covers nightly bathroom needs. The early morning will be discussed next. These tasks can help:

1. Take your dog out one hour before bed and again 20 minutes prior, allocating the 15-20 minutes previously covered.
2. Don't feed him anything after two hours before bedtime.
3. However, never restrict his water.
4. Place him in a confined space so messes don't appear all around your home. The playpen mentioned earlier is a terrific idea. If you don't know he needs to go, he'll likely use the pads provided.
5. He needs enough activity and exercise throughout the day, so he'll sleep when it's time. This means a 20-minute walk each day and a 20-minute cardio session (playing fetch or something similar).

He poos and/or pees extremely early some mornings

These tasks can help:

1. Make his last meal an hour or two earlier than normal. It will increase the chance he'll use the bathroom last thing at night. If you do this, give him a small dry snack at his normal dinner time.
2. Sometimes it's the opposite that works. Feed him two hours later in the evening so he may not have a bathroom urge until two hours later than he usually does in the morning. Again, give him a small dry snack at his usual meal time.
3. Give your dog more exercise each evening. Don't do it too close to his bedtime but if you play fetch or take him for a long walk, he'll be more tired and should sleep through the night and not want to go to the bathroom while you're still deep in slumber.

4. Certain noises can wake your dog. It could be birds chirping, a door closing or loud voices outside. Perhaps you have a quieter location for his sleeping area.

5. Your dog barks when he wakes up because he's feeling bored. You might assume he needs the bathroom, so you take him out. He'll pee only because he's outside. However, if he had something to keep himself busy when he woke, he may not have barked and disturbed you. Placing a treat-release toy in his sleeping space after he's asleep can keep him happy when he wakes up and that may stop him from barking.

My dog uses the whole house as a bathroom

1. If he completely empties his bladder and it began suddenly, it could be a urinary tract or bladder infection so it's vet time.

2. If it's only a sprinkle, often in the same spot, he may be marking his territory. Read the "Marking" section for more information on this topic.

3. If your dog simply hasn't understood your rules, you'll need to start from the beginning again.

4. You may have spent months training your Pomeranian, but if you find faeces and urine all around your home, something didn't go according to plan, perhaps a step was missed. If you skip steps to save time, you end up wasting time.

My dog moves or destroys pee pads

1. Use a pee pad holder. You can also buy cat litter boxes that act like good quality pee pad holders.

2. Ensure he has the ideal chew toys to occupy his time; 20 minutes of cardio exercises and a couple of walks each day. This should release all his pent-up energy and stop him feeling restless.

My dog misses the pads

This can happen if his area is too big (e.g., half a room divided with gates). However, his space can't be too small either or he'll feel claustrophobic, causing emotional and physical stress.

The ideal space should be just big enough for a bed area, space for water and food, a toy play space and pee pads. It's rare for a dog to soil his belongings so this sized space strongly encourages his use of pee pads.

A playpen that's 8-foot square and 24 inches high is perfect for a puppy. Once he becomes an adult, you can get extensions.

Marking

A Pomeranian dog of any age may mark their territory. Dog marking is not actually an issue with housebreaking. Instead, marking is a behavioural problem. Dogs of both genders will mark their territory, but it's not because they're not housetrained or don't know where to do their business. Dog marking isn't just a case of peeing when needed. They deliberately spray a small amount to mark their specific territory. Homes with more than one dog will find this is a common occurrence.

There are numerous reasons why a dog may not be able to control his bladder. Here are just a few: bladder stones, bladder infection, kidney stones, kidney infection, urinary tract infection, and diabetes.

If your vet has already told you that your dog has no health reasons for marking, and you're positive he comprehends the housebreaking rules, it's time to focus on what else may cause marking.

Steps to take to stop your dog marking

It's important to understand that these tips should only be used if all health problems and other possible causes have been eliminated by you and your vet:

- If not already done, consider having your dog spayed or neutered because that will prevent him from marking, and stop him doing everything in his power to announce himself to all potential mates.
- Thoroughly clean any area that your dog has marked. Use a good quality enzyme cleaner to eliminate all traces of urine.

- Block possible sightlines to other dogs such as fencing off your yard at the front and back to avoid your dog seeing other neighbourhood dogs and any that may be going past your home. Inside, close curtains if you can, especially at the front where dogs going by may be visible.
- Watch your Pom and, if you suspect he's about to lift his leg, distract him by calling his name, loudly clapping your hands, or tossing a ball or toy at him. Then take him directly outside to his bathroom area. If he does his business outside, praise him and give him a small reward to acknowledge good behaviour.
- If you're unable to watch him or keep him inside when you go to work, keep him comfortable in a pen or behind a gated area.

Re-assess the dog's hierarchy and make sure that it's right. If it's incorrect, you can improve it in a few ways:

- Don't give him anything to eat unless he obeys the "sit" command.
- People must go in and out of the house first.
- Ensure he obeys the "heel" command.

Behavioural marking patterns when you have two or more dogs:

- Dogs may mark because they're trying to establish the canine leader. Until the alpha dog is determined, there will always be some sort of battle going on. If both think they're the alpha, it will help you know who's trying harder to be the alpha dog.
- After you know, you'll be able to help your dogs by doing everything for your alpha dog first. At mealtime, feed your alpha first. If you give them treats, you'll give the alpha a treat first. At exercise time, put the leash and harness on your alpha first. Following these steps helps your dogs appreciate that you (as the human leader of the "pack,") comprehend that strong "pack hierarchy."
- It's also critical that your beta dog(s) feel just as loved

and important as your alpha. You'll decrease the stress felt by your dogs if they know their place in the pack.

How to Talk to Your Pomeranian

Most people confuse their dogs because they use vocal and visual cues that often change. The same visual cues could mean different things. Words can be used in varying contexts so it's surprising that dogs don't go crazy trying to interpret what their owners want. However, dogs are intelligent (for the most part) so they manage to figure out what you're trying to tell them. Make it easier for your dog to know what you want and he'll love you for it.

Body language

The trouble with using body language is that what a human may think something means is different to the way a dog interprets it.

Here are some guidelines you can follow to help with better communications:

- Never stare at your Pom. He thinks that's a threat and if he's about to bite, he may attack in what he sees as self-defence. Staring can also scare a dog to the point where he pees on himself or runs away to hide. You can look at a point near him but not directly at him.
- Protect your Pomeranian from strangers who may approach him quickly. When strange dogs first meet, they tend to creep up sideways in a circular move so they can check each other out. If a dog doesn't do this, he's sending a message he may possibly attack. If a person does this, they feel threatened.
- The dog may react in one of three ways: try to escape, crouch down or bite in an act of self-defence. If you see your dog is scared, walk up to him and stop with your side towards him. If somebody wants to pat him, tell them to scratch under his chin. Patting on the back or head is regarded as being dominant. A dominant dog would do

that to one that's submissive. If you have a submissive dog, scratching under his chin is the best technique.

- If you want to make your dog follow you, turn your back on him and walk, while calling his name. To make him stop, face him (making you seem big) and take one or two steps in his direction.
- A dog views you walking towards him as a message to follow in that direction while keeping out of your way. A dominant wolf behaves this way when leading his pack. It's common for a person to call a dog while facing him and then get annoyed when the dog walks away. He's only doing what you told him to do.
- Don't hug your pet. Dogs don't hug each other. The only similar behaviour is when they hump and the one on the bottom doesn't like it. So, he sees a hug as being dominant and tries to squirm out of it.

Champion Dochlaggie Debonair. Photo by Michelle Doe

Use verbal commands correctly

It's normal to talk to your dog and it would be odd if you didn't. However, your constant babbling may be confusing. Also, as he cocks his head and seems to listen, he's only really trying to hear words that actually mean something to him such as: eat, walk, food, treats, etc.

How you talk to your dog is just as vital as what you say. Your volume, tone and language are all key elements so remember these points to be an effective communicator:

- Choose a single word for each command and then stick with that word. If you want your Pom to come to you when you call, just say "come."
- Don't use variations such as: come here, here boy, over here, here and various other options. Choose one word and only use that word, even in training, until you have him obeying you easily.
- Choose words that are unique. Don't use similar words for more than one command or your dog will get confused. If your pet's name is Sid, don't use "sit" because it's easy to get the two confused.
- You need to be consistent with the sound of the command as well as the word itself. Dogs are more in tune with sounds so keep your voice steady. Never yell because he has much sharper hearing than you do. Yelling may frighten him (unless he's a long way from you, perhaps off his leash in a dog park).
- If you want to tell him off for something, use a low tone because it indicates leadership, aggression and power. Most species use low tones, often as threats. They make the animal being scolded stop and listen. If your dog is about to run into the path of a car, the word STOP! in a low, but loud, tone will make him stop dead in his tracks.
- A high-pitched tone denotes playfulness. The dog will feel happy and ready to play. People speak to dogs much like they do to babies because it's not a threatening tone and it's easy to ignore if the pet or baby is stubborn.
- Think about rhythm of what you say. It's natural for people to alter their cadence to get the response they desire.

These are just a few examples:

- A low tone that's abrupt will stop your dog from doing whatever he's doing.
- A set of short, high-pitched, repeated sounds that keep rising higher in pitch usually makes your dog go faster.
- A monotonous, long talk calms or slows your pet down.
- If you want him to come running to you, say "go, go, go, go, go, go in short bursts. Once he's there, say noooo in a low tone to stop him.
- Then draw out the words "settle down" to calm him.

Learning to understand your Pom

While you teach your dog how to understand you, it's also essential that you put effort into learning what he means by the different things he does and the sounds he makes. He doesn't speak English, so you have to be smarter when working out what he means.

What is your Pom's body language telling you?

Take your time and learn properly. Observe your dog doing all the things he normally does. Watch how other dogs behave as well. Then watch how your Pomeranian interacts with other dogs. You'll quickly notice numerous facial expressions and body language. Piecing it all together will take time but it's time well spent because your bond will grow stronger as you learn more about how to communicate with your beloved pet. Eventually it will all become second nature.

The Language of Pomeranians

Every movement has a meaning so get to know these to start with.

- Leans forward: interest and confidence.
- Stands with stiff legs while leaning forward: aggression.
- Leaning backwards: Submission or fear.
- Lowering his head or crouching down: submission, anxiety or fear.

- Lowering the body, twisting his head to one side, especially if he's crouching: submission.
- Lowering his front end until his elbows touch the floor while his butt is waving in the air: he's feeling playful.
- Rolls onto his back: depending on the situation, this may be fear or submission or it may simply be that he wants a tummy rub.
- Rolls around while lying on his back: He's having fun!
- Putting his head or a paw on the back of another dog: trying to dominate.
- Slams into another dog with his hip or body: playfully dominant.
- Turning his head away: truce or submission.
- Head held high: Perhaps challenging another dog. Make him turn away before trouble starts.

What's your Pom saying?

Dogs don't just bark. They also howl, growl, pant, yip, whine and sneeze. Each sound has a different meaning. New owners are often worried if their dog growls like a tiger. However, that's just part of their language and can mean different things. When he growls, don't scold him. Listen to see if you can decipher what he's saying.

Interpreting your Pom's language

- A yip or single brief bark: he's demanding something. He may want food, to play, to go for a walk or something else.
- One low-pitched bark: A warning to stay away from him.
- Staccato barks: intruder alarm.
- Repeated yipping: he's excited.
- One soft bark: he wants you to play with him or it's an uncertain warning.
- A low growl: warns another subordinate dog to stay away. That's ok, but not if he growls at you.
- A low growl combined with some yips: could also warn an equal to go away but not acceptable if he's doing it to you.

- An undulating, high-pitched growl: uncertainly or fear.
- High-pitched growls that are short and often repeated: Let's play.

Taking Training to the Next Level

Everyone enjoys the company of a Pomeranian that's well-trained and obedient. While some will be easier to train than others, the actions of the owner are much more important in training than the difference between individual Pomeranians. Keep in mind that having a one or two syllable name, combined with using one or two syllable commands, will make training much more successful.

Once the Pomeranian has a complete understanding of potty training and the correct purpose of living behind a gated area or within a crate, some simple commands can be added to the routine. The puppy should be very comfortable with the person giving the commands and a loving relationship with lots of playtimes, bonding and attention should be developed prior to attempting additional training.

"COME" is one of the first and easiest commands to teach your dog

The best way to start is during playtime, away from distractions and other animals and people. Simply walk a few steps away from the dog, turn and say *COME* in an even, calm voice. Hold out a treat and reward him for being good. It will be necessary to do this several times to get the animal to associate the word *COME* with the action required. A treat and an extra hug or show of attention should always accompany the proper conduct.

After the Pomeranian has learned the command consistently, adding their name to the command will help him understand the owner is speaking to him.

Any time there's unacceptable behaviour, using the words NO or *STOP* in a very demanding voice will help the Pomeranian understand he's doing something wrong or dangerous. Be patient and consistent while using these commands and either remove the temptation or remove the Pomeranian from the temptation so the dog will associate the inappropriate action with the word.

The successful application of these two commands can save your Pomeranian's life if he understands that he shouldn't run out on the road, pull away from a leash, chase a car or chase or engage with another animal. Using his name with the command in a totally different voice than used for any other commands will help the Pomeranian to understand unacceptable, and even dangerous, actions and avoid them.

Training the Pomeranian to SIT

This is also within the realm of training by an owner, usually without the help of a professional trainer. There will be more steps involved, but a solid foundation with the use of the commands *COME, NO* and *STOP* will help you to achieve success with patience and practice. Treats, praise, and extra attention are all acceptable rewards for proper behaviour. Many dogs will sit naturally when a person walks up to them but, as a preferred behaviour to having a dog jump or run around at a person's feet, the act of sitting must be associated with the word *SIT*.

The owner should always have a pocket full of treats before starting any training session. Allow the Pomeranian to see the owner with a treat in his hand. Hold the treat above the Pomeranian's head but not too high or he may jump for it. (This is an entirely different action that the owner will want to associate with the command *JUMP*.) While holding a treat and calming the dog so he'll listen, say his name and the word *SIT*. While saying your Pom's name and the word *SIT,* slowly move the treat above and behind his head.

Hopefully, your Pomeranian will sit, rather than turn around to see the treat. If he sits, immediately say *GOOD SIT* and give the treat. Try to get him to associate the act of sitting with the words *GOOD SIT* and the treat. If the desired goal isn't accomplished, keep the treat and wait a bit before trying again.

Remember...reward good behaviour; don't punish undesired behaviour, and do NOT reward it. Don't confuse the puppy. Just be patient and continue to try and achieve the desired results.

While some trainers will say it's acceptable to force the Pomeranian to sit to get him to understand, force may confuse the whole process. Take the time to notice when the Pomeranian sits and use the term *GOOD SIT* and give him a treat. Continue with patience and confirmation that *GOOD SIT* is the description of the desired behaviour to be attached to the command *SIT*. Try to achieve the desired goal without stress or forcing the puppy in order to own a happy, eager to please Pomeranian.

It has been noted that attempting the command *SIT* in different locations helps the Pomeranian to associate commands and behaviours. Two of the most common places for the association of the *SIT* instruction are: close to the front door or any entry door into the home, and close to the feeding area. In this way, your Pomeranian will begin to associate sitting as an acceptable action when guests are arriving, or while his meals are being served.

STAY is often a difficult concept to get the puppy to understand

When teaching one-word commands, adding his name before the command helps to prepare the puppy for the command that's coming.

Using the same even voice for all commands, except for *NO* and *STOP* will help the puppy to understand. When attempting to teach the Pomeranian to *STAY*, hold out a treat and firmly say his name and then *STAY*. If he doesn't come towards you, give him the treat, back away from him and try again.

Remember to reward good behaviour and simply ignore, rather than punish, improper actions. The puppy loves you and will do the best he can to please you and receive rewards. The owner's goal is to remain consistent and keep the commands, and resulting actions, as simple as possible, so the puppy can understand what's being asked of him.

Training a puppy to walk on a leash is very important, especially in suburban and urban areas where traffic can be a problem. Many small dogs, including Pomeranians, don't work well with a collar and leash. It's often best to use a harness and leash to keep from injuring their neck or shoulders. It should be a slow process reinforced with treats, just as all of the other training has been.

Teaching the puppy to grow accustomed to wearing the harness from a very young age is helpful. When the leash is added, allow him to drag it around for a bit, just to get used to the extra weight. Then apply pressure by holding the leash without tugging or yanking on it. Ignore your puppy if he pulls or tugs on the leash and reward him when he walks beside you without barking and without pulling against the leash.

This training saves lives and is some of the most important training an owner will share with his dog. If the Pomeranian is to be a show dog, proper lead training will mean the difference between overall success and failure in the ring.

Dealing with Behavioural Problems

Aggressive behaviour

Pomeranians tend to be good-natured and aggression is extremely rare in this breed. Never try to reassure your puppy when he's doing something wrong.

One easy way to get the attention of the Pomeranian is by snapping your fingers or making a loud clap with your hands. When you have his attention, you should make a very demanding *STOP* or *NO* command.

If your dog resumes the aggressive conduct, repeat the same procedure until he understands his actions are NOT desirable. When your Pomeranian has completely calmed down and stopped, he should be rewarded with a treat or extra loving attention.

Only reward the Pomeranian when he has completely stopped the snapping, nipping, growling or whatever aggressive actions he's doing. Patience and consistency, as with all training, is the key to success.

Why Pomeranians bark and how to control excessive barking

In the same way that you try training your Pomeranian, he also has a language he wants the owner to understand. The language for most dogs is barking. It may seem like noise, but often it's your dog's attempt to tell you something. Dogs rarely bark for no reason, so try to understand their end of the conversation and find a solution to the problem.

There are several different types of barks Pomeranians commonly use to let their owners know something is happening. Sharp, loud barks often mean they have sensed an intruder or commotion and are trying to warn you of possible danger. They're also trying to notify the intruder that it's their job to protect the area and they're doing it properly.

Pomeranians are often owned by elderly people who have more free time to spend with their Pom. These owners are often retired and spend more time closer to home or on short car trips where the puppy can come along.

The more accustomed the Pomeranian is to having people close by, the more difficult they'll find it to be alone.

Separation anxiety is often noted with a high-pitched bark or a whining sound. In many cases, if this anxiety isn't properly handled, it can lead to destructive actions. Being able to soothe and comfort a Pomeranian and let him know he hasn't been abandoned is very important. A good owner will respond when he hears these types of sounds from a puppy.

A Pomeranian may also bark if he's: happy, excited, sad, bored, seeking attention, sick, or responding to other animals. By spending as much time with your dog as possible, you'll learn the different types of barks and you'll be able to react with patience, love, and attention.

Shouting doesn't help the situation and often makes it worse. If the owner can remove as much anxiety as possible, has tried to deal with the situation patiently and attentively, and still can't achieve positive results, a veterinarian or professional trainer should be consulted.

All dogs bark, but excessive barking for no apparent reason can be a signal that something is seriously wrong. It's your job to pay attention and try to understand what your dog is trying to tell you.

It's both unfair and unrealistic to expect your Pomeranian to become mute, but here are a few simple steps to teach him to only bark when appropriate.

How to stop your Pomeranian's excessive barking:

Try to determine why your Pomeranian barks because eliminating the stimuli will increase your chances of success. Have your Pomeranian's favourite treat within reach.

Praise him for barking once he starts by saying, "Good job" and then, "What's the matter?"

Tell the Pomeranian to "be quiet." Wave the treat in front of your puppy's nose. Most Poms will instantly stop barking because they'll be concentrating on smelling and attempting to lick the treat instead. Keep praising the Pomeranian and tell him that he's a good dog for being quiet.

Let the dog have the treat after 3 seconds of quiet time.

Wave another dog treat in front of your Pomeranian if he starts to bark again. This time try not to let your dog have the treat until 5 seconds of quiet time has elapsed. Your Pomeranian should learn that after each successful quiet-time interval, he'll be rewarded.

Scold your puppy every time he makes a mistake. If he barks, even for an instant, as you're waving the treat in front of his nose, say "Be quiet," in a louder voice. Then reward your Pom immediately after he stops barking. Increase the quiet-time intervals by 3 seconds each time: from 3 seconds to 6 seconds to 9 seconds and so on. It's possible to continue to a couple of minutes of quiet time during the first session, which would mean significant progress in curbing your Pomeranian's barking habit.

How to deal with nipping or biting

Barking isn't the only way a puppy may try to communicate his feelings to the owner. Nipping or biting is a normal instinct from birth to establish an order of dominance within a litter. If a Pomeranian learns that nipping or biting gets the attention of the owner, he may use this behaviour for that reason. The owner must set reasonable parameters and show the dog that nipping, and biting are not acceptable.

Never allow a puppy to do something you wouldn't want him to do as an adult. Nipping your hands or feet or refusing to give up toys may all be amusing in a tiny puppy, but this might encourage negative actions, which can be difficult to stop. The puppy must be confident of his role in the *pack*. The puppy's human family is his *pack* and his position below human family members must be established from day one.

Destructive chewing

Excessive chewing and gnawing are other intuitive puppy habits. When a puppy is young and teething, he'll learn that chewing and gnawing will soothe his gums. When he's older,

he'll often seek the same sort of comfort if he feels deserted, bored, alone or unloved. While it's healthy for a puppy to chew to clean his teeth and exercise his jaws, excessive chewing can be destructive, expensive and even dangerous. Again, this situation calls for the owner to step up and control the situation before there is a problem.

The best defence is a good offense. Providing proper chew toys that taste good helps a dog understand what's acceptable to chew and what's not. Getting plenty of attention from the owner, through play, exercise, and cuddling, can help puppy avoid loneliness and boredom.

Keeping a puppy in his crate or gated area during the day with only acceptable, chewable toys will help avoid dangers. Make sure all electrical cords, pipes and other household items that could injure or poison the puppy are always out of his reach.

This also means crawling around on the floor or laying down

and looking to see things from your puppy's viewpoint because it's easy not to notice a danger if you can't see it, but your puppy can and may harm himself.

Jumping on people

Another behaviour some people think may be cute in a small pup (such as a Pomeranian) is the habit of jumping up on people to show they're happy to see them. The best way to deter this action is to ignore it. Don't reach down and acknowledge or talk to an uncontrolled puppy.

Don't allow others to encourage uncontrolled behaviour. Turn your back to the puppy and, once you have his attention, make a loud clap and say SIT. Be firm and don't let your emotions supersede the training. Reward sitting and ignore the rest.

Continue this lesson every time you walk up to your puppy until he recognises your raised hands prior to clapping and sits before you make the command, then rewards all around for a job well done.

Remember, during the day, to watch and acknowledge when your Pomeranian is just sitting peacefully, by saying *GOOD SIT* and giving him a treat or a hug. Dogs want to please you, so remember to reward them when they do.

Dogs often possess territorial aggression

Having a small dog that tries to defend you is great but there are many Pomeranians who take this responsibility more seriously than others.

They'll bark at visitors, at neighbours in their yards, and anybody walking past your home. They may also view your car as something to protect. Poms may also try to defend you from other dogs in the vicinity.

There are some elements of this territorial behaviour that you can teach your pom. For example, if the postman enters your yard or even stops at your letterbox, your Pom may bark and keep at it until the postman is gone.

Then your dog is happy because he believes he was successful in getting rid of the stranger. Eventually, your Pomeranian may believe he's the toughest dog on the block.

The general behaviour is that a dog will bark whenever a stranger enters their territory but as soon as you tell him to be quiet, he does so. However, you can't always make him stop barking and some owners think it's fantastic that he's such a fearless watchdog.

However, a dog who tries to protect you too much can easily become a pest and a danger, in that you could fall over him while walking or trying to stop him barking. This is the case with dogs of any size.

Barking can be extremely annoying, and he can also trip or nip strangers while protecting his territory and you. Here are some tips to help you stop these things happening:

Stop him from behaving in a territorial manner by moving him away from:

- Your front fence if you know people may walk past.
- Your front door if visitors are expected.
- Seeing the mailbox when the postman arrives.

Give him treats if he behaves by sitting and not barking at visitors.

Ask visitors to bring treats.

It's common for a dog's aggressive tendencies to be reinforced by distracting him or reassuring him because he views it as rewards for such aggressive performance. Don't yell at him because he wrongly believes you're simply joining in.

Train him not to beg

Your dog will beg for food more often than you would like and you can't give in all the time. Otherwise, he'll keep doing it because he'll understand that if he does that, he gets rewarded. His pleading puppy dog eyes are almost irresistible, and you may even give him small pieces of your meal. He can make you feel guilty every time you eat a mouthful of food.

A dog learns actions that benefit him. If he barks while you eat, and you give him a treat, he'll associate that action with food and will keep at it until you stop him doing it. If you refuse to give him food at all, except for his scheduled meal time, he'll soon stop barking because he'll know it doesn't help him. If you relent and give him treats while dining, even only occasionally, it weakens your resolve and tells him to bark more and more.

Here's a good example. If you insert a coin in a soft drink machine, you expect a drink will come out. If the machine refuses to give you a drink after inserting the coins, you'll be unhappy, but you may try again. If you still can't get what you want, you'll likely give up and assume it's faulty.

Now think about a slot machine. You feed it coins and more coins, hoping to hit a jackpot with the next coin, but usually, you don't. If you do reward your dog sometimes when he begs, you'll become a slot machine and he'll become addicted to gambling. Be the soft drink machine and use the all or nothing method.

How to reduce your dog's reaction to guarding food

No owner wants their Pom to be a food-guarding dog. You want to train him, so he understands that your hands will give him food, not remove his bowl.

There are four ways to do this:

1. Feed him smaller amounts, wait until that's finished, and then put treats in his bowl.
2. Give him treats as part of his meal, to begin with.
3. Feed him with kibble, one piece at a time, dropping the next one into his bowl while he eats the one.
4. Never remove food unless your plan is to give him better food.

Eventually, he'll beg you to come close to the bowl

If you have multiple dogs, each one may guard their bowl and treats from the others. You need to feed each dog separately and give treats when they're alone in a room or in individual crates.

Never drop a treat between two dogs or they'll fight over it, or one could swallow it so fast he chokes on it. Don't let treats be left somewhere. If they're not eaten in a reasonable time, pick them up. Later discovery can cause trouble, perhaps when you're not even home.

You Can Do Lots of Activities with Your Pomeranian

Some of the greatest times you spend with your Pom are when you're both relaxing and watching TV or fooling around at home where nobody can see the silly things you do together.

However, it's also great fun being outside, whether you're walking your dog along a path, around a sports field, or sharing good times in a doggie park with other people. These are just a few of the activities you can do with your Pom while outside.

Playing in the park

Letting your dog run free in a dog park is great fun for both you and him. There are different types of parks. Some are open to anybody while others require a membership. Some parks request a payment each time you visit, and others will keep the big and small dogs separate for safety. Certain parks will have equipment you can use.

Avoid places where your puppy can play with big dogs you don't know or those who aren't controlled by their owners. Never let your Pom go anywhere prior to receiving all vaccinations.

Dogs love playing fetch

Most dogs love playing Fetch. You should have a ball that's small enough for your Pom to grab but still big enough, so it can't be swallowed. If unsure, bigger is better. As an alternative, you could use a cat toy, or a stuffed toy filled with feathers or fur. The other option is a Frisbee, a round plastic disc you can throw, and your Pom can retrieve.

Pomeranians don't naturally retrieve things because it wasn't part of the main goal of their ancestors. However, if you start playing early enough, you can quickly teach your puppy to play and have loads of fun.

These tips will help you teach your Pom to be a super retriever:

Stand in the centre of your hall at home with two toys or balls.

- Throw the first toy in one direction and encourage your dog to fetch it— once he has it, call him back to you.
- Toss the second toy in the opposite direction the moment your pom is by your side.
- Repeat this process a few times but stop while he still wants to play.
- Then start again, but this time click when he takes a step towards the ball and give him a treat.
- After doing this a few times, only click and give him a treat as he gets closer to the ball, touches it, picks it up, and brings it back to you.
- This may sound hard but it's easy once you get the hang of it.

Smell the way

Although Poms aren't known to have as good a sense of smell as dogs used for search and rescue purposes, they still have an amazing sense of smell, enabling them to find wild animals, crooks, buried people, and any treats you have hidden. However, you should stick to only looking for treats.

Follow these steps:

- Let your pup watch you hide a yummy treat in an obvious place.
- Take him to a different room for 10 seconds - then back to the treat room and encourage him to look for it and eat it once located.
- Hide the treat in a spot that's not as easy to find, with him still watching you. Repeat the process in step 2.
- Next, don't let him watch as you hide another treat. Make him sniff his way to the delicacy and follow step 2.
- Do it as often as you want but make each time a bit

harder for him to find it.

Most Pomeranians will enjoy this game and it's a fun way to get him to work for his food, in the same way his ancestors did. If he's carrying too much weight, hide the kibble piece by piece so he burns off calories looking for his food and eating it.

Outdoor excursions can be fun

If you thought your new Pom would be great for long, mountainous hikes, you'll find that he will, but only if you carry him most of the way. However, short hikes may be great, as will walks around the block or the local park.

Whether it's walking or camping somewhere, always keep his harness and leash on. If you're in a campground, also pack an exercise pen so he can be confined and safe.

Boating is another fun activity. Because a Pom is so small, he's great on a boat, as long as he knows how to swim and also wears a dog's life vest. If he falls overboard, a strong net can scoop him up, but swimming may just save his life.

Be a good citizen dog

Your dog should be a model citizen. He must behave when strangers are around, even when touched, and he shouldn't jump all over them or act resentful. He should be easy to walk and not freak out or jerk his leash when he sees or hears distractions.

One test is that he should be attached to a 20-foot line. He must stay, lie or sit still and then come to you when called. He must allow a stranger to hold him for three minutes, when you're not in sight, and not behave badly.

You're permitted to talk to your Pom during the test, but toys and treats can't be used as bribes. You're not allowed to force your puppy into a specific position, but you can gently guide him.

If your Pom does his business while participating in a test, he fails automatically, so make sure he has done it beforehand. The test is ended if he snaps, bites, growls, or attempts to attack another animal or person.

Meet and greet

If your Pomeranian enjoys making new friends, you can take him to an organised event, where one or two different dog breeds meet members of the public. Rescued dogs gain a lot from such events and people get to see how great these dogs really are. Make sure your dog has been bathed and is behaving properly.

Everyone loves petting Poms so ensure you're in control. These pointers will help you:

- Set up a table so he can sit on it instead of on the ground, surrounded by people.
- Restrict the number of people who pat him at the same time, or he could feel overwhelmed.
- Never let a stranger hold him because they may get startled and drop him.
- Have a lot of small treats so people can use your "safe" treats instead of whatever they bring.
- Let him show off some of his tricks for the audience's amusement.
- Contact a Pomeranian club, kennel club or rescue group to see if they have events planned. If not, recommend it and offer your help.

School is good

Although you may like to teach your dog everything he needs to know, attending dog school will help with things you can't do. He gets to socialise with other dogs. If he's a puppy, this is a critical part of his learning. If you only own one canine, it's an ideal way to meet other dogs of the same breed in a structured setting where everybody behaves.

Your Pom learns how to behave despite distractions. Sitting in a room full of other dogs will be a challenge when compared to sitting at your feet in front of the TV.

Experienced trainers will watch him and may offer extra information on how to help him be more obedient. You also get to socialise with other owners and their dogs.

There are classes for dogs that cover all aspects of their life including kindergarten for puppies, agility, obedience, therapy work, behaviour at home, and much more. Information on classes may be obtained from your vet, grooming shop, kennel club or local shelter.

Always ask questions prior to signing up for any classes. Lesson numbers and cost shouldn't be the only factors in your decision. What training methods are used? Phrases such as positive reinforcement, clicker or reward-based training are good. Don't go to trainers who use choke collars or use language such as dominant or alpha.

Here are some basic questions:

- How many dogs per class?
- Are big and small dogs segregated?
- Are dogs controlled?
- If your dog is allowed off his leash so he can exercise, is the space fenced off or indoors and secure?

Your Pomeranian can help others

Owning a dog can be cathartic. Imagine not being able to have pets and receiving that unconditional love 24/7. If you enjoy it so much, why not help others who can't have pets for whatever reason? It could be an elderly neighbour, someone in a children's hospital, a nursing home, or somewhere else. Many people would benefit greatly from contact with a loving dog.

There are lots of places where people take their dogs. Your Pomeranian can even be trained to be a therapy dog and this extra set of skills allows you into places where regular dogs are forbidden. Therapy work is the most rewarding activity you and your dog can enjoy and offer to others.

Agility competitions

Maybe you're physically fit and want to get your dog to be more active. If so, think about agility competitions. An obstacle course is a great way to do it, as a timed exercise. Both you and your dog would tackle each obstacle along the way, and they may include: tunnels, ramps to climb over, a see-saw, jumps and so on.

There are various organisations that have obstacle courses set up for this purpose so contact your vet, local kennel club or pet shop to see if anybody can give you information.

Become a member of a flyball team

Flyball is one of a mere handful of team sports for dogs. It's a relay race for dogs, one by one they go, each one eventually passing a ball to the next dog and on they go until all have completed it. It's one of the craziest, funniest, most enjoyable activities for dogs.

Poms aren't too small. The height of all jumps is set by the height of the smallest dog, so there's no excuse to miss out on all the fun in the world.

Part 8 – Behaviour

©Pomeranian.Org

Pomeranian Intelligence

You obviously know your Pomeranian is very smart. However, you may sometimes wonder how smart the Pomeranian dog breed is in general, when compared to other dog breeds and also to people.

An overall picture of dog intelligence

When trying to work out how intelligent dogs really are, there are a number of elements that must be considered.

Language comprehension

This is a huge part of assessing the intelligence of our canine friends. Most dogs living in a home where there's lots of interaction will comprehend approximately 165 words. So, your assumption that your dog only knows a few simple commands and greetings, is wrong. Some dogs know less and others know more. Breeds that are considered to be in the top 20% when it comes to being smart can comprehend up to 250 different words. However, even if they know 165 words, that's about the same as a two-year-old child.

Memory capacity

This is much more than just memorising different words. It also covers the way a dog will look at an object and, weeks later, he can still remember the same object. People do it this way too. There are tales of dogs who get separated from their loving owners for a long time. When reunited, they're ecstatic, proving this to be factual. Assuming dogs have a short memory is a myth.

Awareness

This covers how a dog can understand what's around him and his environment. He clearly demonstrates his intelligence when you take him to the dog park or into a pet store (both places he visits regularly). If you grab the brush and he runs off because he doesn't like it…that's smart. If he walks to his leash and gets excited, that's also being smart. These are all clear examples that your Pom is aware of what's going on around him.

Perception

In some ways this resembles awareness but is significantly more because it includes how your dog uses his five senses to work out what's going on. Sight, touch, sound, smell and taste can all help him identify what objects are. This (surprising to some) actually includes using the Earth's magnetic field.

Scientists have verified that dogs can sense this field (known as Magnetoreception. They carried out studies on dogs and their use of this magnetic field which had to be calm. The dogs had to be off their leash and in an open space.

Their studies concluded that the dogs preferred to line their bodies up along a north-south axis and then urinate and/or defecate. However, why they did it this way wasn't known.

They studied 70 dogs from 37 toy breeds including Pugs and Yorkshire Terriers (but not Poms) over a two-year period. The totals were 1893 defecation incidents and 5582 urination incidents. In every single instance, they were lined up in a north-south direction.

While it's a wise idea to have your Pom on a leash for bathroom breaks, if your yard is fenced off, try not using the leash and see what he does.

Social cognition

This can be a good way to tell how smart your dog is. It relates to how well he interprets certain social cues. One example used in numerous studies was to put an item under a bucket. There are two buckets, and the dog should be able to tell you which one it's under. The idea is not to pat the bucket but to try pointing or looking at it and seeing what the dog does.

The study concluded that dogs were smarter than chimps and human babies. It's essential to understand that dogs are always learning from the things you do and they never stop learning.

The smallest of gestures or looks can tell convey what you're thinking or about to do. They can tell him what you feel and what your expectations are of him as well. Appreciating this can assist you in finding the best ways to handle your pet's separation anxiety.

Problem solving

You can teach your dog how to solve problems. For example, if he presses a button with his paw to reveal a hidden treat. Some games are useful for dog and owner to play together as they help sharpen his skills. More on this subject later in the article.

Emotional intelligence

To test the intelligence of a Pomeranian or any other dog breed, you need to test the range of his emotions. Testing can help compare the emotional ability of a Pom when compared to a person. People's abilities to feel and express emotions expands as they grow older. For example, a child can be excited from birth but generally can't express contempt until around the age of five years.

Studies on Pomeranians have proved that emotions are at least comparable to a 2.5-year-old toddler. Obviously, some will be more and others will be less. Studies have proven the existence of these canine emotions: excitement, distress, contentment, disgust, fear, anger, joy, suspicion, shyness, affection and love.

What's more important to know is that the emotions generally develop in this specific order. By the time your Pom is four months old, he has the ability to express all of them.

Studies further reveal that dogs stop just short of developing guilt, shame or pride. However, they can still walk proudly and a dog obviously feels guilty if he does something wrong. So how does this happen?

People develop pride at around the age of three years. Canine overall development stops at "around" the age of 2.5 years and these are only rough figures. Dogs have proven they can feel shy and so, by definition, confidence is the opposite so they should also feel confident.

Some people believe pride and confidence are the same but there is a clear distinction between them. A dog can feel confident but not pride. People can feel proud and that can lead to ego which can affect the way the brain works. With guilt, if your puppy has chewed up your slippers, can it be possible that he feels no guilt?

Emotional intelligence in dogs is a very controversial topic because most dogs have at least some appearance of emotions, regardless of where they live and how they're treated.

In one study, dogs were left alone in a room with lots of things they could shred. Later, the owners did the shredding but made the dogs watch and then the owners looked at their dogs with a very unhappy face. The dogs behaved the same as if they had done the shredding themselves. It's believed that dogs sense their owners' non-verbal cues that tell them how they should behave, feel and react when something like this happens.

Some scientists claim that, if a dog tucks his tail, lowers his ears, poses in a specific way and has other indicators of shame, it's actually because he's fearful, submissive or, perhaps, both.

How do dogs learn?

A dog learns in order of rank or priority. If he feels superior to another dog or a person, he generally ignores them. Puppies learn by watching adult dogs. Dogs of all ages learn through commands given by owners. However, there are occasions where a dog might do something after seeing a subordinate do it. As an example, an adult dog may check out something a puppy is playing with or checking out. However, most of the time when a dog is learning something new, it's generally more readily learned when coming from a higher-ranking dog or person.

This is why it's crucial for owners of Poms to quickly and firmly establish their identities as leaders (aka Alphas) before trying to teach or housebreak a Pom. If your dog doesn't acknowledge that you're the alpha, you won't accomplish much.

How Intelligent are Pomeranians?

There are two elements that must be considered:

1. Overall intelligence. We have already covered the myriad of ways to test the intelligence of dogs. That included: memory, language comprehension, emotional capacity, problem-solving skills, social understanding, awareness and perception.

Consider all these factors and the result is that dogs are, on average, as smart as toddlers between 2 and 2.5 years of age. Obviously, some Poms will be lower and others will be higher.

The bottom line is that your Pom is like your toddler, with similar levels of intelligence. Lots of people do treat their dogs as children, sometimes better than children.

2. Stanley Coren, a Canadian author and professor of canine psychology, wrote a book called "The Intelligence of Dogs," in 1994 and revised it in 1996. Because there weren't other supporting sources to back his claims, his book was highly controversial at the time. However, it discusses a method of ranking 80 different dog breeds in order of intelligence.

A large number of people disagreed with the rankings for numerous reasons including the following:

- He never saw or interacted with dogs.
- The dogs involved were only measured in terms of obedience and work.
- Judges were all from the US and Canadian Kennel Clubs who assessed dogs during trials in the show rings.
- Only 199 people provided information on which to base the assessment and information published in the book.

Later on, owners of some dogs were asked for their assessment of canine intelligence of their own dogs. Some breeds matched the other list and others didn't.

The Pomeranian is number 23 on the intelligence ranking list which is good. It puts them in an "excellent working dog" group. Dogs above them on the ladder were considered the "brightest dogs." It's vital that you understand that not all dogs in any breed will have the same level of intelligence.

Tips to help your Pom demonstrate how smart he is

Dogs need the opportunity to learn. If you found a neglected dog living in a crate by the side of the road, he wouldn't have many skills. He *could* learn but isn't given the chance. If he was taken home by some kind soul and cared for, he would be a much happier, healthier dog and would become much smarter.

These tips will help your Pom learn more:

1. Dogs have the same five senses that humans do, but they're much sharper. Spend time in the garden, the local dog park, in a specific room in your home or anywhere else you think of where he can do a bit of investigating, using his senses.

After a while, hide a treat in your home and see if he can locate it just through smell. Use other nonverbal cues such as nodding or shaking your head as he gets closer or further away. Each time you get him to do these types of things, it helps his mind become sharper.

2. Train your Pom to understand words. Commands help but there are more words to use than *sit* or *heel.* A dog generally understands 165 words, the same amount as a toddler. Your pet is keen to learn new words so teach him!

You can start teaching him words by grabbing a few objects and, one by one, hold each item and say its name. Do it over and over again, until he knows what they are.

Once you have accomplished that, put them in a line and tell him to choose one.

Did he do that? If so, praise him and give him a treat. Repetition is the key to learning for dogs as their long term memory is much stronger than their short-term memory.

Once you have done this enough times with those three items, start again with a different set of three.

When a dog is given the opportunities to demonstrate his intelligence, life is more enjoyable for you both. Keep a list of all his words to see what the end result is. You'll be quite surprised.

3. Play different games that help your dog learn. Fetch is a good game because it's great exercise and helps strengthen your bond with your pet.

Mind games are as essential as physical ones. Hide one of his treats under one of three upside-down cups and see if he can choose the one it's under. If he figures it out, shuffle them around to make it harder.

Your Pom really is your child in many ways. Let him enjoy a long, healthy life by appreciating how smart he is. He reads nonverbal cues correctly, can sense your emotions and knows what you're saying, even if it's not every word.

Dogs have such a wide range of emotions including love. You know how much you love your pet but isn't it truly amazing to know that feeling is reciprocated? Share as much of your life with your dog as possible. Avoid emotions such as suspicion and fear. Focus on happy emotions such as joy and contentment.

Australian Supreme Champion and Canadian Champion Shallany's Rebel With A Cause.

Why Do Pomeranians Spin in Circles?

Pomeranians are very adorable, partly due to their size, and partly because they may have odd little quirks. Their fun-loving demeanour and great personality appeal to lots of owners who may wonder what they'll get up to next.

One typical quirk they may have is a love of spinning in circles. Owners commonly ask why this happens and if it's normal behaviour.

The habit of spinning in circles is a Pomeranian breed trait and is often referred to as the Pomeranian pirouette. Judges will often make allowances for this engrained Pomeranian habit in the show ring. Poms often like to give a little spin in the show ring, much to the embarrassment of their handler. Let's look at the reasons for this to see if you need to be worried or not.

Reason 1. Spinning is the Pomeranian's way of telling you he's enjoying himself and is happy. When you come home and walk in the door, your Pom will be so happy that he'll start spinning in circles. It's his way of saying, "hello Mommy, you're finally home at last and I love you."

Reason 2. He wants your attention! The Pom is one of the friendliest, most charismatic dogs in the world, as well as being a terrific companion and lap dog.

Over the generations, these qualities have become deeply inbred and have enabled Pomeranians to really love their human family and spinning to get your attention so they can demonstrate how much they do love you. Spinning is a rather unique way of getting you to stop whatever you're doing and pay attention to your beloved Pom. It works very well.

If your Pom acts like a shadow, going wherever you go, it's not something bad. However, remember to do your tasks because he's an easy distraction. If you're busy and he's spinning around because he craves attention, take a few minutes each hour to pet and talk to him. Then he understands that you know he's there, and it gives him positive reassurance that you're not ignoring him.

Your Pom is also trying to help you, even if you don't realise it. Taking a few minutes away from your busy life each hour will enable you to reduce your stress levels and, ultimately, it also helps you get more done. So, he's not being entirely selfish.

Finally, he needs at least one walk every day. It helps him to burn off excess energy and keeps you both healthy in the process.

Reason 3. Excitement. If your dog spins while you make dinner, when you try to play with him or when you grab his leash because it's walk time, this is because he's excited. You should not be concerned because another side effect can be "excitement urination," not a problem you want to have.

Reason 4. Playing on his own. Think back to your own childhood. You may have gone outside and literally spun around, just for fun. Canines can be a lot like humans in many ways, including finding their own ways of enjoying themselves. After all, a dog is a bit like a child.

It's normal to expect him to find funny, silly, even odd, ways to enjoy himself…and this includes spinning. If your Pomeranian is spinning around, there's no cause for concern. It's typical behaviour and isn't dangerous in any way. It's just that he's telling you how much he loves you and craves your attention.

How Long Can Pomeranians Be Left Alone?

It's impossible for us to spend 100% of our time at home with our Pomeranians, despite wanting to do so. It's also not possible to take them along wherever we go, including work and school, places where the whole day is usually spent. Therefore, it's essential to ask, "how long can Pomeranians be left alone?" Poms are social dogs, but you might be surprised at the amount of time they can handle being on their own.

How long can Pomeranians stay home alone?

The age of your Pom and his state of health are the two main factors that will help you make this decision because it's not black and white. Depending on his age, you'll have to consider not leaving him on his own for long periods. A quick trip to the post office or store is generally fine but spending all day at work could cause problems in the initial stages.

Adult Poms (12 months+) can be comfortable on their own for 6 - 8 hours. If your Pomeranian suffers from anxiety disorders, particularly separation anxiety, he shouldn't be on his own for longer than 5 hours prior to you giving him extensive training so he can cope for 6 - 8 hours.

When your Pomeranian puppy is still very young, it's vital that you never leave him on his own for more than an hour. At this age, he hasn't yet learned how to control his bladder. Lack of potty training can mean little messes if you don't get him to his toilet spot in time.

Pomeranians and their Toys

It's essential to find good quality toys because they'll help your Pom deal with separation anxiety and accepting that he'll be home on his own when you have to go out. Sheer boredom and the stress he will feel when waiting for you to return home may cause him to nervously chew almost anything he can find if you don't provide him with something suitable that he loves to chew and play with. Chewing is his way of dealing with stress so you can ease it by getting the best toys for him to chew as you can.

There are several different types of toys to satisfy this need:

Toys that encourage puppy to play independently. If your Pomeranian doesn't feel like chewing, he should still have a reason to play with each toy he's given.

Toys for bored Pomeranians. If the toy isn't liked by your Pom, it can just lay there doing nothing and your pet will still be bored. The ideal toys are those that can keep him interested and focused when nobody else is around.

Here are a few ideas:

- Colours: dogs love brightly coloured toys to help them focus.
- Textures: A toy with a few different textures will make him more curious and keep him enthralled for longer.
- Teasing toys: There are some amazing toys around that contain small treats. Once your dog has done some work, he'll get a treat. It's critical that you buy high quality toys so they last longer and you'll have comfort in knowing pieces can't break free, especially if you're not home to rescue your dog if something does go wrong.

Comforting toys for Pomeranians. When any age dog is all alone at home with no other people or animals for company, he'll cope better if he doesn't feel as isolated.

The ideal toys for these times are ones that provide an element of calmness and comfort. Poms love large, soft stuffed toys that emit a soothing, peaceful heartbeat. This toy provides a sense of companionship and security and older Poms may start to mother the toy. Puppies may regard it as a type of mother.

Boxes and dispensers. Dispensers are perfect for those times you need to leave your dog alone for a few hours. However, they're not cheap. Toy boxes are great fun and offer a place where your Pom can "hide" his favourite toys. Dogs should know they own their toys and they can always rely on finding them, wherever they leave them.

If you can't afford to constantly buy new toys, it's a great idea to have two boxes of toys. Only let your puppy play with toys in one box at a time. When he gets bored with those toys, you can bring out the new set and hide the first set again.

By rotating the boxes, you can keep your puppy occupied for a long time because he'll feel as though he has new toys each time you change the boxes. However, you have to let him keep his "favourite" toys or he may get upset if he loses them suddenly.

There are lots of toys designed for owners and their pets to play with together. It's a lot of fun and it's also cathartic for you because it releases your stresses and makes you relax more.

Having fun with your dog creates a "magical" bond that keeps him occupied and decreases any destructive behaviour or boredom in the quiet times. These toys actually increase your dog's intelligence.

Playing with your Pom is fantastic fun

The best way to bond with your puppy is by playing with him in an interactive manner. You'll be able to stimulate him and that's all part of your overall care plan.

There are lots of toys designed for owners and their pets to play with together. It's a lot of fun and it's also cathartic for you because it releases your stresses and makes you relax more. Having fun with your dog creates a "magical" bond that keeps him occupied and decreases any destructive behaviour or boredom in the quiet times. These toys actually increase your dog's intelligence.

It's important to note that anybody can make a cheap plastic object and claim it's a dog toy. That's not what your puppy needs. Cheap toys can be easily pulled apart; pieces may be chewed until they fall off, and the toy may contain chemicals hazardous to your puppy's health as well. A caring owner will only buy good quality toys their puppy can enjoy.

Dochlaggie Winter Wolfe.

Dochlaggie Winter Wolfe.

Pomeranians And the Outdoors

A Pomeranian is a toy dog and, because of that, it's not recommended that he should be treated as an outdoors dog, even though he can moderately tolerate the cold and hot weather. He's much better off living inside your home with your family.

How old should your Pomeranian be before you take him outside?

This question has three answers:

1. Letting him outside in your yard. If other factors are covered, you can take your Pom out into your back yard when he's eight weeks old. However, this is only if no other dogs can get into that part of your yard, and this includes other dogs you own.

It's also essential that your yard is clean. i.e., you have treated the ground for weeds and fleas, etc. with necessary chemicals and how long those chemicals remain at a toxic level. If you don't know how long, consider using a canine playpen so he's still outside but protected from everything on the ground.

2. Carrying your Pomeranian in public. At eight weeks of age, you can take your puppy outside as long as you hold him at all times. This includes being out in your front yard, when walking along the footpath, at the shops, in parks, in yards belonging to neighbours and so on. Until he has had all the necessary shots, his feet can never touch the ground outside except in your back yard if safe.

3. On the ground in public. Vaccination periods may fluctuate from vet to vet so it's critical that you ask your vet if every needed shot has been given BEFORE allowing your Pom to put his feet on the ground in public.

Even after he has been given all the shots, it's best to wait an extra two weeks in case he's still susceptible. So, it means he'll be 12-16 weeks old before he can safely be taken outside. Then you can put him on the ground and let him explore, as long as you have him on a leash at all times while he's out.

Can I keep my Pomeranian inside 100% of the time?

Some owners do keep their dogs inside all the time but it's very unhealthy. Unless you live in a spacious mansion, your home won't have sufficient space for him to run around, enjoying himself and burning off all that energy so he's tired enough to have good quality sleep.

Regular exercise is essential for your Pom. If you take him for a 30-minute brisk walk, he'll burn off lots of energy and that helps prevent the urge to bark and/or chew things. Plan your walks to happen at the same time every day (if possible) so he looks forward to it. Exercise helps him fight off diseases, smell, hear and see new things, is heart-healthy and balances out his muscle tone.

How can I stop my Pomeranian's fear of going outside?

Your dog will usually be wary of new things and may react when facing something new by ignoring you and/or barking. Don't be in a hurry to expose him to everything outside the home simultaneously and don't go from 0 to 100 without stops in between. Take baby steps when introducing your Pomeranian puppy to new elements that will be in his life. Then he won't feel bombarded. Take him for short walks and avoid possible triggers such as heavy traffic. Then gradually change the places where you walk him and include noisy areas.

Don't keep him inside all the time; It's only by going out into the real world that your Pom pet will learn what he can/can't do. Over time, it means he'll respond less frequently to loud noises or other distractions that may previously have greatly annoyed or alarmed him to begin with.

How can I encourage my Pomeranian to go outside if it's raining?

Dogs either love running and playing in the rain OR they refuse to get their paws wet. Obviously, you don't want your Pom to get drowned in a torrent of rain so it's wise to slowly teach him that rain can't harm him.

Take baby steps at first. Put a dog raincoat on him and/or keep him under your umbrella so he feels safe. If the weather is warm and it's only drizzling, encourage him to go outside because the rain won't feel so bad. The more often he gets wet, the less frightened he'll be when it comes to rainy weather.

If my yard is fully fenced and dog-proof and I have a doggie door, can I let my Pomeranian go outside when he needs the bathroom?

When first considering how to train your dog to do his business outside, it may seem logical to train him to use a doggie door so he can come and go when he wants. However, you should consider a few other elements as well.

1. Choose one part of your yard for him to do his business. If you let him roam and do it wherever he desires, that can hinder the learning process. A Pom faces numerous distractions (and potential dangers) and this can prevent him from indicating to you that he needs to go outside when he needs the toilet. With no structure, your Pom won't automatically associate going outside with his need to go to the bathroom as two aspects of the same event instead of two separate events.

2. If you're not able to supervise your Pomeranian when he successfully does his business in the right area outside, you won't have extra chances to praise his actions and even reward him, which all helps strengthen the training you're doing with him. Otherwise, he can easily forget what he has learned. The ideal method to teach your pet anything is to acknowledge and reward the moment he does his business and that's impossible if you're not outside when it happens.

3. When your Pomeranian is outside, there are lots of possible dangers he may face. Some owners claim they always let their dogs play or do bathroom business on their own and never had any problems. However, they're fortunate and are in a small minority. If your Pomeranian is left on his own outside whenever he wants to go out, it's most likely that, at some point, he'll have a problem with one or more of these potential dangers:

   - Poms are attractive and small so they're potential targets for dog thieves. Even if your yard is secure, there's still the potential that you'll lose him.
   - Pomeranians are small so they can be viewed as prey for hawks, eagles, owls and other wild birds. If you're outside with your pet, he's safe, but if he's alone, he has little chance against large birds of prey.
   - If your yard is securely fenced in, meaning your dog can't burrow beneath it and he can't jump over it, it still doesn't guarantee that aggressive dogs and even coyotes may somehow get in. Poms are courageous and will often try to protect their territory. However,

they're also small and, when faced with a much larger creature, they don't have much chance.

- Leptospirosis is an animal's disease and is spread through the urine of creatures such as: raccoons, deer, skunks and other animals. If you allow your Pom to wander the yard alone, he may sniff out areas that you would never let him get near if you were outside with him. Not every dog gets all the possible vaccinations. Vets generally only vaccinate against Leptospirosis if you live in a risky area. For example, your home may back onto a forest. If not diagnosed early enough, this disease can kill your dog. Even if you 100% supervise your Pom when he's in the yard, if you believe there's a remote risk of this disease, talk to your vet about your pet having the vaccine.
- Insect stings. All stinging insects have the ability to affect your Pom when he's outside. Bee stings may be painful, can cause dangerous allergic reactions and, if not diagnosed and treated quickly, they can cause fatalities.
- Mushrooms and plants. Yards often contain toxic flowers and plants. There are currently 96 potentially toxic weeds and plants listed.
- Running away. Jumping fences isn't the only means of escape for dogs. Some can burrow under a fence, either by digging or pushing through a weak area. Poms and other small dogs don't need much space from which to escape. Regardless of whether your Pom is the most loved dog in the world, there will still be possible reasons for running away, and this includes sexual canine instincts.
- An un-neutered male can smell urine of an "in heat" female up to a distance of five kilometres. Females that haven't been desexed may feel powerful urges to escape and locate males, including those that have been fixed, if they feel curious or bored, a feeling of something scary or a chase trigger.

How quickly could a Pomeranian succumb to hypothermia?

This depends on whether the dog has any protection, the weather temperature, and length of time out in the cold. If he's soaking wet, he would rapidly develop hypothermia. If anybody (dog or human) is outside in a temperature lower that their own body temperature for enough time, they would face hypothermia.

If a Pomeranian remains outside, can he get frostbite?

Of course, he can! But he has to be outside for a long period in the winter weather and his ear tips, tail, nose and paws will be his main affected parts. How long he can last before suffering frostbite will vary according to wind chill and temperature. If you take him for a walk or just to do his business, that won't be enough time.

If a Pomeranian remains outside, how long would it take before he gets heat stroke?

In summer, heat stroke is a serious problem. How soon it happens depends on variables such as the dog's activity level, humidity and temperature. Many people think a thick coat (like the coat of a Pomeranian) increases the risk when the reverse is actually true. Shaving your Pom isn't always wise in Summer because the coat helps protect against direct exposure to the sun.

Heat exhaustion is the first indicator and symptoms include: weakness, panting, vomiting and confusion. When heat stroke starts, extra symptoms include diarrhoea, disorientation, pale or red gums, heavier panting and an increased heart rate. If untreated, heat stroke can lead to a coma and even death. Heat stroke may occur in less than 30 minutes, depending on the variables.

Can a Pomeranian safely drink from puddles?

No! Puddles can contain all sorts of nasties, including water-borne parasites, road salt and ice melt chemicals.

Dochlaggie Winter Wolfe. Photo by Ffire

Dochlaggie Winter Wolfe. Photo by Ffire

How to Avoid Pomeranian Dog Park Dangers

It would be absolutely wonderful to have a park especially for pets and that it would be a safe, friendly, fun place for your Pomeranian to run around in and maybe even find some new friends.

At a minimum, it would be great for fun and would help your Pomeranian improve his social skills. Sadly, there are some dog park dangers that owners must watch for and every park is laid out differently so you can't assume that if one park is safe, the others are just as safe. The main reason owners take their Poms to parks is so they can meet other dogs and play in a safe environment. This is a terrific idea in theory, because once a Pomeranian has been faced with various potential triggers (and this includes meeting other dogs), he'll be calmer when he meets the same dogs and others down the track. Unfortunately, dogs have faced horrific, and sometimes deadly, attacks whilst in a supposedly safe environment.

How to Avoid Dog Parks Dangers

Find a dog park for small dogs. If a small dog park is not available in your area, choose a dog park that has fenced off areas for little dogs. A lot of dog parks are doing this to help prevent attacks from occurring.

Parks should also have a rule that leashes are required when walking on the park's trails. If both of these aspects don't apply to a park, never go there again.

Your Pomeranian may be playing with small dogs but don't assume toy dogs are always calm. Some can attack other dogs, although fatalities won't generally occur as they would be more evenly matched. However, such attacks can still leave physical and emotional scars that can last for a long time.

Keep your eyes open for warning signs that a dog may attack. Signs include baring his teeth, raised hackles and an icy glare. If this happens, remove your dog from that part of the park. However, you shouldn't let an incident like that prevent you from using the park because it can happen often.

Socialising and playing with other dogs of a similar size are great benefits and outweigh the odds of a fight happening. Instead of visiting an actual dog park, go to a park where you can simply have your pet on his leash and take him for walks.

Some won't have signs saying dogs are permitted. However, there will be rules governing the use of a leash at all times and that all droppings must be picked up.

Parasites

Your precious Pomeranian can catch roundworms and fleas from other dogs in a couple of different ways. Fleas can jump from one dog to another, a maximum of six feet in a single jump.

Keep your Pom dog safe and use flea protection all the time. This will protect him when he's playing in a park or taking you for a walk around your home block.

Dogs may sniff or eat faeces before other owners can scoop them up. Whenever he's on his leash, don't let him even sniff faeces. If he's roaming free, keep an eagle eye on him to ensure he doesn't do this, and race to stop him if he tries.

When shouldn't you take your Pomeranian to a park?

If your female is in heat and isn't spayed. Every male who isn't neutered will go for her as quickly as possible. This can be dangerous for your pet and you when you try to separate them. It can be hard to read the signs that she's in heat. If she's not spayed, keep the leash on her and observe her behaviour around other dogs. If her tail goes up, offering herself to the males, it's time to quickly remove her from the park and take her home.

If your puppy hasn't had all the necessary vaccinations, he should NOT be mingling with other dogs. Wait a couple of weeks after he has finished all the injections before you take him anywhere public, especially a dog park full of animals who may have all sorts of problems.

If your Pomeranian is very shy, a park isn't a good idea at first. He needs more training to lift his confidence and then try to socialise him with one or two dogs at a time. Taking a very shy dog to a park is like throwing him in the deep end of a swimming pool if he can't swim. It won't work. Do it gradually and he'll adjust to the idea.

Why Does My Pom Eat Poop?

Pomeranians are very cute and adorable in every way. So, it can be upsetting when we see that our Pom is eating poop. This is frustrating for owners and it may cause your Pomeranian to pick up bacteria and parasites that can cause diarrhea and other health problems.

This behaviour is often embarrassing for people who own Pomeranians and it's also extremely bad for a dog's health. Let's look at all this in greater detail so you'll know what to do if this happens to your dog.

Your dog might be eating low-quality commercial food containing lots of indigestible "fillers." This causes lots of poop and it smells exactly the same as the dog food your Pom has consumed. You'll know whether commercial food is good or bad by the consistency and amount of poop your dog produces. I would recommend changing to a healthier diet.

One of the most common reasons why a dog may eat his own poop or that of other dogs is because his food is missing essential nutrients. If your dog's body craves something specific, his canine instincts will make him eat it, wherever he can find it, including in poop.

Your first course of action is to examine what you're feeding your dog. Some of the manufactured foods are ok to eat, but many contain fillers.

What exactly are fillers? They're ingredients that manufacturers add to dog food to make it bulkier. This is done to give the appearance of more food than there really is. It "fluffs" the food up so it looks like a lot of food when the fillers have no nutrients or calories at all. If your Pomeranian eats these foods regularly, he may still feel hungry and he'll eventually become deficient in various vitamins and minerals.

If you need to use manufactured food, it's a wise move to also feed your dog the best vitamin and mineral supplement you can buy to help balance out his diet and keep him healthy.

Your other choice is to make his food at home. This is the only guaranteed way to know your pet is getting healthy, wholesome, fresh food for his meals and snacks. Another benefit is that Pomeranians love homemade food. Owners often find that making the food themselves solves any problems with the dog being a picky eater and will stop him eating poop while he's outside.

The answer is that he may simply be curious and that can become a habit. Some owners claim their dog eats virtually anything. Some dogs will sniff and taste most things, so they can work out what it is, if it's edible, and whether they do (or don't) like the taste.

It's difficult to imagine a dog enjoying the taste of faeces because it's a repulsive thought to us. However, it can depend on what foods are digested and then expelled. If your dog is eating poop, there must be something in it that he likes, or he wouldn't do it.

If a Pom eats poop once and isn't taught that he shouldn't do so, he may keep looking for poop and eating it. You must remember that if a wrong behaviour isn't corrected, your dog will simply assume it's ok and he's allowed to do it.

There are a few ways you can prevent your Pom from eating poop:

- When you housetrain your Pom, just pick one specific area. Then your dog can identify his exact spot. That spot must not be used for anything except for the bathroom area. It should never be used as an exercise or play area. Ensure your dog's environment is kept clean. After your Pomeranian has done his business, scoop it up and lead him away from the area.
- Watch him closely when you take him to parks and anywhere else other dogs play and walk. Eating faeces from other dogs may cause an infestation of worms.

- The moment you notice your Pom walking towards faeces, clap your hands loudly to get his attention. Then change his focus to something else and, when he complies, reward that good behaviour.
- If your yard has an open area in which your Pomeranian can run, you must go outside first and collect any poop.
- Make sure your Pom is now eating homemade food.
- Ensure his poop tastes really bad. If you add small amounts of meat tenderiser to his food, this can deter him from eating his faeces.
- People have suggested adding pineapple, pumpkin or a stool deterrent supplement as other options. Your vet can also give you medicine to make the poop taste very bitter.
- It's important to only use a single additive to avoid overwhelming your dog's digestive system. Talk to your vet before trying anything because too much may cause other issues and some dogs could also be allergic to certain additives.
- Make sure your dog has plenty of exercise and play time. If a dog is bored, he may damage property and develop unwanted behavioural patterns.

Traveling with Your Pomeranian

Pomeranians are such a big part of your family that you'll find it tough to leave them at home when you go on vacation. That means you'll need to plan how to occupy their time and keep them safe, whether they're in a car, on a plane, at a hotel, on the beach or in any other place that's out of their comfort zone.

No matter where you're heading, your Pomeranian must be protected. Initially, it's a good idea to take him to the veterinarian just to be certain he's in good health for traveling. He may need booster shots, too. Just as people need certain additional shots when traveling to certain parts of the world, your dog may need them as well.

While you're at the vet, ask for a copy of your Pomeranian's shot records, just in case. If he doesn't have a microchip, now would be a good time to insert one. Other health certifications may be required by airlines, so checking their requirements before traveling is wise.

If plane travel is your goal, make sure you know your airline's rules regarding pets. Call in advance so you aren't surprised. It's likely you'll need proof of your Pomeranian's vaccinations, as well as health certificates. Should the weather be extremely cold or hot, the airlines might tell you they can't safely transport your Pomeranian. Another option may be for you to have your Pom in a carrier under your seat rather than in the cargo hold.

For any road trips, your Pomeranian's comfort is a must. Even if he whines and tries to cajole you into letting your lap be his seat for the ride, don't give in. Instead, crate your dog in equipment that provides space and security. Put soft material with a certain amount of absorbency at the bottom of the crate.

Even if your Pomeranian is sleeping, wake him up to take a leashed walk and potty break every two hours or so. This will keep him from getting too bored or stiff during the time you're on the road. Bring bottled water, a toy or two, and treats. If your Pomeranian is prone to car or air sicknesses, don't feed him right before you leave.

However, do keep him well hydrated. Additionally, ensure there's an abundance of fresh air; Pomeranians, like all dogs, love to sniff and smell new places.

One word of caution—*never* leave your dog unattended in your vehicle with the windows closed. Pomeranians and other pets can quickly succumb to the devastating effects of heat, even if the weather seems cool to you.

Before your trip, make sure that overnight stays (e.g., at a motel, hotel, bed and breakfast or rental property) have been informed you'll be bringing a dog with you. The last thing you need is to have your vacation marred by hearing that you can't bring your Pomeranian into a facility.

Every overnight company has its own pet policies. Some allow your dog to sleep in your room in a crate. Others have an optional kennel service. If your room is in the former category, remember to be respectful to other visitors in the establishment. If he begins to whine or bark, respond to the situation immediately. Don't leave your Pomeranian alone in any hotel or motel room. Finally, when you're at a hotel, motel or similar place, always pick up after your Pomeranian. This will show you're a caring, responsible pet owner.

Tips to help your Pomeranian combat travel sickness:

Travel sickness medication is available from your vet. This medication is best reserved for extreme cases of motion sickness. Preference should be given to trying the following natural techniques first:

- Prior to travel, enjoy a few play sessions with your Pom in your stationary, but running, vehicle.
- Taking your Pomeranian on short, frequent car journeys will get him used to car travel.
- Pomeranians that suffer travel sickness often tend to be much happier in a dog booster car seat.
- If you're planning on using a pet crate, ensure your Pom is familiar with the crate prior to travel—position the crate on the front passenger seat facing forward.
- In the event your Pomeranian is traveling in a dog crate, always face the crate in the direction of travel, not in the opposite direction.
- Avoid feeding your Pomeranian large meals prior to travel.
- Ensure your Pomeranian is totally free of internal parasites; intestinal worm infestations can contribute to nausea and vomiting.

Selecting the ideal car seat for your Pomeranian

It's extremely dangerous having a puppy or dog in your car if he's not secured. He may end up sitting in your lap and distracting you while you drive, potentially causing a serious accident. It doesn't matter how well you believe your dog behaves, not securing him before driving is simply stupid and dangerous.

You may also be the "best driver in the world" and you've never had a car accident until now. But anybody can have an accident, whether it's your fault or if the other driver is to blame.

Therefore, you must have a car seat for your Pom so you can focus on driving and nothing else.

55% of the people who use dog car seats aren't sure if their seat choice is the best one and if they're actually using it the proper way. 8% of people don't care enough to even restrain their pet while they drive.

A dog car seat is essential for these reasons:

1. Unsecured pets will be tossed around in your car when you have an accident, even if you're driving slowly. If you're moving at 60 kph and hit another car or something else, your dog will be affected in several ways.
    a. A Pom that weighs 2.26 kgs will be tossed as though he weighs 102 kgs. If he weighs double, he'll be thrown at double the force.
    b. Because of this, he may suffer from broken bones, brain damage, injuries to various internal organs and even a fractured neck.
2. If the car seat is too big for your Pom or if you haven't restrained him correctly, he may face the same serious problems. Research has shown that if your car is moving at 24 kph or more, your dog will be thrown from his doggie seat.

Characteristics of the ideal Pom car seat

There are several aspects to a car seat you need to look for when making a purchase. They help keep him comfortable and safe if an accident was to occur:

- Size matters. You can buy different size seats for all dogs ranging from the Chihuahua to the St. Bernard. Some use a hammock or a belt as well/or instead of a seat. Because a Pomeranian is a small breed, he definitely needs a seat that secures him.

- Never borrow a dog car seat from a friend or family member, unless it's for the same size dog and never use a generic seat. If a seat is too big, that eliminates its safety features. This assumes that buckles and the belt can't be adjusted to suit your dog's safely. You'll likely want him to have a toy to play with, and perhaps a blanket, but the seat must match his specific size.
- The right material and comfort level. You need to get the right seat to fit your dog, but it should also be made from comfortable material or he won't sit still. The outer casing should be durable and strong. The inner padding must be comfortable and not abrasive.
- Seats that have padded foam are good and they have removable covers you can wash so you're able to keep it clean as well. Most options have Velcro strapping to adjust them and will be made from environmentally friendly products and no hard dyes. These factors are very good because your Pom may decide to chew the seat. This way he won't get sick if he does so.
- Height. Bigger dogs can put their noses out the window to get some air. Smaller dogs will usually feel more confined because they can't see over the door panel. If your Pomeranian is small, a safe and secure booster seat is a logical choice to purchase.
- Another reason why having their nose out the window is vital is to avoid getting car sick. If a dog can't see outside, his body feels as though it's moving but the interior of the car isn't, so that apparent contradiction affects his inner ear and motion sickness can be the result, making him feel dizzy.
- It's easy for nausea to overwhelm your Pomeranian if he can't see and smell the outside world. He may start whining, get restless, struggle against the seat and, in worst case scenarios, vomit.
- When an animal has a bad experience such as this, he'll remember it next time you want to take him for a drive, so it will be harder to get him into the car. Think before

you buy and choose the ideal seat for your dog. Get a booster seat for your Pomeranian so you can open a window, depending on the weather conditions, of course. Even if you can't open it, at least he can see what's happening outside and his inner ear will remain balanced.

Extra tips. After you have bought your Pom's ideal seat, there are other elements to consider when travelling:

- If your vehicle has an airbag in the front passenger seat, the safest place for your dog is in the back seat. The other option is to move the front seat as far back as you can, so it lessens the impact if it's released. If your Pom is too close, he could sustain serious injuries when the bag is deployed.
- Regardless of how comfortable his car seat is, most canines can't handle long car trips without a break. Avoid possible problems and take breaks when you think he needs it. Dogs do vary with some needing a break several times each hour and some can last longer. Regardless of how often you stop, always do it safely. Let him stretch and walk around a bit, on a leash, and do his business. Have some cold water for him to drink and a few little snacks.
- Some Pomeranians hate travelling in a car. The right seat will reduce this hatred. You may need to slowly get him accustomed to being a passenger by starting with short trips and slowly increasing the time and distance. A blanket and his favourite toy will help him relax a little. If he's very edgy, start by simply going up and down your driveway. Poms will eventually get used to longer drives if you slowly build up to them.
- Understand the dangers of a collar and seat. The car seats for a small breed are set up with a safety strap that you connect to his harness or collar. However, never connect it to his collar. Even if he's only tossed a short distance during an accident, it may be enough to severely hurt his neck. Put his comfortable harness on first and then join the safety strap to it.

Boarding Your Pomeranian or Using a Pet Sitter

Not sure you want to take your Pomeranian along with you, given all the parameters involved? You can always board him instead. Sometimes, your vet may offer, or know someone who offers boarding services. There are even posh pet resorts in major cities for pampered pooches like yours.

Of course, it's necessary to visit any kennel before choosing where to place your Pomeranian.

Ask plenty of questions, such as:

- What services are available?
- Do you walk the dogs?
- Do you have dog runs?
- Do the dogs socialise?
- Do you groom the dogs?

As you did when choosing your veterinarian, rely on your gut. If a place smells bad, or the staff seems unfriendly, don't leave your dog there. You want your best friend to feel comfortable when he's not with you.

Always send your Pomeranian with a special blanket and a little toy from home. Be aware that they'll want records of your dog's vaccinations and, possibly, his health certificates.

When you drop your Pomeranian off, do so without too much emotion. If you cry, you'll upset your dog. Instead, give him a cuddle and leave. You can always shed tears outside.

Okay, so you don't want to leave your Pomeranian with anyone but family. That's always an option, too. This may give you peace of mind that you simply would never have at a kennel. Just be certain that your pet sitter, no matter if they're family or not, understands how to care for your Pomeranian. And make sure they're introduced in advance of the overnight "play dates."

Important Tips to Follow if Your Pomeranian is Lost

You would never expect your dog to escape but even the best owner can't always anticipate every scenario. So, it's essential that you know what to do if your dog does run away.

Here are some possible situations:

- Your fence may be unlocked, and he might have dug a hole beneath it or found a way to get over it.
- A door could be left open or ajar, perhaps while you bring.
- in your groceries.
- Your dog could jump out of the car window.

Most dogs that get lost are quickly found. However, you need to arrange a search for your dog as quickly as possible, to increase the odds of having your Pom brought back home safely to you.

Start by checking out the number one place where your pet will go. Also, check the most dangerous place (usually on the main road) and call his name, but be wary of calling your dog and forcing him to cross major traffic on his own. If several hours pass with no luck, you need to make extra efforts to locate him.

Enlist the help of neighbours, family and friends and anybody else you know if they have seen your dog before. Also, carry recent photos of him at all times.

Ring local vets to determine if they have treated a small, injured dog recently. Contact local shelters daily because people come and go, and some are more likely to help than others. Ring the local police station direct and ask if officers on patrol can lookout for your Pomeranian.

If he hasn't been found by the end of your first day, make big posters and plaster them everywhere possible. All members of the search group should also put them on their vehicles. Ask pet shops because they generally have a noticeboard. Add them to every notice board you can find.

Ensure you write a vivid description and add photos because a photo truly is worth a thousand words. Most people don't know enough about every breed, so you can also say your Pom resembles a "puffy-haired chihuahua."

Don't reveal everything about your dog. Keep some identifying markers secret so you can question people who claim to have found him and, if it's really him, they can identify him through the secret questions.

If your Pomeranian hasn't been found within a few days, create postcard size handouts that can be delivered to homes in a larger area (e.g., a 2-to-5-kilometre radius of your home or from where he escaped) and to all animal shelters, vet clinics and anywhere else deemed practical.

If he becomes lost during a visit away from your home, take a familiar item with you. This could be a favourite toy, his bed or crate, or an item of your clothing that has your scent. Return to the place where your dog last saw you. It's common for dogs to go back to the last place where they were still with you. If practical, park with your car door open in that location as he may see or smell you and come running.

Refuse to give up hope. Dogs are extremely intelligent and often have been found weeks or months after getting lost. Having said that, the chances are greatest within the first 24 hours. If your dog does get lost, it's critical to raise the alarm as quickly as possible and always be prepared for this possibility.

Lastly, always ensure your dog has a microchip. On his collar, you should have your name and contact details, as well as the name of your Pom. This information will help strangers locate you quickly if they do find your wandering pet.

Looking After A Rescue Pomeranian

A big thank you to people who open their hearts and homes to a rescue Pomeranian. Many of these poor dogs spend their days, and sometimes years, in cages, in backyard breeder properties or puppy mills. Others get left at kill venues when they get too old, have health problems, if the owners moved, if they barked or peed too much, needed lots of money for vet bills, or simply didn't fit in with other pets or new relationships/households.

Your newly adopted Pomeranian may have been left to live on his own in a crate in a garage or under a porch for a while before even being taken to a shelter or left by the side of a desolate country road. It's sad to think what conditions these dogs struggled to live in before coming to you.

Many were fenced in with packs of dogs, trying to survive in the harsh elements with little or no contact with human beings. They have never lived in a nice home or felt grass underneath their paws. Many rescue Poms have poor teeth and may need some pulled out.

They'll often need a shave to get rid of hair that's become deeply matted. They'll usually have fleas or tics or other skin problems that need correcting. When you bring your new Pom home, he'll need a complete vet exam and blood tests so he can truly start his brand-new better-quality life.

If you adopt a Pom through a rescue organisation, he may already have had some attention from a vet. Either way, you will need to invest lots of time and effort in welcoming him into your life and making him feel safe and happy.

Tips for a new life

Here are a few tips to help guarantee your new pet understands he's about to start a good quality life with a loving owner.

The best way to make your Pomeranian feel welcome is to have a big exercise pen in a quiet part of your home where he can feel safe but he can also hear and see you. Put a dog bed, carrier or crate in one corner and add lots of soft bedding, fresh water, pee pads and some fun stuffed toys. Then he'll start to feel at home.

From his safe haven, he can slowly get to know you and your family and your routine without getting in your way, feeling unsafe or making a potty mess. Let him sleep in this space, stay there if you have visitors, stay there when you go out, feel safe when the TV is blaring and if fireworks or storms happen. All dogs, especially rescued Poms, need a safe, comfortable, clean space to live in.

Nutrition

Nutrition is crucial to a rescue dog. Because he has lived in rough surroundings, he may be malnourished and have a sensitive digestive system. Work on the "less is more" principle. Choose good quality food and small kibble as he is a toy dog. Feed him twice each day, in small amounts and don't offer treats until he starts adjusting to his new life.

If your dog has no teeth or bad teeth, use wet, canned food and remove the gel before you feed him. Put the food in a container in your fridge and let each meal sit in his dish for 10 minutes to warm a little before feeding him.

It's common for rescue dogs to weigh less than they should and one part of your caring should be to help him slowly gain a little weight. Feed him small meals four times each day. Slowly increase portion sizes and reduce the number of feeds per day as he gains weight and strength.

If he happens to be overweight, use a low-fat food. Boiled chicken with no skin can be shredded into tiny pieces. Add a little boiled skinless yam. These are well tolerated by dogs and will help him lose weight.

Talk to your vet about digestive enzymes, prebiotics and probiotics if your pet has diarrhoea or an upset stomach.

Vet care

Your new Pomeranian may need to have blood tests to see how healthy he is and to check if he has worms or ticks. A dental and wellness exam and a stool sample to test for worms is also suggested.

Although your dog does need good quality vet care when you first get him, work out a prioritised action plan. Not everything has to be done at once. Vaccinations, grooming, tests, medications and more can be overwhelming for your dog and your bank balance as well.

First on the list should be tick, heartworm and dental issues. But it should be done according to your dog's current level of health.

If your rescued Pomeranian needs a deep shave, you must watch for overheating and chills as well as any drafts in his sleeping space.

Blankets he can crawl into and out of are useful. A sweater is handy for outside trips but should be removed when inside, so he doesn't overheat.

If your Pom is in good enough health, microchipping, ear cleaning and nail clipping can all be done in one go. This avoids your dog having to be stressed about lots of things happening at once.

Protect your Pom

When taking your Pom in the car, use a strapped-in carrier so he doesn't move around inside. You never know what could make him react differently to normal. Even taking him to the vet, the carrier will help prevent him trying to escape. The carrier is his safe place where he feels protected.

Don't ever leave your Pom in the carrier unattended. He can fall off a bench or table. He can be stolen. He can get overheated or stressed in your car. Other dogs who are loose and/or are aggressive may bite him or even try to take him away.

Dog-proof your home and garden to stop him escaping. If you open your door to a friend, he may run through your legs and out onto the road and then get hit by a car. He can get out and get lost easily. Ensure he's microchipped and that he has tags and your phone number on them.

Use dog barriers to stop him getting to your front or back door. They can limit his access to parts of your home. Keep him in his safe space when you have guests over for parties.

Rescued Pomeranians can exhibit fear-based aggression or they may be timid and shy towards other dogs; both behaviours may cause problems.

This also applies when you're taking your dog for a walk. If you see an unknown dog, pick yours up to protect him. Your dog won't win a fight so avoid that happening.

Pay attention

A key component of looking after a rescued Pom is really getting to know him. He becomes a member of your family and has his own unique personality. You'll learn what is "normal" and what seems "off" for him. Rescued dogs often hide their fear, discomfort and pain but you'll learn to see through that and, once he feels confident that you really care, he'll relax more. So, you'll be able to treat anything that's wrong when it occurs.

Your home is a brand-new environment for your rescue Pom. Know where he is at all times. Is your home "dog-proofed?" Did food fall on the floor that he shouldn't eat?

Did the kids leave the front door wide open so he could run out? Rescued dogs don't know what they should and shouldn't do until you teach them. They rely on you to dog-proof your home to make it safe for them to live in.

Have realistic expectations of your rescue Pom. He may be terrified, shy, detached or aggressive. Barking, pacing, spinning and stress-related panting may happen. These are normal signs in a rescue dog. If he doesn't want you to touch him, sit down and relax and let him come to you. Talk to him kindly and feed him with no pressure. He needs to trust you and you must work to earn his trust, even though he's a dog. It's well worth it!

Rescued dogs may not understand what toys are, but if you get him some squeaky ones and some playful ones, he'll quickly learn and become interested. Hand feed him canned food and don't pat him. That's a way to let him feel safe with you.

The peaceful space helps him relax and bond faster. Give him an aromatherapy collar to calm him and stop the pacing, spinning and panting. Bach Rescue Remedy for Dogs is a good one. (Don't use the human version as it has alcohol in it.)

Many rescued dogs are so excited they're free that they run

around the house in a crazy way. They want to go outside and they don't want to be held. Leave this type of dog with plenty of toys and don't try to hold him. Eventually he'll settle down.

A Pom might be an arm, bed and lap jumper so be careful when you hold him.

A Pomeranian who had been abused or neglected may be very clingy as he gets used to you. This means he'll be stressed when he can't see you. Talk to him so he knows you're still there. Eventually the sounds of your movements will calm him. You might have to pat him, hold him and let him sleep in your lap or bed. Do this for a while and then have small sessions where you leave him alone. It will take a while for him to appreciate that this is his permanent, safe home.

Many rescued dogs may never have been forced to hold "urge to do" potty. They just go wherever they are. It will take time to train him to go outside or to ask when he wants to go out. Soiled drinking water or a lack of water may have caused urinary or kidney issues. Older dogs are harder to train.

Most Poms from backyard breeders and puppy mills go in their cage so they lose their instinct to separate bed from toilet. They may toilet if they're bored. They mark everything and may never unlearn this habit.

Invest time and patience and you'll teach him how to go outside. Don't reprimand him if he makes a mess inside. That scares him and he doesn't know what he did wrong.

Diapers and bellybands can help but need to be used properly. You only use them between frequent outside potty breaks, such as time spent on the carpet playing to discourage the marking.

Misuse of belly bands can cause urine burns and also confuse the dog.

Use a sanitary pad cut into half (or something very absorbent) and softly wash and dry your dog's skin when the diaper/band is taken off if peeing or marking has happened.

It's not wise to use a crate because small dogs can't hold their pee for long and being in a cage is all some have ever known.

Being confined is damaging and traumatic.

Their peaceful space will change their way of "thinking" and behaving. It also protects your home from little accidents. Throw in pee pads, belly bands and outside walks on a harness and you can eventually overcome all the obstacles.

If you leave the crate open and it has loads of toys and bedding, he can come and go at will. If you ever do have to crate him for a short time, he'll be ok with it.

Love will heal both you and your rescue Pom. Rescued Pomeranians have an amazing capability to live for the present and overcome past abuse. Watching them run, jump, bark, smile and play for the very first time is an overwhelming joyful experience.

Because of you, they have a chance to lead a normal life, filled with love and caring, in a comfortable, safe home. They'll feel such happiness that they'll soon forget their tragic past life. There's no greater gift you can give a rescued dog.

Part 9 – Breeding and Showing

Breeding and Exhibiting Pomeranians

As you watch your Pomeranian puppy scamper and play, you may be tempted to imagine the fun you would have with a litter of such adorable pups but be cautious. Breeding Pomeranians, or any dogs, can be costly and takes tons of time, money, emotion and patience.

Unless your dog is Kennel Club registered, is of exceptional type, and you're prepared to mate her with the best possible male in an attempt to produce superior offspring that will be an asset to the Pomeranian breed as a whole, please think long and hard before you contemplate breeding a litter of pet-quality Pomeranian puppies.

To be a responsible, reputable Pomeranian breeder, you must be prepared for the ups and down and the realities of breeding such as: Pomeranians often require caesarean sections, which means whelping can be a life-or-death situation if you're unprepared.

If you feel you're ready to take the plunge, it's best to touch base with your Pomeranian's breeder and, if possible, other Pomeranian breeders, too. That way, you'll get the best advice to help you make the smartest decisions for you and your Pomeranian family.

Wise breeders will have their vet check for any hereditary problems, prove their Pom 's abilities in competitions, learn all they can about this particular breed, and promise to love, support and protect the puppies forever.

Pet puppy buyers will often have to spay or neuter their dogs. This is often monitored by a few options such as: providing a specified refund amount when done, not signing over complete ownership until it's done and the proof is supplied, or having the dog registered on Kennel Club limited registration. These are considered as steps to help prevent all the problems caused by poor dog breeding.

If you decide that breeding and exhibiting Pomeranians is for you, here are a few tips to help you get started:

- Go to dog shows. Pay special attention to the Pomeranians in the ring.
- Become a member of your regional Pomeranian Breed Club.
- Attend Pomeranian breed specialty shows to network with other breeders and exhibitors.
- Observe which Pomeranian types seem to be more desirable than others and which types appeal to you the most.
- Learn the Pomeranian Breed Standard. The more information you have, the smarter your breeding decisions will be.
- Recognise that whelping and other problems have dubbed Pomeranians "the heartbreak breed" amongst Pomeranian breeders.

As a new breeder, it's smart to focus on females until you have garnered a lot of experience. It's unwise to buy a male within the first few years. Studs to the best males are usually available at a fee. Look at your female dog and find the most compatible mate. Retain the best puppies for yourself and go forward from there. The strength of any kennel is the quality of their females.

In an ideal world, you should have two females, to begin with. Two puppies living together grow up better than one living alone. They are great company for each other.

It's vital to choose breeding stock with well-bred parents on both sides. Females can often set the type in their puppies, so you need excellent females and a superior quality male if the puppies produced are to be of the highest quality.

Balance, type, movement, correct conformation and a good temperament are all crucial in the makeup of an ideal dog. If these can all be identified in a couple of females, grab them quickly. If you plan to find a female puppy that will breed you good stock in the future, select one that's good enough to show, from a successful lineage that you can easily access. It's also best to choose for type and soundness.

Exaggerations in breed type may be impressive, but if you need a dog for breeding, correctness is the most valuable attribute and makes breeding top quality dogs a lot easier to accomplish.

Try to find an above average, good type of female with no major faults or exaggerated points and, most importantly, is sound. This type of female will be suitable for sires of many different lines.

Spend lots of time at shows learning everything that's involved. If you can locate a breeder who consistently produces the type of dog you most admire, go and talk to him and ask as many questions as possible. That's the only way to learn.

Novice breeders need to be cautious of pedigrees that have quite close breeding. Only very experienced breeders with an intimate knowledge of their stock and breed history should attempt this. Mismanaged close breeding, known as inbreeding, can become catastrophic.

It's very handy to have lots of champions behind breeding stock but it's even better if their pedigrees have some line breeding to known good quality dogs. When line breeding is done properly, it consolidates the best points of the dog's ancestors, and this often leads to even more improvement.

Champions who come from unknown lines may not always be ideal for breeding. It's quite unlikely that good breeding material exists in a litter without first-rate dogs in their pedigree. It's a rare situation when very good quality stock surfaces from ordinary ancestors and, if this rarity does occur, the puppies rarely breed on.

Become a full-time apprentice. There's an enormous amount to learn when it comes to Pomeranians and this includes: grooming, feeding, breeding, training, soundness, conformation and breed type.

If you can find a good mentor, your apprenticeship will be much shorter in duration. There are lots of experienced breeders who are genuinely happy to mentor newbies prepared to listen and learn.

The stage is set. You own a wonderful Pomeranian who comes from a fabulous family. Now it's time to breed. But wait. It's not that easy. Your Pomeranian's breeder has likely been breeding for a long time, and it probably took many years of study and trial and error to create your Pomeranian. So, for you to breed a similar Pomeranian, it will take some serious consideration and much research.

First, study your dog's pedigree. An important part of reading a pedigree is knowing what each of your Pomeranian's ancestors looked like. Helpful information on your dog's lineage can often be obtained from long-time breeders who are willing to share information and offer advice.

Ask other Pomeranian breeder friends who they would suggest in terms of mating your dog. Above all, you want to produce a dog you'll be proud to be seen with in the show ring.

Next, proactively evaluate your dog's strengths and weaknesses. After all, you want to know which ones to "breed out." The whole point of breeding is to keep improving the breed. A good rule of thumb is to try to avoid "doubling up" on the weakest characteristics.

Understand that a certain amount of "line breeding" or "inbreeding" went into producing all dog breeds as we now know them.

Breeding

Puppies tend to resemble their total pedigree more often than the immediate sire and dam. It's almost impossible to improve quality via a single outcrossing. Often more than one breeding to the same outcross line is required.

The breeding together of half-brothers and half-sisters, grandfather to granddaughter or grandmother to grandson, is thought to be ideal, especially if you're doubling up on the specific female or dog you think is the superior animal in the pedigree and outcrossing the inferior sections of the pedigree.

You need to outcross every few generations to keep the vigour of that line strong. Inbreeding and line breeding can result in diminishing vigour. The more times you outcross, the less chance there is of a uniform quality. A knowledgeable breeder knows when to inbreed when to line breed and when an outcross is required.

Some outcrosses can disappoint you. However, if the resulting litter has no major faults, the outcross progeny should be retained and bred right back into the original line you want to copy.

Every aspect of a dog is inherited: personality, type, markings and, most important of all, showmanship. The unwanted qualities won't be fully bred out, but they can be masked or buried. They can come back to haunt you over and over, for many years, often when least expected.

Take care to avoid breeding dogs together who share common faults. There's no such thing as a perfect dog. Mother nature influences dogs in a multitude of ways.

How do we move forward? Be guided by your conscience and only use dogs you believe are worth duplicating. Use the ones that have the qualities you want and keep working towards improvements.

What is the Pomeranian Breed Standard?

The Pomeranian breed standard is the criteria which identifies the ideal qualities, personality, character and visual appearance of the Pomeranian. The prime objective of all dedicated Pom breeders is to produce Pomeranians closely resembling the "blueprint" of the Pomeranian dog, the breed standard.

Without breed standards, we wouldn't have purebred dogs. The Pomeranian dog was created over 100 years ago by Pomeranian fanciers, who selected and bred for specific characteristics and traits.

The modern Pomeranian is the result of over 100 years of careful breeding and selection, using the breed standard as a guide.

Without careful selection for the traits and characteristics described in the Breed Standard, the very essence of the Pomeranian dog is often quickly lost.

Breeders need to compare and evaluate their breeding program by participating in dog shows.

Pomeranian puppies purchased from preservation breeders (often referred to as show breeders) usually conform very closely to the breed standard. Prospective Pom owners should familiarise themselves with the breed standard prior to purchase.

Characteristics of the Pomeranian

General appearance:

The Pomeranian is the smallest member of the Spitz family. He's a small, compact, dainty dog. He displays character and glamour. His crowning glory is a dense, double-coat, made up of long, harsh, standoff guard hairs and a soft woolly undercoat. The Pomeranian's coat contributes tremendously to the breed's visual appeal.

His tail lies flat, straight over his back. The tail has a profuse plume reaching to the back of his head.

The Pomeranian's symmetry and balance are in the right proportions to each other, and this is crucial to his overall appearance. His carriage, gait, style and temperament are also elements to be kept in mind.

A perfect Pomeranian should appear to fit into a circle. You need to have a square in the circle. The square represents the dog's body. The circle is formed by the Pomeranian's double coat that's harsh and trimmed merely to keep it neat. He's a short backed, compact canine and his body is well rounded. Because of his huge double coat and short back, he seems to be a floating fur ball.

He's a square breed. His back is short and his ratio of height to body length, at the withers, is 1 to 1. To calculate the proportions, two measurements are taken. The first is from the ground to the highest point of his withers; the second is from his buttocks to his prosternum.

The Pomeranian dog is well-proportioned. His body is balanced in that his legs are very much in proportion to the rest of his body. A Pomeranian needs a certain amount of leg but he shouldn't be too short or tall. He needs to have a well-balanced, symmetrical outline that's also dainty, glamorous, alert and pretty.

The Pomeranian has a short, compact body, a short neck, and tight cat-like feet. He should move soundly with grace and style.

Size:

The Pomeranian ideally weighs 4 to 5 pounds (1.8 to 2.5 kg) but may weigh 3 to 7 pounds. In contrast to most dog breeds, the female Pomeranian is preferred to be larger than the male.

Pomeranians experience their share of whelping difficulties. Breeding with larger females is encouraged, in the hope of decreasing whelping complications.

Oversize and undersize are serious flaws. If the dog is oversize, he can lose the dainty look and type common to the breed. If he's undersize, he may lack sufficient coat, body and soundness. He may look weedy and lacking in substance.

Temperament:

The Pomeranian is a delightful family member. He's playful, energetic, loyal, loving, lively, outgoing and intelligent. He won't be in the least bit timid or shy and bounces like a ball whenever he hears a sound.

The Pom should be so light and dainty on his feet that he seems to dance. A show Pomeranian needs to be stylish, glamorous, intelligent and outgoing. Whenever he enters the ring, he'll be full of life and self-confidence.

An ideal Pomeranian possesses an exaggerated sense of his own importance. He's sure of himself and quite cocky. He's beautiful, with exceptional style, and he knows this.

A show Pomeranian needs to be vain enough to show off his beauty to its best advantage. If he doesn't have this vanity so he can be a show-off, it's as serious a problem as owning a Pom with no good qualities that can be displayed.

Despite the Pomeranian's classification as a toy breed, the words *placid* and *toyish* do NOT describe him in any way. He was bred from the Spitz and has the enormous spirit you would expect from that breed of dog.

Because Poms are intelligent and playful, they require lots of mental stimuli to keep them busy. They're fiercely independent and succumb to "small dog syndrome," a trait they share with numerous other small dog breeds. They require plenty of training to help them be social and to ensure good behaviour.

Poms respond well to training and enjoy learning, so it generally becomes easier to train them as you add new elements to the training regime.

Average life expectancy:

The average Pomeranian lifespan is about 12 years, but it's not unusual for some to live a happy life well into their mid to late teens. Keeping your Pom trim and active will help prevent many health problems and enable him to lead a long life.

Head:

The head is wedge-shaped with a short fine muzzle. He has medium- sized almond-shaped eyes, tiny pricked ears, and an intelligent sweet expression.

The Pomeranian Breed Standards make mention of "foxy in outline" and "expression" and may be referred to as "fox-like." However, this description has caused much confusion. Some assume this reference means a longer-nosed type of Pomeranian but it's not the case.

The Pomeranian originated from the Spitz dog and the word "spitz" means pointed. The Spitz acquired their name because of their fox-like, pointed head.

A Pomeranian's head must be in proportion to the dog's body and any exaggerations are incorrect.

An ideal Pomeranian head is wide behind the jaw and graduates to a fine muzzle. An incorrect long muzzle means the essential wedge won't exist and the Pomeranian will have a German Shepherd look. If his muzzle is too short, it will resemble that of a Chihuahua.

The Pom's skull is slightly flat and shouldn't be shaped like a round dome. Pomeranians that have a lot of dense head coat can give the impression their heads are rounder than desired. Lightly run your fingers over his skull to learn the real shape of his head, which should have a moderate stop.

As a standard guideline: from the tip of the nose to the stop and from the stop to the back of the head will measure 1:2 in most Pomeranians. The stop is dog terminology for the small indentation between a dog's eyes.

A Pomeranian's eyes are almond shaped, medium-sized and dark in colour. If the Pom's eyes aren't the correct almond shape, he loses that distinct Pom expression.

When evaluating the size of a Pomeranian's eyes, consider the total size of the dog. If his eyes appear too small for his head, he'll have beady eyes and a cunning expression. If they're too big, he'll resemble an owl; yet another negative feature.

A Pomeranian's ears are covered by shorter hair which is generally trimmed for appearance. Small ears should be positioned high on the head. The Pomeranian's ear placement can't be too high, nor can the ears be too tiny.

Bite:

His teeth meet in what's described as a scissor bite, where his top incisors sit just in front of his bottom teeth. A Pomeranian's mouth must never be wry, overshot or undershot.

In a wry mouth, neither set of teeth are set square in his jawline. This causes his mouth to look twisted. In an overshot mouth, the Pom's upper jaw protrudes a long way over his lower jaw. If he has an undershot mouth, it's the lower jaw that protrudes over his upper jaw.

Forequarters:

A Pomeranian's shoulders are laid well back, sloping back so the point of the withers sits a little bit higher than the line from the back. Each shoulder blade and upper arm usually measure the same length. His elbows sit well in his sides. The tips of his toes and his throat should be in a perfect straight line.

A Pomeranian's legs are the correct length to enable his elbows to sit midway between the high point of his shoulders and the ground. A Pom's forelegs and pasterns should be straight and parallel.

Body:

The ideal silhouette of a Pomeranian depicts a stylish, compact, well-balanced, sturdy, dainty small dog. His back has to be short. His barrel is well-rounded and his well-sprung ribs provides enough space for his lungs and heart. The Pomeranian is short coupled and well-ribbed.

A Pomeranian possesses a deep brisket and well-developed chest. His body has lots of substance and is very well defined. Serious faults such as long couplings and slab side bodies spoil the Pom's shape, type and outline.

Hindquarters:

From his side, the buttocks sit way behind the tail. If you view him from the rear, his legs should be straight and parallel.

Feet:

The Pomeranian's feet must be small, compact and resemble a cat's paws with strong, straight pasterns. Standing well up on his toes, his compact feet point straight ahead. Long thin feet with spreading toes or down on the pasterns are undesirable. When trimmed, the feet should look like an extension of the legs with only small definition.

Tail:

The tail is a unique characteristic of the breed. It's profusely covered with long, harsh, straight hair and should be carried high and flat over the back. Check the tail set by positioning the palm of your hand up against the dog's rear. If the tail set is correct, a hard bone won't be felt.

If the tail is set extremely low, it will sit in an upward "circle" shape. If the root of his tail has a twist, it will fall to the side instead of lying flat, regardless of the height of the set and plume. It should never fall or curl to the side. A low set tail spoils the Pomeranian's outline. His tail is strongly hereditary.

Movement:

The Pomeranian has a smooth, balanced, vigorous gait. He possesses good reach in his forequarters, with strong drive in his hindquarters. The front leg extends forward in a straight line, with his opposite rear leg taking the same action. Each rear leg will move at the same time as the front leg on the opposite side. To keep balanced, his legs will slightly converge inwards to a centre line under his body. As he moves, none of his legs are thrown out or in. His topline stays level and he maintains his outline and balance.

Coat:

A Pomeranian's coat is a breed major characteristic. The coat has two parts: the top coat is straight, long and harsh and the undercoat is dense and soft. His thick undercoat causes his outer hair to stand out from the body, making him look like a little puffball. His coat is heaviest on the front part of his shoulders, chest and neck, whereas his head and legs have the shortest hair.

As a Nordic breed, the requirements of a harsh double coat should never be ignored. A soft, cotton type coat is undesirable on an adult Pomeranian. Despite the quantity of his coat being essential, it's also vital that it has a correct texture. His double coat has to be luxurious.

The Pomeranian's coat must meet the quality and quantity correctness for the breed's ideal appearance. A Pom puppy's coat may be dense and shorter and may (or may not) show guard hair.

Dochlaggie Show Team. Photo by Pedini

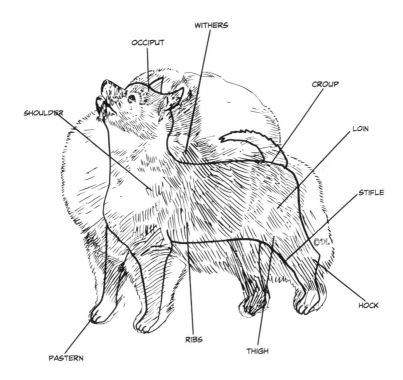

Points of the Pomeranian.

Pomeranian side movement

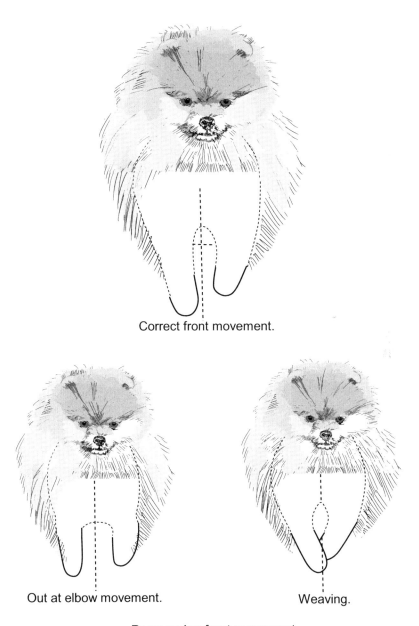

Correct front movement.

Out at elbow movement.

Weaving.

Pomeranian front movement

Correct front.

Out at the elbows.

©Pomeranian.Org

Fiddle front

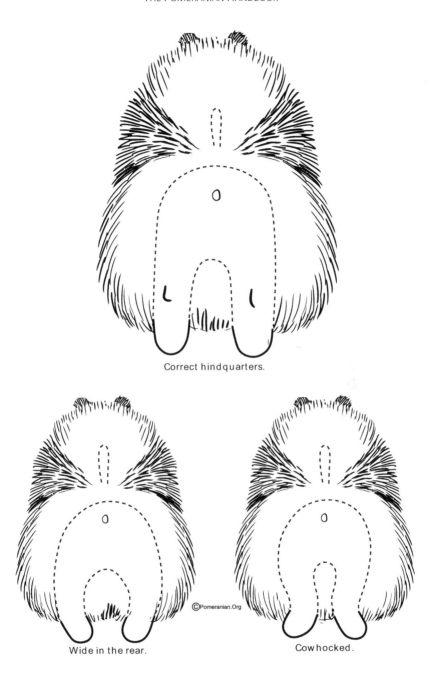

Correct hindquarters.

Wide in the rear.

Cowhocked.

©Pomeranian.Org

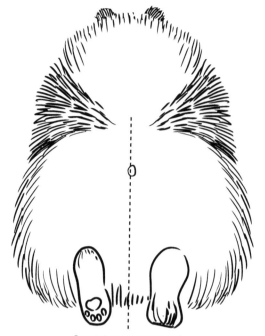

Correct rear movement.

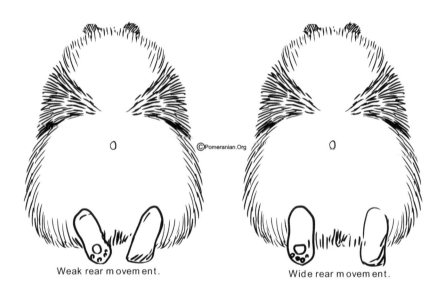

Weak rear movement.

Wide rear movement.

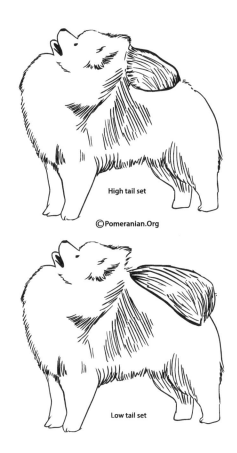

High tail set

©Pomeranian.Org

Low tail set

Pomeranian Colours and Patterns

Colours:

Pomeranians come in many different colours and it's important to understand the diverse colours. To clarify, one element mentioned throughout, "points," refers to the rims of the eyes, lips and nose and the pads of the feet.

Red

A red Pomeranian is a deep, rusty red colour and his points must be black.

Orange

Orange Pomeranians may vary from a deep, rich orange right through to a light orange shade. Breed Standards dictate that an orange must have black points the same as the red Pom.

Cream

Cream is an extremely pale orange. Creams should be self - coloured, with no white breechings. Because of the harsher texture of the guard hairs, the top coat may appear darker. Cream Poms must possess black eye rims, nose, lips and pads. Cream puppies typically appear white at birth.

Sable

Sables have at least three colours shaded through the coat. This shading must be as consistent as possible with no areas of self-colour.

Sable coats usually have the best textures. Red sables have black tips and red hues. Orange sables have deep orange guard hairs with black tips and the undercoat is cream to light orange in colour. Cream sables are creams with sable tipping.

Wolf sable

Wolf sables have a light grey undercoat and the guard hair is a darker grey ending with black tipping. The grey undercoat and guard hairs can vary in colour from silvery off-white to light grey. The wolf sable must not have any hint of orange in his coat.

Beginner breeders sometimes mistakenly register a puppy as a wolf sable. Orange sable puppies often appear greyer than orange at six weeks. However, as they mature, the orange comes through. Experienced breeders know to check behind the ears. The actual colour of the hair behind a puppy's ears is a reasonably accurate guide to the Pomeranian puppy's adult coat colour.

Chocolate & blue sable

Chocolate sable Pomeranians have a chocolate base coat with darker chocolate guard hairs. A blue sable has a blue base coat with dark blue guard hairs. If you find the colours reversed, this is called a reverse sable.

White

A white Pomeranian should be a solid white with no lemon or cream shadings. The guard hairs and undercoat are also white. He must have black eye rims, nose, lips and pads. White Pomeranians are born ice white with pink points. By the age of six weeks, the points should have darkened to black; however, the coat will remain ice white. Cream and light orange, very young Pomeranian puppies are often erroneously described as white.

Blacks

The black Pomeranian's coat consists of black guard hairs with a black undercoat and should be a "coal black" colour. A black Pomeranian's coat should be free of red, white-coloured or brownish fur. The points must also be black. The guard hairs on a black Pom should be precisely the same colour throughout his coat. Exposure to sunlight can cause red tinges on the fur of dogs who spend long periods of time outdoors. The black Pom's undercoat may appear a lighter shade, especially preceding shedding.

Black Pomeranian puppies often will have greyish tones to their coat during the coat change or puppy "uglies" stage. This is nothing to be concerned about because when the adult coat comes in, your puppy's coat will usually be a bright black colour.

Brown (chocolate)

Brown is a very diverse colour and ranges from light beaver through to the darkest chocolate shade. The chocolate colour is rich and is fully self-coloured and may sometimes have lighter shadings. "Sunburning" or a reddening of the colour can occur if the dog spends a lot of time outside. Points are also brown.

Beaver

Beaver is a diluted brown and this colour can range from dark beige to beige-cream. In older versions of the breed standard, this colour was called "biscuit." Beaver Pomeranians must have self-coloured pads, eye rims and nose. Beavers are not simply an orange Pomeranian lacking pigmentation.

Blue

Blue, a solid colour, is a light to darkish grey and sometimes has a bluish tinge. The undercoat colour is grey as well. Blue puppies are usually black or silver when born and, as time passes, they develop the dark slate blue colour topcoat and the silver-grey undercoat. Some blues may appear black until you compare the two colours side by side. The points are dark blue.

Patterns:

Brindle

Brindle can be described as a pattern that has striped overlays on a base colour. The base colour can be: red, gold or orange and the brindle has strong black stripes. It may also be combined with other patterns on a dog's coat; for example, black and tan or parti. The points should match the base colour. Stripes may be thin or broad and may only appear on parts of the dog's body or the entire width. Stripes on adult brindle Pomeranians' coats may appear to be broken, due to the length of an adult Pom's coat. Brindles often have an extremely dark dorsal stripe.

Tan points

Pomeranians with tan points appear in three base colours: blue, brown and black. The three colours share the same tan marking pattern. The tan points are on the cheeks, above both eyes, inside the ears, on either side of the muzzle, the throat, on all feet and legs, and under the tail. On both sides of the upper chest, there's either one big, or two small, spots called "rosettes."

There may be a line in the main colour that runs along the length of the toes. The tan colour itself varies from a dark mahogany rust colour through to a pale cream colour (often called silver). Sometimes the tan pattern doesn't appear, so some markings may be reduced or lost completely.

Dogs with tan and white markings (except for the aging grey colour around the muzzle area), in places not mentioned here, or with no markings in the necessary areas, need to be called brown, blue or black with tan markings parti colour.

Black and tan

As the name suggests, these are black coloured Poms with rust or tan markings. The undercoat's base colour may be lighter than the main colour and points will be black. If you have two dogs of the same quality, the dog with deeper coloured markings is the preferred option.

Brown and tan

This is generally called chocolate and tan and covers all shades from beaver with rust or tan right through to the darkest chocolate. The points will match the base coat.

Blue and tan

This is a blue coloured base coat and has rust or tan markings. The points will be blue and match the coat's shade.

Parti-colour

This is white with any other colour distributed in patches. A white blaze on the head is preferred. Markings on the head should be symmetrical.

Excessive ticking should be regarded as a fault. The points on parti-coloured Poms should match the colour of the patches. This means black, red, cream, orange, brindle parti Poms, blue and red merle and sable parti-colours should have black points. Blue sable and blue must have blue points. Brown merle, brown and beaver must have brown coloured points.

Merle

Merle can influence most coat colours. Along with modifying the base coat colour, merle additionally changes eye colour and points. Dark pigment in the eyes is also changed by the merle, sometimes altering dark eyes to blue, or a section of the eye may be coloured blue.

Because the merle gene triggers different changes, dark-eyed, blue-eyed, and odd-coloured eyes are a possibility. The colour of the points in the merles is influenced by the base colour of the Pomeranian, e.g., orange merles should have black points; and blue, brown and beaver merles should have self-coloured points.

Chocolate or liver merle is a chocolate-coloured dog affected by the merle pattern. The nose is chocolate. The pattern and pigment will be a mix of silvery chocolate and regular chocolate. The genetically-altered eyes may be blue, have flecks of blue or be brown in colour.

Sable merle

This one is a sable dog with the merle gene mainly affecting the coat's black hairs. If the dog is heavily sabled, the pattern will clearly stand out.

In a light-coloured sable, you may not see the merle at all. The merle pattern is obvious when the puppy is born but may fade within a few weeks. The pigment colour will be black. The eyes may be blue, have flecks of blue or be brown in colour.

Variations

Merle may dilute chocolate and black and this includes black & tan, black, chocolate & tan, blue & tan, diluted black (blue), brindles, sables and diluted beaver. The merle pattern may appear in coloured areas of dogs that are parti-coloured. Cream, orange and red display little visible effect. The eyes may genetically be blue, have flecks of blue or be brown in colour.

NOTE: The Pomeranian Standard doesn't permit blue eyes.

Coloured Pomeranians

Attention to all the Pomeranian colours will also undoubtedly benefit the Pomeranian breed in general.

The original Pomeranian colours happen to be the actual colours we currently refer to as the exotic colours. Imagine the incredible excitement the appearance of the first orange and orange sable Pomeranians caused amongst fanciers of that time.

Orange and orange sable quickly, and completely, overshadowed the original colours to become the most popular in the show ring.

Although the orange Pomeranians seem to be the easiest to win with, I have observed many disadvantages when breeding clear orange with clear orange.

This practice may result in a softer coat texture than is required by the standard, coat colour may appear faded and lack depth and pigmentation often fades.

Even if your only interest is in producing oranges, using some of the exotic colours in your breeding program occasionally can be an advantage.

Adding a black or black and tan to the orange and orange sables will improve pigmentation and often produces wonderful deep orange with coats of amazing texture, depth, and clarity.

Whites bred from parti-colours will always be a parti Pom, even if you can't see the parti patches as they're so small and the dog looks to be white in appearance.

It's very hard to predict the finished colour of a Pom puppy until at least 7 months of age. A "true cream sable" may appear to be a very light grey or even orange sable as a baby puppy. Both the cream sable and wolf sable must have no orange at all in the adult coat.

These are the two most useful colours to use as an out-cross colour in a white breeding program.

Colour breeding

To carry out in-depth research into the colours of dog coats, you'll require an accurate book on canine colour genetics containing loci placements, genetic codes and how they interact with regards to dominance.

Record details of breedings and capture the results in two ways: Pictorially, and in a document, illustrating a minimum of the last three generations of colour.

Snap a photo of the newborn litter, have it printed and include it in your notebook for each litter's case study. Years from now, when you need to refer to this information, you won't need to rely solely on your memory.

One critical element to remember with colour breeding is the order of dominance. It's believed that genes are either dominant or recessive, but in these different categories, there will exist an order of dominance. In recessive genes, some will still be dominant over others.

You need a rudimentary understanding of the different terms, and their genetic definitions, involved in determining the colour and pattern of a dog's coat.

Then you can arrange your breedings, record them correctly, and create a level of consistency in colour predictions for each of your puppies.

Here are a few recommendations related to colour breeding programs:

White: When mating for white, the ideal to pair are: white with white; White with black (as long as the black has white close in its pedigree; white with cream; white with parti (preferably black parti), and white with wolf sable or a cream sable.

Don'ts: I don't suggest you breed white with chocolate, white with orange, and white with beaver.

Chocolate: When you want to mate for chocolate, the best pairs are: chocolate with chocolate; chocolate with black (ideally by having chocolate close in its pedigree); chocolate with beaver; chocolate with chocolate sable and these same colours if you want to mate for a chocolate parti-colour.

Don't: Don't breed chocolate with cream or white.

Blue: When you want to mate for blue, the best pairs are: blue with cream or white; black & tan.

Black and Tan: If your aim is for black & tan, the recommended pairs are black & tan, orange sable (ideally having a black and tan close within its pedigree), and blue & tan (if you wish to have a possible blue dilution).

Don'ts: Oranges without black and tan in the pedigree will create oranges and sables, not black and tans. It's not a completely bad idea because there are times when this pair can cause improvements to the quality, and sometimes the marking pattern will be inherited by the offspring. However, this mating won't create black and tans.

Black: When you mate for black, what you want will determine what you do. If you want to keep the intensely dark black pigment, don't mate with dilution genes. The ideal choices are other blacks, black and tans, dark orange sables, red sables, and intense reds.

Don'ts: If you plan to breed black with black for numerous generations without including sable genes, it's likely that the texture of the coat will be lost but the black intense pigment will remain.

Orange: When you want to mate for orange, the best outcome will be achieved if you add black or heavy sable. They'll help keep the pigment intensity and improve the coat's texture.

Don'ts: If you breed orange with orange for numerous generations, it's possible that there will be a pigment loss and the coat will lose its correct texture.

Merle: To mate for merle, it's wise to mate to darker colours because the merle gene affects those dark colours to produce the pattern. This means the recommended pairing colours are: Black, chocolate and blue and each of their tans: You can also breed merle solids with partis in any of the chosen colours.

Don'ts: It's unwise to breed merle with white, cream, or extreme white piebald pattern parti-colour.

Brindle: If you wish to mate brindle, there aren't many limitations. However, if you want deeper, richer colours, use chocolates, reds, and oranges. You may decide to use the colours with a tan marking pattern, meaning you'll sometimes end up with a chocolate and brindle or black and brindle within the tan pattern. If you choose creams or whites, the brindles could be pale and a little grizzled, but you will achieve a defined brindle stripe, sometimes on a cream background.

Dog Stud Services – Contracts, Compensation, Fees and Stud Selection

A "dog stud service" covers everything related to the use of a stud, all written in a contract that clearly covers everything, including all terms and conditions, so both parties know what's expected. It covers the using or lending of a particular stud to mate with a female dog. The dog's semen is exchanged for an agreed amount of money, the first choice of her litter, or anything else both breeders agree on.

In the breeding world, the term "stud" is a male that the owner agrees is ideal for breeding with a female (called a "dam"). The female also must be ideal for breeding.

Both dogs will go through complete health check-ups conducted by a vet. The dogs shouldn't have any genetic defects and need to be in great physical health. The partners need to be chosen because they conform closely to the breed standard.

What's a stud service?

A stud service is the phrase used for the mating process that occurs between the dam and stud with the goal of producing a litter. The stud's owner is the advocate for his sire by networking at events and running advertisements. Dam owners can make contact and express their interest in that particular stud.

Both owners will have their own expectations of a dog stud service:

The dam owner wants to ensure the stud is healthy, has good genes and pleasing looks so the dam will produce a quality litter.

The owner of the stud will be seeking the most well-matched dam for the stud. After the stud has serviced the dam, the stud owner needs to be compensated. This might be financial, or an alternative is often the guaranteed first choice of the litter, if the mating has been successful.

Owners of dams will usually have a particular profile of the type of stud they want to father their litter. Traits such as good pedigree and excellent health will be high on such a list.

Contracting a stud service

A stud owner provides the stud service contract which is a written agreement between both dam and stud owners. This contract should ensure that both parties will uphold their side of the agreement, while protecting the welfare and health of the dam, stud, and all offspring. Both owners are required to sign this contract.

Compensation

Because both owners allow their dogs to mate, there's a level of compensation expected in return. This is formalised in the contract of the stud service:

The stud fee is the first item on the agenda. It's listed early on the contract because it's a major point to be agreed on. Before the signing of the contract, you would expect both parties to have discussed details such as this, so there are no surprises when it comes to signing day.

Health screenings

Several conditions must be complied with prior to the contract signing. The stud should be in excellent physical health, and a vet should have supplied certificates confirming this, as well as current vaccines and a negative test result for brucellosis.

The stud owner needs to have a pedigree chart that goes back at least three generations as this provides the owner of the dam with the family history of the stud.

Apart from the dam owner paying for this service, he still needs to satisfy all other requirements of the contract, so the process is as smooth as possible. The dam must be in season, be healthy and free of brucellosis, and have all current vaccines, with the required certifications.

It's common behaviour for the stud owner to be fully paid before servicing. Owners of dams need to accept the agreed period of notice about a non-pregnancy.

Breeding attempts and failures

The owners must choose an appropriate period of time in which both dogs are together and the number of matings. Both owners should discuss and agree to terms if no pregnancy results.

After a successful mating, the stud owner is obligated to provide the dam's owner with a completed stud service certificate. Information that must be covered includes: where and when the mating took place, the name of both parents, listing the stud as the father of all puppies.

A Week-by-Week Guide to Your Dog's Pregnancy

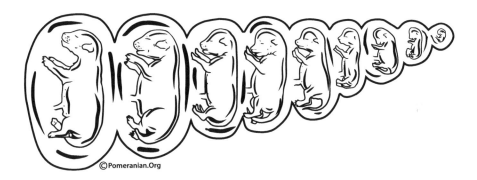

Female dogs usually have their litter approx. 63 days after fertilisation. The numbers are between 56 - 70 days because there are a few variables regarding the time the female was fertilised and how it relates to the mating process.

This guide will help you learn what you can expect while your female is pregnant and some useful information to assist you during the whole process.

Before you consider allowing your dog to become pregnant, you have certain factors to think about. The dog should be current with all vaccinations during the pregnancy along with the lactating (feeding) period. Discuss your thoughts with a vet as he will be able to give you advice related to your specific situation.

It's inadvisable to get your female Pom pregnant until she's mature and fully grown. This means the female needs to be at least two years old. It's also unwise to breed a female that is too mature. Most vets say she should be between 2 - 5 years of age. However, the maximum limit may depend on other variables such as: the breed, your specific dog herself, her reproduction history, and the vet's opinion.

Before making the big decision, talk to your vet, a breeder of your type of dog or Kennel club for advice regarding precautions and screening plans applicable to your dog breed.

Mating

The mating period sometimes begins with a courting, playful time. Penetration can happen quickly, often in less than one *minute.

The male dog will mount the female to enter her, triggering a specific reflex in her vagina that grips him tight, and this may be 15 - 30 minutes in some cases. It may appear weird to the onlooker, particularly if the male dog spins 180 degrees. NEVER attempt to separate the dogs as it may cause harm to one or both.

Even after all that, fertilisation may not have occurred. Her fertility may not have hit its peak. The sperm may survive inside her uterus for a week, so the fertilising may happen two or three days after the actual act.

To improve the odds of the female becoming pregnant, the dogs often mate with a couple of days break in between. There are breeders who use progesterone blood tests (supplied by most vets) to calculate the perfect fertility window, before even trying to get her mated.

Fertilisation

Gestation will start once the eggs get fertilised by sperm from the male. That fertilised egg is the initial stage of a brand-new puppy. Embryos begin at the high point of her uterus but by the first week's end, they move down to the horns of her uterus and they float within the liquid found there.

Maintenance

Once your dog has finished her heat period, you can return to her usual grooming routine. Her embryos are protected inside the uterus so gentle grooming won't distress her.

During the early gestation period (lasts from the mating through to day 35), you need to control her weight. A gain in weight isn't a good thing when it comes to her health. Within the initial 42 days, she shouldn't gain more than 10% of her ideal weight. Her energy needs will stay stable until this time, so you don't need to make changes to her food, unless you have been advised to do so by the vet.

If she's being fed a well-balanced diet, she won't need added minerals or vitamins (unless ordered by your vet). Her embryos get imbedded in the lining of her uterus where they will start growing and developing. Gradually, they will be covered with a protective membrane designed to supply vital nutrients.

Confirm gestational pregnancy

On the 25th day, take your female Pomeranian to the vet for an ultrasound that can confirm she is pregnant. This scan can also indicate the approx. number of puppies to expect (but the exact number can't always be identified yet), and also see if there are abnormalities.

A different method to diagnose pregnancy is via a blood test to identify the amount of a specific hormone that exists as only the placenta can create this one. Regardless of method, the sooner you know, the better you can prepare.

Foetal stage

When the 35th day comes, it means the initial phase of gestation is finished (embryogenesis). Organs are forming and now the "embryo" name is gone, replaced with the new name: foetus. Throughout this new phase (particularly from day 40), the weight of each foetus will grow by approx. 75%.

Turning point

Day 42 sees the start of the last phase of gestation. Each foetus develops fast. Claws appear, the skeleton solidifies, and the weight increases.

Because of all the changes, your female Pom's nutritional needs alter significantly because she must be fed a diet rich in minerals, protein and energy. Despite this, her appetite may wane because her abdomen becomes distended so eating her previously scheduled meals becomes more difficult. It is critical that she eats the right foods and breaking it all up into smaller meals through the day may help her get enough nutrition if she can't get through two large meals.

By the 45th day, hairs start appearing, the skeleton solidifies even more, and the bones and coat start to form.

Get ready for whelping

Do not get caught out. Prepare for the whelping process as early as possible because birth can happen any day now. Choose a place where it's quiet and out of the way of the rest of the people in the house. It needs to be heated as puppies require warmth. It must be a floor that is easily cleaned. The female and her litter will spend a few weeks in this quiet space, away from any form of excitement, so the puppies are not disturbed while suckling.

Scan

Around the 50-day mark, the foetus's skeleton will be solid, and you can seek advice from the vet regarding whether a scan would be useful. In a lot of situations, a scan can tell you how many puppies your female will have so you can prepare adequately for the whelping process, and that you won't leave any puppies still inside the mother. Pomeranians often have small litters, and it's not unusual for a female to be only carrying one puppy. This one puppy often will be larger than desired and may require a C section.

Check her bedding

Make certain you have enough linen so you can regularly change her bedding within the whelping space. Linen should be fully dry before you can use it again. Ensure you have a spare heater so the space can be kept warm but without any chance of burning puppies or causing draughts. The room must be at a perfect temperature when birth takes place and for the first week. That temperature is 24-26°C because the puppies are unable to control their own body temperature when born. The room should also be set at a good humidity level and then maintained.

Milk

Mothers-to-be often will have milk in her teats roughly one week before the whelping commences but this is not a reliable indicator to tell you the correct birth date. Despite feeling comforted by the fact that the mother will have the ability to feed the puppies, always ensure you have bottles, teats and a quality milk replacer available. Having enough milk prior to the arrival of fresh puppies will make life much simpler for you if you are faced with the task of feeding them yourself.

The final countdown

Your female will have instincts that make her find a quiet area to create a nest and might appear edgy, but don't be alarmed. If not done, it's time to set up the whelping nest in the pre-chosen quiet place, far from any form of excitement, and a place easy to get to and that she has already adjusted to sleeping in.

It is wise to acquire a whelping box and line it by using multiple layers of sheets or towels. Have a LOT of prepared materials as they will need to be replaced regularly after birth has occurred.

It's recommended that you clean the mother's teats and butt and make them easy to access so she can give birth and then feed the new puppies in an exceptionally clean environment. If her hair is long, use round tipped scissors to clear away the hair near the teats and vulva.

To prevent any surprises, check the female's temperature thrice daily. If it has dropped by 1°C when compared to the previous day's average, it's an indicator that birth is imminent as this reduction means whelping usually happens within 48 hours.

The check list of things to be done prior to birth

Her whelping nest is already pre-set in the quiet chosen place.

Check the temperature in the whelping room. Sources advise a range of ideal figures, so nothing is set in concrete. Many people say that a minimum temp of 30°C is perfect for the initial 24 hours after birth and then decreased to 26°C.

Giving birth

Most females can give birth on their own, while you provide a comforting presence and a suitable bed. If you have any questions beforehand, ask your vet because there may be something you don't expect so be prepared for all eventualities.

The labour process may only last a few minutes or could take 2-3 hours. Check how she is going every 15 minutes, making sure she remains calm and never showing your concerns (if any).

After puppy number one comes out, the female must rip open that foetal sack. If she does not do that, you must do it, whilst having clean hands and using disposable gloves.

More puppies will arrive within a few minutes or not until 3 to 4 hours has elapsed. Each puppy will be born within several hours of the previous puppy emerging. However, this may change significantly.

As some puppies are born, their rear feet come out first. The wrong, but often used, name for this type of birth is a "breech."

The right use of the term is to describe a puppy that comes out with his butt first and his back feet are pushed forward.

What you should do:
- Check her progress frequently.
- Contact the vet if contractions do not produce any puppies, or if you're worried.
- If you must stimulate one of the new puppies, use a towel to rub him softly.

What you should NOT do:

Never pull a puppy's paws to assist in getting him out because this can cause serious harm.

Putting Together Your Own Whelping Kit

As a breeder, you shouldn't interfere with your Pomeranian during the birthing process unless your help is necessary.

However, it's essential that you always have a "whelping kit" so you can assist your dog while she's in labour or shortly afterwards.

Here's a comprehensive list of essential products in a whelping kit so you don't even have to think if there's a problem.

Keep it handy near the area you have reserved for her labour, so you don't have to go and find it when you have no time.

Your first task is to discuss the pregnancy with your vet and tell him that he'll be your first phone call when needed.

He can also advise you on what components are needed in the whelping kit, which should always be fully stocked.

Before you go shopping, there are a few simple things you need:

- Your vet's number in your phone's speed dial and the phone fully charged.
- A vehicle fuelled and ready to go if needed.
- A friend who can help if you have an emergency - ideally a dog lover, but it's not crucial.

"The Box"

Whether you call it a whelping box, a nest or something else, this is the next essential item. You can buy a good quality one from numerous sources or, if you're a handy person, you might wish to build one yourself.

It must be in your home at least several weeks prior to the anticipated birth date. Whether you have a Pomeranian or some other small dog breed, you need to get the mother to be familiar with it because she will live in it for numerous weeks with her litter.

The whelping box must have plenty of space for your mother dog and the puppies. It needs to be dry, warm, clean and comfortable, especially during the birthing process.

You'll also need:

- Several hot water bottles or heating pads.

315

- Plenty of clean sheets, blankets and towels.
- Rails to protect the puppies from getting squashed on the inside walls if the mother starts stretching out.

Ensure all these items are ready at least a week prior to the big day.

Essential supplies for the whelping box for D-day:

Round-tipped scissors. While regular scissors may be used, using round-tipped scissors is better because you're handling fragile, tiny puppies and, if you have to snip their umbilical cord, it's a cleaner way to do it.

Haemostat. This is a tool used in surgeries, predominantly used to prevent excessive bleeding by crimping the umbilical cord.

Dental floss. After you cut the umbilical cord and clamp it to stop bleeding, you might need to tie off the cord. The best tool to use is unwaxed dental floss.

Lubricant and Surgical Gloves. While the dam is whelping, keep away but supervise the process. If you need to get involved, always wear surgical gloves so everything remains sterile.

Scales. Another aspect of caring for the new Pomeranian puppies is to ensure you weigh them regularly and track their weight as they grow. Ask the vet for "typical" weight figures for the breed for the initial few weeks so you can compare. You will need good quality dog scales. Once you have finished with the litter each time, disinfect the scales.

Pen and paper. Even if the entire litter seems healthy, you must monitor their weight because Pom pups can't control their body temperature and so they rely on their parent to keep them warm. Keep a record of the exact time each puppy arrived in a notepad for that specific purpose. Use a different page for each puppy.

Preemie and dog milk substitute bottles. If the dam can't feed the puppies for even a short time, you need a backup plan to feed them until the dam can take over again. Talk to your vet and have plans in place if this occurs.

Calcium Supplements. Used during whelping, calcium is like a super booster for whelping mothers, because it assists her parathyroid gland to release more of the parathyroid hormone from her bones. This provides her with extra energy and strength so she can push harder when the time comes.

Good quality flashlights. You may be in the middle of helping her give birth and suddenly your power goes out. While this may "never" happen to you, be prepared just in case.

Weaning

Weaning is the transition process of moving a puppy from solely the dam's milk (i.e., a liquid diet) to solid food. This generally begins when a puppy is three weeks old. The dam won't be producing the same amount of milk, and it may soon be time for the puppy to go to a new home.

Because the puppy won't have enough liquid to get his nutrition, and he needs to get ready to a new life away from his mother, his gastrointestinal tract and body needs to slowly adjust to eating solid foods.

If you wean a puppy too early and the transition from liquid to solid food isn't smooth, the puppy may face intestinal distress and/or develop food allergies.

How to correctly wean your puppy:

The aim is to make gradual steps towards eating solid food. A blender is perfect for doing this. Mix puppy formula that matches the brand of food consumed by the dam. This way you're restricting new ingredients that may potentially upset his stomach and, (particularly at the start), hot water.

If I have been bottle feeding these pups, their milk formula will be added to canned puppy food and this mixture is fed at a warm, not hot, temperature. The goal is to avoid any tummy upsets if possible. If the pups have not been on a milk replacement formula, goat's milk is used. I have had excellent results with goat's milk, often successfully rearing new-born orphan pups solely on goat's milk.

Goat's milk is readily available at most supermarkets. It is advisable to keep using the same brand of goat's milk.

Start the process at the beginning of week 3 by feeding a mixture that seems very "soupy" in substance. You can use a shallow dish for this. You might have to pick up your puppy, carry him to the dish and encourage him to drink a little.

During the next two weeks, slowly make it with less water and a thicker mixture. Then with no water and less of the milk replacer.

By the sixth week and usually to a maximum of 8 weeks, puppies should eat solid food a minimum of 4 times daily.

Tips:

1. To get weaning started, I pull the mother away from the litter for a few hours, morning and night. Mum needs a break and it's easier to get puppies eating solid food when access to the milk bar is limited. Once they're finished eating, you can allow the dam back in with the pups for some nursing.

2. Another part of weaning is that it separates puppy from the dam. Pups who are not fully weaned onto solid food often retain maternal antibodies for a longer period of time, which makes vaccinations for deadly canine diseases completely ineffectual. Before considering vaccinating the puppies, ensure they are independent of their mother.

3. Separation from the dam is necessary for a puppy to become independent and adjust to his new world. By the 5-week mark, I kept the mother away from the puppies during the day and only let her sleep with her puppies at night. I encourage mothers to sleep with their babies as long as they want to. Mothers are often quick to let me know when they have had enough of their babies and I allow each mother to make her own choice.

4. It's not normal for puppies to maintain or lose weight

while they're weaning; their appetite should be robust and weight gain should occur steadily. If a pup struggles, it's time to consult the vet immediately.

Denise Leo and Dochlaggie Debonair. Photo by Pedini

The Different Stages of Puppy Development

Similar to the ways that humans develop, puppies also have a predictable pattern of steps, although there has never been any official agreement regarding the exact ages a puppy may be when each step is taken.

Small dogs develop quickly, many reaching maturity prior to bigger dog breeds. Although development of puppies is quite predictable, every puppy and breed are unique and differ a little at each stage of their development.

The previous rule that stated that one dog year is the same as seven years for a person is simply not true. Most dogs have a lifespan of around 16 years. Smaller dogs mature earlier than big dogs and the females are only 6-7 months of age when experiencing their first heat. They're usually ready for breeding by the age of 12-13 months.

Numerous changes occur in a puppy's first year of living. He starts as a relatively helpless neonate, unable to hear, see or go potty on his own. By the end of the first year, he has become fully grown, is agile and a sexually mature dog.

When do these steps actually happen?

There are a total of seven acknowledged steps of the puppy's development:

- Stage One = 0 - 3 Weeks.
- Stage Two = 3 - 7 Weeks.
- Stage Three = 7 - 12 Weeks.
- Stage Four = 12 - 17 weeks.
- Stage Five = 17 - 40 Weeks.
- Stage Six = 40 - 52 Weeks.
- Stage Seven = 1 year and older.

Let's look at each step of development week by week.

Puppy Development – 1 – 2 weeks. The Neonatal period.

Milestones:

- Touch, taste and smell are all working. No hearing or

sight.
- Recognises pain.
- Sleeps and eats most of the time.
- Can't regulate their own body temperature.
- Can't eliminate on their own. Needs mother to initiate defecation and urination.

Needs:

- Dependent on mother for food and elimination.
- If canine mother isn't available, human interactions must occur and provide warmth, food and elimination.
- Dependent on breeder for warm environment.
- First worming at the end of this stage.

Puppy Development – 2 - 3 Weeks. The Transitional Stage

Milestones:

- Eyes and ears open so puppy can hear and see what's going on.
- May be able to eat solid food by the end of this stage.
- First significant learning time happens.
- First few steps.

Needs:

- Still needs to be warm.
- The start of interactions with mother, others in the litter and people.

Puppy Development. 3 - 4 Weeks

Milestones:

- Puppies start knowing dogs and humans aren't the same.
- Mother dog teaches puppy canine manners.
- Play fighting may happen with others in the litter.
- Eating solid foods but continues to nurse.
- Starts to eliminate without assistance.
- Is more stable when standing.

Needs:

- Introduced to loud noises and other sounds within the environment.
- Introduced to different textures and allowed to walk on different floor surfaces.
- Second worming treatment at the conclusion of this step.

Puppy Development. 4 - 5 Weeks

Milestones:

- Teeth may start appearing.
- Curiosity about everything is a big thing at this stage.
- Plays with other puppies in the litter.
- Puppies each take turns in being the dominant one.
- Weaning carries on.

Needs:

- Needs to have plenty of new experiences.
- Puppies need time on their own to stop separation anxiety.
- Needs to be around people more than ever.
- Needs excellent quality food because they nurse less frequently.

Puppy Development. 5 - 7 Weeks

Milestones:

- Weaning begins.
- May get first set of shots.
- Very curious and may venture away from litter mates and mother at times.
- Begins to understand boundaries and impulse control.
- Mother will spend more time away from puppies.

Needs:

- Good time for their first car ride and first bath.
- Not ready to leave litter mates and mother just yet.
- Socialisation, human interactions, variety of experiences.

Puppy Development. 8 - 11 Weeks

Milestones:

- Good motor skills and coordination.
- Most curious phase. A puppy will move further away if his interest is piqued.
- This is puppy's first time for fear to become imprinted. Traumatic events may make a permanent impact.

Needs:

- Puppy must be protected from all forms of trauma.
- He must be prevented from wandering too far away.
- This is the time for puppy's second round of injections.
- Not fully vaccinated so the owner must strike a fine balance between health risks and socialisation.
- If puppy goes to a new home, he should start being trained immediately.
- Puppy needs to hear his name called as often as possible.

Puppy Development. 10 - 16 Weeks

Milestones:

- Puppies are taken to their new homes.
- They have moved past the initial fear stage.
- Puppy doesn't mess his bed anymore.
- He chews everything in sight as he continues teeth cutting.

Needs:

- Good time for socialisation training to begin. Expose puppy to different things without overdoing it. Stress can be felt at this age.
- Good time for potty training to begin.
- Provide lots of chew toys and bones to chew on.
- By the end of this time, puppy is ready for puppy classes.

Puppy Development. 16 Weeks to 6 Months

Milestones:

- Puppy is now more independent than ever.
- This is the "preteen" period.
- Demonstrates signs of a "big dog" attitude within a small dog.

Needs:

- More socialising.
- More training is needed.
- Owners must have a great deal of patience.

Puppy Development. 6 – 12 Months

Milestones:

- The dog starts as an adolescent and, by the end of this period, he reaches sexual maturity.
- Very independent. Likely to possess a mind of his own and be stubborn.
- The second fear stage starts at around six months and can last a few days to a few weeks.

Female dogs face their first heat period. Males get extra testosterone which can make them be hard to control. Although their development is responsible for this problem, many people think the dog is simply badly behaved or doesn't obey instructions.

Needs:

- Reinforcement of rules must be followed up, as should ongoing training.
- Dogs should be spayed or neutered.
- You can feed your dog adult food once this period is over.

An Overview of Puppy Development

When a puppy is first born, his ears and eyes are shut. Only his senses of taste, touch and smell work, but they're not fully functional yet.

He can respond to discomfort and pain as well as minor disturbances and he'll cry or whine to let you know. His body's temperature is far lower than that of a mature dog and he can't handle cool weather.

To help with ideal development, the room should be kept quite warm (around 80 degrees) and breeders achieve this through the use of heating pads and/or heat lamps.

Puppies of this tender age need their mother to stimulate the defecating and urinating process as they can't do it for themselves.

Their first goal in life is to find food and warmth. Although they don't yet have any teeth, their nails are fully grown and might need to be trimmed within the first week of being born. Their main activities are to look for nourishment from their mother and also to sleep as much as possible.

Newborns spend most of their time sleeping, sometimes twitching or moving a little to change position. The twitching happens because their main sleep is REM sleep, a level that's caused by higher brain activity. Apart from that, they don't interact with others in the litter or their surroundings, except to huddle as close as possible to their mother and litter mates to keep warm.

Puppies rely on the mother to supply their nourishment and to help them go potty. The mother also has to clean up the potty messes, which she happily does.

Puppy's eyes start opening when they're about two weeks old. A couple of days after that, their ears also open. Their sight is blurry at first but soon settles and they can take in their first view of the environment around them.

Sight doesn't get very sharp even as they start growing into adulthood. After their ears open, they may get startled by different sounds around them. Even from the moment their ears start working, they can hear the ultrasonic range and their range is almost twice the capacity of humans.

At the three-week point, puppies will become a bit adventurous and will start to move around, albeit in a clumsy manner. This can be likened to a human infant's crawling period.

At this time, progress happens quickly. By 3 ½ weeks, the majority of puppies are stable and can move around easily on their own. Hearing and sight improve each day. They can start to drink liquids and eat mushy solid foods.

They will have some interaction with others in their litter but most of this will be deciding who will act as a blanket as they sleep in a pile and cuddle up underneath. However, they don't mind either role.

This is also the time when they first start socialising. With open ears and eyes, they crawl a lot more and even begin trying to stand up and walk properly.

By the time they're four weeks old, they know what "real" food is, eat more of such foods and reduce their nursing. They're not weaned at this stage. Puppies sleep less and spend more time moving around.

This is the point where they begin to socialise with the world around them. They should start listening to sounds such as the vacuum cleaner, dishwasher, can opener and hair dryer. They should listen to the TV or music as well.

This is the perfect time to give the puppy chances to walk on different textured surfaces such as grass, tile, wood, dirt, carpet and concrete. Additional textures can be added to his bedding and the breeder can wear different textures in clothing so the puppy can snuggle up and feel them for himself.

Puppy is starting to control his own body temperature as well as do his business without stimulation from the mother. However, she'll keep on cleaning up after him for a bit longer.

At the five-week point, he's now considered a toddler and will spend a lot of time mixing with his litter mates and humans. If he has toys, he'll explore them but they won't be an object of vigorous play until he's a bit older. The mother will encourage her little ones to wean by not being as available for drinks whenever they desire.

Puppies begin to "play fight" with their mates but they're still too young to work out their pecking order and temperament. Some mothers regurgitate food for the puppies but this doesn't often happen in dogs that are domesticated.

At six weeks old, several wormings will have taken place and it's time for puppy's first shots. Tiny breeds may not have shots until they're eight weeks old.

Play time changes dramatically at this stage and toys become objects of pure fascination and delight. Puppies will find different ways to explore every possible corner of their surroundings. Breeders should offer plenty of stimuli in terms of smells, sounds and textures and vary the environments where puppy can safely explore.

The mother will keep teaching manners, particularly when it comes to "bite suppression." Puppies will gradually learn what is and isn't appropriate canine behaviour. These behaviours will carry on repeatedly for two weeks until they're completely weaned and can be taken to their permanent homes.

Smaller breeds such as Pomeranians might need extra time with the litter and mother. At six weeks, a puppy is outgoing, friendly, curious and eager to learn.

If socialising is handled properly, the puppy will be keen to please his new owners when that time arrives.

At the eight-week-old mark, many of the smaller breeds are prepared to be taken to their permanent homes. Other types may need as much as four more weeks in the care of the breeder and mother, especially if the puppies are the tiniest toy breeds.

When the puppy is eight weeks old, he starts to exercise caution in his behaviour. Prior to this he would be reckless and exuberant, running headlong into any adventure fearlessly. During the following two weeks, he becomes more cautious as he investigates everything around him. New owners must let him go through this stage because then he'll move past it quickly.

During this time, owners shouldn't "baby and cuddle" the puppy. Instead, they can assure his safety without moving in to rescue him when it's not needed. Anxiety and fear issues may arise in puppies who get rescued too early and these issues can be difficult to correct down the track.

When a puppy is taken to his new home, his first few nights can be hard because he hasn't spent much time on his own before. Socialisation is critical during this period and should be maintained until he's 12 weeks old. Even before he's brought home, it's essential for the home to be ready for his arrival.

Puppy should be exposed to as many new smells, sounds, sights and other sensations as possible. The more stimuli and experiences he faces, the easier it will be for him to handle changes as he gets older.

This is also an ideal starting point for training. Potty training is the first essential focus, followed by basic commands. Teaching basic obedience skills is best commenced in the home, and down the track he can be enrolled in an obedience school, after he has been immunised and is ready for that next phase.

Immunisations are critical to the health of all young puppies. They must be top priority, even over socialising attempts. Puppy can't be allowed to go into a dog park until he has received his shots. Consider a puppy in a similar vein to a newborn infant baby. If you wouldn't do something to an infant, why would you do it to a puppy?

The puppies are now in the "tween" phase where they exhibit some examples of independence. It's likened to the pre-teen stage in humans and is demanding in nature. Instead of puppy sticking to you like glue, he'll start wandering off.

Puppy's behaviour is more erratic and he may be a cute little baby one minute and the most stubborn of tweens the next. This is the point when teething sets in and he'll look to find anything he can chew on, including toys, a wooden chair and even a person's toes or fingers.

He should start to be potty trained now. It's also time for the basics of obedience training such as how to walk properly on a leash. At this point his growth spurt should slow down and he may eat less food.

At the end of this stage, puppy must have had his third round of shots and a Rabies shot as well. Once vaccinated, it's a perfect time to take puppy exploring. Take him whenever you go out (if possible). It's also good to start teaching basic commands.

Congratulations, your fur child has finally reached his teenage years. His attitude is everything now. He'll try breaking rules and testing boundaries when he sees chances to do so.

Provided that you have been training and socialising with him, he won't turn into a juvenile delinquent. He can go to puppy classes and learn more commands. His baby teeth will fall out, to be replaced by a full mouth of adult teeth.

Dental care is critical from this point on. Puppy will be at sexual maturity stage at some point in this time. It's wise to have her spayed or him neutered. Most vets recommend doing this by the age of six months.

Puppy needs lots of chewing toys, exercise and discipline. Patience will be your new best friend. At the conclusion of this stage, puppy is now a dog and is sexually mature. Smaller breeds will be their full weight, size and height.

If spaying or neutering hasn't taken place, there will be visible signs of sexual maturity. Females will often have their first heat between 6-7 months old.

If the males haven't been neutered, they generally start marking their territory. Males may be fathers when they're as young as seven months of age.

There won't be visible changes immediately and many of the smaller breeds retain the playful personality for most of their life.

Over time, their youthful exuberance will fade and (provided you did socialising and training properly), the dog will become calmer and behave more predictably with habits that stay the same.

Selecting a Pomeranian Show Puppy

Despite other breeders protesting that they have a 100% success rate, I have never believed in the "pick your puppy at birth" theory. During this period, the priority is to ensure puppies are born safely and quickly commence feeding on their mother.

I'll very quickly check markings in coloured litters. It's always exciting to look at the markings on newborn parti-coloured Pomeranians. As a puppy develops, narrow blazes may completely disappear, and wide blazes will often narrow.

Solid-coloured puppies born with white toes shouldn't be passed over as being only pet quality, as these white markings will often "grow out" as the puppy grows. The puppies' birth weights are documented.

Despite all my experience in keeping records of growth rates and weight, I can't find anything that significantly correlates between the puppy's weight at birth and their eventual size as an adult.

Observations: 0 - 3 weeks

At this age, I focus on the mother and her puppies' health. It's important all pups commence nursing quickly after birth and receive a share of their mother's colostrum. The dam has her temperature checked daily for a few days after the birth. I monitor the litter closely during the next few days. Pups should gain weight daily and be firm and plump to hold. If a puppy doesn't gain quickly, or if the skin pinches up with your fingers, the pup may be dehydrating.

Pups who are firmly latched onto the teat and actually drinking are easy to detect as these pups will be holding tiny tails high. Another good sign to see is a puppy twitching while sleeping. This twitching is activated sleep and the pup's muscles are getting stronger as he twitches.

A puppy with colic will scream in pain for days. Plain yogurt often helps ease the pain. A puppy in trouble will feel cold to touch, lays limp and refuses to nurse. This puppy needs your assistance.

Observations: 3 – 8 weeks

The litter will develop quickly. Pups start eating solid food, eyes will now be open, and they'll attempt to stand and begin to play. I spend lots of time playing with pups of this age. It's an ideal time to commence socialising and to observe overall behaviour and note any changes.

Often a stylish puppy has caught my eye and it's quite usual for the same puppy to keep catching my eye. I can't help myself; this is the puppy I always pick up and cuddle first.

As his head starts to develop, I begin looking for correct head proportions. If I can look at a puppy at nose level, that helps me get a clear picture of the under-jaw and his head in general. Don't choose a puppy with a narrow under-jaw because, as an adult, his lower incisors will require adequate space.

I don't pay much attention to the length of legs or height during these early stages, because most puppies seem to be chubby and short anyway. However, it's advisable to be alert if a puppy seems extremely up on leg or has very little depth of ribs at his elbow. Coats grow quickly, and the pups are starting to resemble cute little fluff balls.

At the 5 to 6-week mark, it's time I start stacking pups to give me an opportunity to make better assessments. I do this on a table, using a bath mat. I spend a short time every day playing with, posing, and handling the puppies.

This early training is a vital element that contributes to show training later. I look for overall balance instead of conformation details at this point. I'm looking for a balanced puppy with a high tail set, good topline, and a short back.

The topline firmness generally won't disappear later, but it may develop later. A long-backed puppy will never develop into a short-backed adult and a low tail set rarely improves. I focus on rears and fronts when stacking. Avoid puppies if they're too narrow or too tight between their legs. Never position the legs. Let the hindquarters move into the natural position.

Fronts are often less reliable to assess. A better idea is to know your lines. However, I can identify puppies that will be out at the elbow and have straight shoulders. At this age, if the puppy's toes are out, this problem could improve as the chest develops. If the puppy is too wide in the chest, this won't improve as this pup develops.

It's hard to determine the colour of eyes at this age. I try to select a puppy with eyes that aren't too small or too large and are the correct almond shape.

It's handy to analyse the amount of stop on a puppy, but this can change as he develops. However, don't think for a second that if he has hardly any stop now, he'll ever get a moderate stop. A puppy with very large ears will always have large ears. While you're evaluating the heads, remember to keep an eye out for the right occlusion of both lower and upper jaw. Although the jawline can vary due to different factors, it's good to know what you have to start with.

One of the many habits I have during the assessment process is to take lots of photos. Having a library of photos of your past puppies at various stages of development is an amazing tool.

By this time, I hope you have possibly "sorted" your puppy litter. Remember to be aware of the weaknesses and strengths of the parents and the immediate grandparents. When the focus may be on one problem in a breeding, never forget about the whole dog as the big picture.

The litter is now 10 to 12 weeks of age

Small litter sizes in Pomeranians don't allow many choices. So, breedings should be meticulously planned. Puppies that are obviously pets should be placed with people who understand how to care for, and genuinely love, Pomeranians. Then it's time for a more meticulous assessment of the puppies that are left.

Is there that special puppy with the potential to be Best in Show or Group winner or do you have some dogs who could easily gain titles that you may run on?

While you're thinking about your choices, consider these criteria: overall balance, soundness, structure, and attitude. If you have these elements and include correct care and training, you'll ensure that your puppy will develop to his full potential.

Eye appeal and balance: Look for the puppy that will be pleasing to the eye because he has indescribable class. The puppy you always pick up first. This is the puppy that won't receive comments like: "I love that head," "what an amazing tail set," or "check out the short back."

Such comments suggest the puppy isn't well-balanced due to one overpowering element. Choosing a puppy with great balance can be hard after eight weeks and before eight months.

The higher limits vary according to different lines, but experience has demonstrated that Pomeranian pups are best assessed at eight to nine weeks. Then you can stop stressing during growth periods or while the puppy is teething. This is the best time to take a large selection of photos of profiles, rears, and fronts.

Soundness and structure: When evaluating a puppy, it's essential to differentiate parts of his structure that could change and the parts that will most likely stay constant. Here are some of the elements that should maintain consistency. In other words, what you see is probably what you'll get.

Temperament: When selecting your show puppy, look for a bold, outgoing, relaxed, confident temperament. Avoid keeping a puppy with a less than desirable temperament in any breeding program.

Low on leg: It's rare for a low-to-the-ground, short-legged puppy to become correct. Their loins are usually too long, and they should not be retained in any breeding program. Keep the ideal Pomeranian proportions in mind when selecting your puppy.

Loose shoulder assembly: This is a serious issue and it's rare for this problem to improve significantly or correct itself. Shoulder layback can be difficult to predict but it's unlikely to improve if it's poor. A little looseness in the puppy's front can sometimes tighten with the right diet and proper exercise.

Low tail set: These are usually pretty well set at the eight to nine-week point and low tail sets should be avoided. A high tail set is such an important breed feature, so to consider retaining a Pomeranian for show or breeding with a low tail set is a serious folly. This fault is almost impossible to breed out.

Hindquarter defects: Another issue is cow hocks, narrow hindquarters or severe weakness in the rear end. Avoid the temptation to retain any pups displaying these defects because these are severe problems that wont improve over time.

Eye size and colour: If the eye is too big, too light, too small or round, it will only get worse when the puppy becomes an adult. Absence of the correct almond-shaped eye will spoil a Pomeranian's expression.

Heavy or fine boned: Avoid keeping a slab-sided puppy lacking bone. It's equally important to avoid the extremely heavy-boned type puppy that shows excessive coarseness.

Good news, that's the negatives

There are also characteristics that may improve as the puppy develops. How much improvement will depend on the particular breeding lines?

This is where you should be completely familiar with the pedigree of your puppy. Understand your dam and sire's weaknesses and strengths. Know the same information about the puppy's grandparents as well.

If you're aiming to achieve a specific quality in your puppy, concentrate your focus on that quality while assessing him but also be objective. It may be difficult to admit but sometimes the litter isn't of the same quality as the parents.

If you haven't made some progress with this breeding, there's no point in retaining a puppy from that specific mating. You have to be ruthless when analysing the potential of the puppies.

Always remember, even if a pup is not likely to be show or breeding quality, he may still make a wonderful pet.

Structure aspects that may alter include:

Head: Some puppies, particularly if they're teething, lose the stop they had when they were seven to eight weeks old and will often have a very "ordinary" head for a month or two.

Be patient. If the head was right as a baby, it should come back. If your puppy had a short muzzle at eight weeks but at five months isn't looking cute, don't despair; it will all correct itself once your puppy has finished growing.

Puppies often look all ears at around five months. Again, if the placement and size of your Pomeranian's ears were correct at eight weeks, relax because puppies often appear to just grow into their ears.

Toplines: As your puppy's muscles build tone and strengthen, a suspect topline may correct itself. However, it's often a matter of how much this problem will improve.

Feet: Pastern problems can generally be corrected by having puppies running on gravel. Remember to keep toenails trimmed short. Ensure diet is a correctly balanced puppy diet.

Size: The final size of any puppy is one of the hardest factors to assess. Birth weight has very little to do with the adult size of your puppy. Puppies born from outcrosses are even harder to predict. Make sure you assess the size over a lengthy period of time.

Growth spurts and plateaus could mislead you enormously if you're not careful. Larger puppies often mature early and have finished growing at an early age. On the other hand, smaller puppies often grow for a longer period of time and may not reach maturity until 14 to 16 months of age.

Coat: A Pomeranian puppy's coat may be dense and short, and may (or may not) show guard hair. If you're looking at Pomeranian puppies with big cotton-wool type coats versus plainer puppies lacking a glamorous baby coat, don't be misled and dazzled by a glamorous puppy with a huge, soft coat that's lacking guard-hairs. This sort of coat may indicate an incorrect coat at maturity.

Short backs: This is related to my previous comments about balance. It's vital to remember your puppy will always be long if he starts out long in the loins. If he starts off short-coupled, he might stay that way but there's no guarantee.

Male gonads: Ideally, these should have dropped by six weeks and be in place by nine to ten weeks. Three months is the upper limit to be holding onto a show prospect puppy with retained gonads and that puppy would have to be extremely special. If a puppy is not entire, it's not wise to allow extra time for them to "come down." Show puppies are breeding puppies. Don't let extra problems get in the way.

Teeth: You must check the bite. Check the placement of all four canines and look for narrow underjaws, particularly if the lower canines are inside the upper canines. Check for proper occlusion. The side teeth should fit together like the teeth on a pair of pinking shears. Misaligned side teeth are frequently the reason for a puppy's mouth to go off.

Ensure retained deciduous teeth are removed. During the teething period, tail sets and ears often do strange things. Don't be concerned if your puppy starts to carry his tail at an incorrect angle or his ears go floppy during the teething period.

You need to add all this information together

Select your puppy based on the reasons you have for breeding, and puppy's overall balance and structure. Nurture your chosen puppy to make sure he develops the best possible attitude.

Training a Pomeranian Show Dog

If you intend to show your Pomeranian, training should commence as early as possible as Pom puppies often have a mind of their own. Before you buy a Pomeranian from a breeder for show purposes, ask what training he'll receive before you take him home.

It's important to start training much earlier than you would for ordinary puppies. In an ideal world, training should have started a couple of weeks before you get the puppy from the breeder.

If you train your Pom early and keep the training consistent, he'll be a quick learner and will be able to do basics from a very young age. Poms are very intelligent and keen to learn. It's important to make training fun for you and your dog.

This Handbook should guide you in the correct approach to puppy training. Positive reinforcement methods are the only way to train a small toy dog like a Pomeranian. I have proved this method produces amazing results repeatedly, during my decades of exhibiting lots of Best in Show Champion Pomeranians.

Positive reinforcement works by you giving your Pom a reward in return for him doing what you have asked of him. A toy or a treat can be used. This style of conformation training for shows will often stop your puppy from learning bad habits.

Choosing a name for your Pomeranian puppy

It's essential that a puppy is named during the first few weeks. Using his name at all times will get him used to his name and that helps with training. Breeders help bolster puppy's self-esteem once they have named the puppy.

They shouldn't wait for the new owner to choose a name. Dogs can quickly get used to a new name if the owner decides to change it a few weeks later. If you plan to buy a specific puppy from the breeder and he isn't named, you should choose a name and ask the breeder to always use it.

Bait training

The single most important thing you can train your dog to do is to maintain eye contact while you give him a command. A good technique is to train him to do it when you feed him. For example, when you put his bowl of food on the floor, repeat the word "cookie," while he begins to gobble it all up.

"Cookie" is a typical word used by breeders and exhibitors to grab their puppy's attention. Of course, you may choose any word you like. Repetition helps make the puppy connect the word to an enjoyable experience, in this case, it's eating his favourite treats.

That same word must be used to catch his attention when offering treats and bait from your hand during a different time when he's in a "stand-stay command." This is called "baiting" and is used in shows to get your dog to stand attentively while being judged.

Younger puppies are given dog food or small pieces of cooked chicken or cheese as bait. Older dogs can be fed liver and hot dogs. Exhibitors can offer their dog bait from their pocket, mouth or hand but just enough bait is to be used to achieve the desired outcome. Never give your dog treats and snacks while he sits. If you allow this behaviour, he'll do the same thing in the show ring. During a show, Poms are always required to stand while in the ring, never to sit. Never allow your dog to eat any dropped pieces of bait during training or at a show.

Standing on the table for examination

Because a Pom is a toy dog, he must stand on a small table in the show ring. He can't sit during this examination. The Judge will check a variety of things including teeth, genitalia and other parts of his body.

The "Stand and Stay" is the command you can use to get your puppy used to remain standing while the judge examines him.

Table training should be started by the breeder prior to the age of 8 weeks. By the time puppy is 4 - 5 weeks old, he should have the ability to stand correctly in show stance on a table.

Using a mirror, practice standing him, so you can check his outline and balance. You'll also be able to see what he looks like on the show side in the mirror. The judge will see that side of your Pomeranian. Practice makes perfect.

While you study your dog, hold him in a safe standing position and then count to 10. As you maintain his upright status, and as he grows older and stronger, he'll have the ability to remain standing on his own.

It's important to get somebody else to touch your puppy while he's standing. When he's older, you'll be able to train him to stand still while being examined. These exercises help make your puppy more comfortable when touched by others.

It's crucial that you train your dog to gait correctly on a lead as this will have an enormous impact on his show performance. Some dogs may not like the lead and so they might gait with tail down or even start either galloping or pacing. So, it's imperative that you create a positive relationship between your Pom and the lead.

Begin your lead training by placing a small collar on your Pomeranian. Entice him with treats while encouraging him to follow you around the home. Let your puppy follow you and offer lots of praise and a small bait when your puppy does as you say.

After he has successfully passed a few days of this training, connect a short lead to his collar and repeat the process again, this time letting puppy drag the lead around as he follows you. Offer copious amounts of praise and treats and stop often to do this. Once the puppy has gotten used to wandering around, following you eagerly, that's when you need to start holding his lead. Formal training can start once your puppy is comfortable with the lead on.

These sessions should only run for 5-10 minutes. Like all babies, Pom puppies only have a brief attention span. Make training fun for both yourself and your puppy and you'll achieve terrific results faster than you may even have anticipated.

End all training sessions in a positive way. If your puppy won't do a specific task, choose one you know he likes doing, so your session finishes in a winning way for you and your puppy.

I don't believe a Pomeranian should be made to wear a collar all the time. It should only be used to train him. If he wears a collar all the time, it may cause damage to his dense coat.

Training your Pomeranian to enjoy grooming

Introduce your new puppy to regular grooming methods while he's still quite young. Always do each element of the grooming the same way every time so he gets used to it all. The list includes: combing, nail trimming, washing, blow drying, cleaning teeth and other grooming practices you want to use.

When your puppy is four months of age, he should have had all the necessary vaccinations. You can begin advanced training elements and also take your puppy on socialisation outings.

Champion Dochlaggie Days Of Our Lives.

Photo by Pedini.

Final Thoughts

There you have it. Thank you for joining me on this remarkable journey into the world of Pomeranians, the cutest canines in the cosmos.

I hope you enjoyed reading this book even half as much as I have loved sharing some of my experiences and knowledge. I've gained this expertise over more than 40 years of proud ownership of Pomeranians, each with their own unique personality.

You might be a dog breeder, a loving pet owner already, or perhaps you have never owned one of these incredible toy dogs before.

Regardless of your situation, this comprehensive handbook is now your handy reference guide for as long as you share your life and home with one or more Pomeranians.

Thank you for purchasing this book. I'm hoping everyone reading my Pomeranian book has all their questions answered. If not, contact me via one of my Pomeranian websites.

Denise's Pomeranian websites

Dochlaggie Pomeranians: https://www.pomeranian.com.au
Pomeranian Headquarters: https://www.pomeranian.org

Pomeranians Australia: https://www.pomeranians.com.au

Thank you,

Denise Leo

Dochlaggie Pomeranians

Printed in Great Britain
by Amazon